STEVE CHRISTIE

Not Really *"Of"* Us

Why Do Children of Christian Parents Abandon the Faith?

WESTBOW·
P R E S S
A DIVISION OF THOMAS NELSON
& ZONDERVAN

WestBow Press books may be ordered through booksellers or by contacting:

WestBow Press
A Division of Thomas Nelson & Zondervan
1663 Liberty Drive
Bloomington, IN 47403
www.westbowpress.com
1 (866) 928-1240

ISBN: 978-1-4908-4846-4 (sc)
ISBN: 978-1-4908-4847-1 (e)

Library of Congress Control Number: 2014915031

Printed in the United States of America.

WestBow Press rev. date: 08/28/2014

Contents

"Steve Christie has written a timely and important book that addresses the challenge of raising children as Christians in a time when society is becoming increasingly secular. Using Jesus' parable of the sower, he analyzes the four kinds of soil (i.e., children), in which the seed of God's word is planted. Although there are practical techniques to address sons and daughters who fall away from the faith, Steve's message is that a parent should start cultivating the soil early and provide them with the reasons why the Christian faith is so compelling. *Not Really 'Of' Us* is an important resource for parents raising children in today's culture."

- Rich Deem, founder of *GodAndScience.org*

For all those Christian parents who loved their children enough to share with them the truth of the gospel and the hope of salvation through Jesus Christ and never gave up praying for them, and for their children that they believe in the truth.

"They went out from us, but they were not really of us; for if they had been of us, they would have remained with us; but they went out, so that it would be shown that they all are not of us."

– 1 John 2:19

Appreciation

I'd like to begin my appreciation to my mother, Darlene, who faithfully prayed to our Lord for my salvation for well over a year - without me even realizing it – until the Holy Spirit finally convicted me in my heart, and I got down on my knees and repented of my sin against God and accepted the truth of the Christian faith and the Inspiration of His Word. Her exemplary, godly model of a Christian parent through her speech, actions, attitude, long-suffering patience, forgiveness, faithfulness, humbleness, consistency, and unconditional love towards me are the godly characteristics that helped me to realize what it *truly* means to be a Christian. If it wasn't for all these things, this book would not have been read nor have touched so many lives.

I'd like to thank my beloved Lucia ('Pusa'), my 'Romanian kitten,' who God put in my life, not once – but twice – at just the right times, and in such significant and specific circumstances that our meetings could only have come by the loving hand of God. She is one of the greatest 'prayer warriors' I have ever known – never doubting that if a prayer is part of God's Will that He *will* answer it. Her 'mustard seed faith' in God's omnipotence, love, grace, and mercy has inspired me to grow even closer in my relationship towards God, which grows stronger each and every day, regardless of the daily tests I endure. Her faithfulness to Christ and to those she loves is second to none. Te iubesc foarte mult din toată inima, Puşa!

I'd like to thank my Bible study teacher, Jerry, of ten years for teaching me 'how' to study the Bible in context. And although we don't always agree on the 'non-essentials' of the Christian faith, that 'Christian liberty' has helped me to discern between personal, *subjective* interpretation of Scripture and proper *objective* Biblical exegesis and hermeneutics. Through his teachings (as well as our disagreements), I have learned to discern when Christians can 'agree to disagree' and continue to remain in fellowship with one another, verses breaking fellowship over essential Biblical and Christian doctrines and truth.

I'd like to thank the countless godly men and women, like Jeanette, who God placed in my walk with Him, who have helped me in different stages through my spiritual journey, at just those 'right times,' aiding me in growing to know Him better and strengthening my faith in the truth of not only His existence and His inerrant, Inspired Word, but also the assurance of His love, mercy, grace, justice, and my salvation.

I'd like to thank everyone at WestBow Press, particularly Gwen Ash, my check-in coordinator and Aaron Hall, my publishing consultant for all their help in publishing my first book, for without them this project would have never gotten past the screen of my home computer. Thank you again for your prayers, Aaron, towards this project, which you can be assured that I, in turn, did (and will continue to) pray for yours.

I'd like to thank Lauri Swisher from Emmanuel Baptist Church, who shared with me some invaluable ideas on how to promote this book, so it could reach as many fellow believers as possible and provide real hope and to aid in the healing of their relationships with their unbelieving children.

Lastly, and certainly not least, I am forever humbly indebted to my Lord, God, and Savior, Jesus Christ for reaching deep down and changing my 'heart of stone' to a 'heart of flesh' – something I would have never done on my own, regardless of who shared the Gospel with me. I am forever thankful for the Holy Spirit Who convicted me of my *need* for a Savior, as well as convinced me of the reality that the Bible is the inerrant, Inspired Word of God, and aided me to accept the truth of all of the godly criteria of Holy Scripture that isn't found in any other religious or secular texts. And, I'd like to thank my Holy Father in Heaven for sending His Only Begotten Son to die in my place, as the *only* way to the Father and Heaven, so that I could inherit eternal life in our Father's Kingdom.

Prologue

The purpose in writing this book is not merely to convince someone that Christianity and the Bible are true or to 'convert' someone to Christianity. Anyone who knows anything about *Biblically*-based Christians knows that they realize that 'true' conversion is the work of the Holy Spirit, not them. Rather, the purpose of this book is to attempt to explain 'why' children of Christian parents walk away from the faith. My desire in this book is to attempt to empathize with and relate to others who either had those same doubts as children as I did, or whether they surfaced later in life and walked away from the faith and 'why.' One of the most distressing experiences a Christian parent can go through is watching their child, who they have loved, protected, nurtured, supported, provided for, clothed, cared for, and – most importantly – told them the truth about Christianity, to one day tell their parent, "I don't believe this anymore," because it's not about being 'unhappy' that their child *disagrees* with them, but because of the reality of the eternal *consequence* of that choice to disbelieve. Unfortunately, children who walk away from the faith, don't fully appreciate or choose to understand what that personal decision to disbelieve does to their parent spiritually and emotionally, and the parent doesn't understand 'why' the child chose to disbelieve, despite being told the truth and reality of Christianity and the Bible. So, in order to help both the Christian parent and the disbelieving child to help understand each other, and at the very least, attempt to reestablish, heal, mend, and strengthen the relationship they would like to have with one other – and hopefully with God – I have written this book. If you can relate to anything I just wrote, this book is for <u>you</u>.

In the Introduction, I purposely explain my own past, including 'why' I didn't believe in the Bible or Christianity throughout my childhood, teen years, and for most of my young adult life, even from an academic or intellectual level. I felt it was important for me to begin talking about not only 'how' I came to embrace and believe in the Truth of the Bible and Christianity, but also 'why' I came to that conclusion, including the 'personal' roadblocks that I set up *myself*, based on my own unwillingness to look outside my personal beliefs. I also wanted to try to empathize and relate with children who are either brought up in a Biblically-based Christian home but walked away from Christianity later in life, or aren't brought up with the Bible but then later either embraced it or continued to reject it. As Ken Ham, President of *Answers in Genesis* (AiG) points out, 'We shouldn't be surprised that two thirds of the young people growing up in the church will leave the church in their 20s".[1] Whatever our individual pasts or exposure to Christianity are, they are largely shaped by our *later* experiences with others, which can be directly,

---

[1] Ken Ham, "Help Stop the Already Gone Phenomenon!" *Answers in Genesis*. Published on December 9, 2011 in Ministry Updates. http://blogs.answersingenesis.org/blogs/ken-ham/2011/12/09/help-stop-the-already-gone-phenomenon/

as well as indirectly, affected *by* our past. So, throughout this book, I'm going to explore the different 'types' of children, as well as their pasts and individual exposures to the Bible and Christianity, in an attempt to explain 'why' children born to Christian parents abandon the faith, by examining the 'Parable of the Four Soils' (or the 'Parable of the Sower') from Matthew 13:1-23. After that, I plan on providing some real hope for Christian parents of children who have abandoned the faith, as well as provide assurance for those children of the Truth that they were taught by their loving Christian parents. Finally, I will conclude this book with some final words, and address what is it that Christian parents, as well as their children who have abandoned the faith, would like to see happen in their relationship with each other, which *is* possible, provided willingness on both sides.

I have no doubt that you may or may not agree with 100% of the theological and doctrinal statements in this book, just as I – a sinner – am more than willing to humbly acknowledge that I may or may not be 100% accurate in terms of Biblical doctrine and theology, since I am capable of being wrong. However, since the purpose of this book is not about defending a particular Christian denomination's doctrines, but about 'why' children of Christian parents abandon the faith, as well as what can be done about it including how they can reestablish that close, intimate relationship they once had, I pray that you can bypass any theological and doctrinal 'disagreements' you might have and be encouraged, comforted, and assured with how this book and – more importantly – the Holy Spirit can aid you.

Introduction

I didn't grow up believing in the Bible. I felt it was important and relevant to bring that fact up first. I think it's difficult for someone who was raised Christian but never abandoned the faith, to be able to empathize with someone else, who was also raised Christian and with the Bible, and to understand why a person with that same exposure to the Truth would abandon the faith. I believe that's because the child of Christian parents who didn't abandon the faith, may not have experienced the exact same doubts that may have led to those uncertainties, as those children of Christian parents who did abandon the faith. Now, I'm not implying that a Christian parent keeping their children in a 'Christian bubble' will automatically prevent them from abandoning the faith when the get older. In fact, I've seen many of them abandon the faith as well – some of them have even abandoned it *earlier* than other children. Rather, I'm suggesting that children of Christian parents who abandon the faith may have been exposed to some *internal* doubts that they don't share with their parents, after being exposed to the same experiences that children of Christian parents who remain in the faith experience, but don't have these same internal doubts. But before discussing some of the reasons 'why' children of

Christian parents abandon the faith, I thought I'd first share my own experiences, which helped shape my own beliefs from childhood to adulthood, including those experiences that did, as well as didn't, involve Christians, as well as other people who didn't believe in Christianity nor the Bible.

CHILDHOOD

I vaguely remember having my great-grandmother's Bible in our home stored away neatly in a shiny, wooden-like box, where we placed the obituaries of loved ones that were cut out from the newspaper, as well as the 'In Loving Memory Of' cards from the funeral homes, and the ribbons from flower decorations from friends and family. However, I never really knew 'what' the Bible was, but I didn't believe it was the 'inerrant, Inspired Word of God.' I had no reason to, since I was never taught much about it. At most, I viewed it as 'just a bunch of stories' that contained some 'moral teachings,' and the life of someone named 'Jesus' who was the 'Son of God' who died on a cross. I picked it up numerous times and when I would attempt to read it, it just sounded 'religious,' and I put it back down. I was raised in a home that prayed and believed in God, and I attended parochial schools – both elementary and high school - which had morning prayers about God. I was even the Treasurer of the Altar Boys of my elementary school parish. However, I don't ever remember *opening* a Bible in school. I learned a lot about my religion, and I believed that what I was being taught was true, even if I didn't totally understand it. I just remember being told 'to just have faith,' even if it 'doesn't make sense' right now. I had no reason to believe otherwise. I had a very comfortable, happy, memorable, and loving upbringing, while that Bible remained in that shiny, wooden-like box – free from dust.

As I got older, I learned that my particular 'denomination' of Christianity wasn't the only one (even though, like many young Christians, I didn't know what a 'denomination' was back then). One of my earliest memories of the Bible was from going to a Sunday School with my mom's friend, Mary Ann, who was not of the same denomination as I was. I was so young that I don't even remember what was discussed. I couldn't have been much older that seven or eight. I just remember that I didn't 'get this whole Jesus and Bible stuff.' I don't even know how long I went to Sunday School, but I know it wasn't long, and when asked by my mom, I said that I didn't really want to go anymore. I was afraid of hurting Mary Ann's feelings, especially since she was such a close friend of my mom. Mary Ann grew up just a few houses down from where my mom grew up. However, my mom never 'forced' me to continue going. I always remember that it was *my* choice whether I wanted to keep attending or not. But, even after I decided to stop going, I still felt bad, despite encouragement, reassurance, and love from both my mom and Mary Ann. I guess that was just the way I was raised. They never made me feel guilty. For the next several years, my understanding of God was based on what I learned in parochial school, while my great-grandmother's Bible remained safely tucked away in that shiny, wooden-like box.

I remember in elementary school, that there were a couple of kids that weren't of the same 'denomination' as me. The first time I noticed this was during Mass, when I went up to receive communion from the pastor, they remained sitting in the pews. I didn't understand why they didn't go up, but I was later told that they didn't 'believe' all the same things I did about the Mass, but I don't remember being told *what* they didn't believe. What I do remember was that I was taught by my teachers and pastors to be respectful of them, and not to 'tease' them about not going up to receive communion, but beyond that it wasn't really talked about. Even though respect for the differences of other people – including their religious preferences – was something that was grounded into me at a young age, as a child I just couldn't understand *why* other people didn't think the way I did, especially since they agreed to attend the same church and parochial school that I did. Without realizing it, deep down, I thought they were 'wrong' for not going up, because everyone else – including me – was going up. I didn't understand what the big deal was. I thought they just didn't want to go. I later found out that the real reason they didn't go up was because their *parents* didn't believe in the same things about communion that I did (even though I didn't really understand *what* I believed, other than the 'surface teachings' that I was taught in my religion classes). When you're a child, reality is based mainly on your 'immediate' surroundings, which, as you get older, your outlook of reality *should* change to form your 'own' belief <u>based</u> on ALL the available evidence.

ADOLESCENCE

When I entered parochial high school, I began to notice and gain a better understanding of 'denominational differences' between Christians by associating with guys from my high school, who were also Christian, but were Protestants. One of my closest friends was Protestant, but even in high school, I didn't know what that really meant. During Mass, I noticed he didn't go up to receive communion either. Somewhere along our high school friendship, the topic came up, and he shared with me that his particular denomination didn't believe the same things about communion that we did, because they had different beliefs about the Bible, and that his Bible had books that were 'missing' which were in my Bible – but we didn't go into detail about it, because I didn't *know* the books that were in 'my Bible.' This was the first time since my Sunday School days with Mary Ann that I was reintroduced to the Bible by someone. But, I'd be lying if I said that I had any greater knowledge of the Bible then, than I did with Mary Ann. The main thing I remember was my Protestant friend telling me about the book of Revelation in the New Testament. As a child, I remember lay-people going up to the pulpit to read passages from the Old and New Testaments, as well as the pastor reading the Homily from one of the Gospels, ending with 'The Word of the Lord,' which I, along with the rest of the congregation, would respond with 'Thanks be to God.' Even though I understood that what I had heard was somehow 'from God,' I still didn't completely understand what all that meant – just that I believed that it was true, because even back then I believed God was honest, so what I heard HAD to be true.

I didn't really gain a whole lot of understanding from my Protestant friend about the book of Revelation, except for a few 'prophecies' that seemed mysterious and intriguing. As a teenager, anything that you find mysterious that you don't understand, you get curious and you *want* to understand it! My Protestant friend told me about a character in the Bible called the Antichrist, which is identified in Revelation as 'the beast' and with the number '666.' He then introduced me to a series of movies called 'The Omen,' which was *very loosely* based on the book of Revelation. We even used my video camera to do a 'skit' about the Antichrist, during a home movie we made (which I'm embarrassed to say, I *still* have!) By this time, my mom and I had moved into our new home, and we now had two Bibles – my great-grandmother's Bible and a 'Gideon Bible.' However, at the time, I didn't know that there was a difference between the two, because my knowledge of the Bible was still very limited, but I remained fascinated about it. But even with my 'religious experiences' and conversations with my Protestant friend, because of my upbringing, I still felt more comfortable discussing religion with my friends, who were also brought up in the same denomination that I was. I think that's just normal. To top it off, my first 'real' girlfriend was also Protestant – a Baptist – which I didn't know what that meant (I thought it meant that they based a lot of importance in their church on getting baptized in water – or something similar). Beyond that, I didn't really know what a 'Baptist' was, and our relationship didn't last much past six months anyways. That's part of growing up.

YOUNG ADULTHOOD - COLLEGE

By the time I entered college, my interest in other people's religions and worldviews increased, while my devotion to my own religious upbringing really dwindled. I never stopped believing in God, even with all the higher-level science and philosophy classes I took at my local public university. I guess at the time, I really couldn't understand how our universe (as well as myself) could exist without a God to create it (and me). This was long before I learned about the universe having a beginning, or the Cosmological Argument, or any of the other historical and modern day apologetics that Christians use to defend the existence of God. I just never bought into the 'theory' that our physical universe could have existed from eternity past, or created by some 'Mother Universe,' because then we would never arrive at this moment in time (even though I didn't really think about it in those exact terms back then). Nor did I ever buy into the idea that the universe somehow created itself out of nothing. That just didn't make any sense at all. However, I never became a deist, since I still believed in a 'private' God – both at a spiritual level, as well as a personal level. I always felt some kind of 'connection' to Something that I just couldn't explain using science, philosophy, or any other knowledge or experience. It was like realizing that you can't explain the color of red to someone who's blind by using your sense of taste – it's the wrong 'medium' to try to explain that to someone. It's also not an emotional or physiological experience, but rather a *spiritual* experience, which is *NON*-emotional and *NON*-physiological, that only someone else who has had this 'Something' experience can appreciate and *partially* understand. However, the level of devotion to my particular denomination of Christianity had diminished considerably by then. Although I still considered myself to be 'Christian' – specifically narrowed to my particular denomination from childhood – I was more of a 'non-practicing theist.' I was open to the idea that if I had been raised in another religion, or even another denomination of Christianity, I would be believing something completely different, and even *denying* what I believed as a child. However, I also believed that 'something' about reality had to be true outside of my *personal* opinion, whether it was based on a religious or secular worldview.

I had the privilege of meeting a LOT of people in college who came from numerous, different backgrounds, religions, and worldviews. As I got to know them personally, I began to admire many of these people. I admired their confidence and assurance of their own religions and worldviews, and many of them were 'ecumenical' in their beliefs (ie: they didn't espouse to just 'one narrow view,' but rather they were 'open-minded' to other people's views that differed from their own). As I met more people, I became more 'open-minded' that what I had believed about God *may* not be necessarily '100% true.' By being surrounded by so many people who thought differently than I did about God and life in general, I began to assimilate some of their own theologies about God and reality into mine. So, although I still considered myself to be 'nominally' affiliated with my particular denomination of Christianity from childhood, I began referring to myself as 'non-practicing,' and I began to believe in a 'god' that was based on my accumulated experience and understanding from my childhood, my friendships, and my college colleagues. The 'god' that I believed in was a mixture of all these experiences, and I believed that since I was only one person out of the billions who are in the world, who feel just as strong about their beliefs about theology as I did or more, that the odds that *everything* that I believed from my youth was '100%

true,' was becoming less and less believable. I also began to believe that there couldn't only be just 'one truth,' since so many people have countless opinions about reality and God. That seemed rather narrow-minded and presumptuous, even though there were people who believed that 'their reality' was '100% true,' and believed that my views about God and reality were '100% false.'

One of my first experiences in college with the Bible was when I was sitting in one of the lounges in the Student Union, and two Christians from 'Campus Crusade for Christ' came up to me to share the Gospel. Since my limited understanding of Biblical Christianity was based on my childhood education (which was 'zilch'), plus what I had accumulated from the beliefs of other people over the years, I really didn't know what they were trying to 'sell me.' I had seen enough 'After School Specials' about cults that try to brainwash you into sharing their beliefs (and eventually taking your money), that whenever anyone of a religious nature carrying religious books or brochures approached me, I would instinctively go into 'on guard mode.' Looking back, they were simply attempting to share with me the Gospel of Jesus Christ, and explain to me 'why' they believed it was true. They weren't really trying to 'sell me' anything or take anything from me. They were just trying to share their beliefs with me and explain to me 'why' they believed what they believed. Unfortunately, I wasn't as hospitable and charitable with them as they were trying to be with me. They never tried to 'force their religion down my throat,' and when I told them I didn't want to talk about it anymore, I remember now that they said they were going to pray *for me* and that God would 'bless me.' Everything that I had learned about being 'open-minded' about other people's beliefs that differed from mine, I failed to be 'open-minded' *towards them*. I didn't even give them a chance to explain 'why' they believed what they believed. Rather, I immediately went on the defensive 'why' I believed what **"I"** believed, and completely *closed* my mind to their beliefs, because they were different than mine, just as I had done as a child thinking about those two kids who didn't go up to receive communion in my church. And to be honest, whenever anyone tested me about my beliefs, I didn't really have a reason outside of my own beliefs, that what I believed was true. Another wards, I knew I couldn't give them any objective evidence or reason 'why' I believed what I believed, outside of my own *personal* and subjective opinion. So, when I got pressed, I got defensive and angry, because I knew I couldn't give them a really good defense for my personal beliefs and worldview – and that infuriated me. From that point on, I didn't know the difference between a Jehovah's Witness, Mormon, or 'mainstream' Protestant Christian, because I didn't make the effort to *learn* the difference, since I unfairly 'lumped' them all together, and I didn't believe that it really had anything to do with me or my beliefs anyways.

YOUNG ADULTHOOD – RELATIONSHIPS AND EMPLOYMENT

The next time I recall discussing Christianity with people was when I was working as a Mental Health Professional. I had graduated with my BA in Psychology and had taken a job in a local hospital. I was dating a woman at the time who had never been affiliated with any church at all. The best way I could describe her was a 'deist' (someone who believes in 'a' god, but doesn't really believe in a 'god' that is personally involved with His creation). Looking back, if you were to ask me about the 'spiritual status' of my life back then, I would describe myself as a 'C and E Catholic' (I attended Mass at Christmas and Easter, but not much beyond that). Another wards, I never stopped being a Catholic. I never renounced Catholicism, but I wasn't exactly devoted to it either. However, I was very hesitant about accepting the legitimacy of any other 'version' of Christianity that wasn't Catholic. To me, there was no other religion other than Catholicism (even if I didn't believe and embrace everything about it myself). Perhaps that hesitancy stemmed from my earlier experience in college from being 'on guard' when I was approached by those Christians from Campus Crusade for Christ, even though I wasn't exactly a devout Catholic then either, nor making the effort to learn about the differences between what they believed and what I believed. We had even discussed the subject of marriage at one point, but I remember she was completely opposed to getting married in the Catholic church, because of an allegedly 'bad experience' her parents had had decades earlier. As a Catholic, it was **vitally** important for me to get married IN a church (even if I didn't spend more than a few *hours* every year in one). Unfortunately, because of my lack of knowledge of anything outside Catholicism, including any real knowledge of the Bible, I honestly didn't know anything about other 'denominations' of Christianity. I remember driving past a Protestant church near her home one day, and we decided to check it out. The physical outlay of the inside was remarkably similar to the Catholic churches I attended in parochial schools, just a lot smaller with a lot less 'visuals' inside of it. Interestingly, I didn't feel completely uncomfortable inside of it and the pastor there, who was dressed in a robe very similar to the Catholic priests I had grown up around, was very pleasant and polite. We met with him a few times, and he had informed me that although I was baptized as a baby, in order to get married in that particular Protestant church, I needed to become a member, which involved making a public declaration of faith before the congregation, while she needed to get baptized as a Protestant before the congregation after she declared her faith, since she was never baptized, and because their particular church taught that you couldn't be a member of their church without being baptized <u>first</u>. Another wards, this particular church believed that the purpose of baptism was church membership, unless you were previously baptized elsewhere. Again, I knew relatively nothing about baptism nor the Bible, so since marriage *in* a church was important to me, and since I didn't consider myself a 'devout' Catholic and what the pastor taught me about Protestantism was similar – albeit not exactly the same – as the limited knowledge I retained about Catholicism, I felt comfortable about converting to Protestantism. However, although we professed our 'new-found faith' in that Protestant church before the congregation, which involved her getting water poured on her head – like it was done to me in the Catholic church when I was an infant – the marriage never took place, I stopped attending church there, and I ended up 'reconverting' back to Catholicism – again, as a non-devout, 'C and E Catholic,' once again, gracing the walls of the Catholic church only a few hours each year. It wasn't until years later when I began to study the Bible, I had learned in the New Testament that *after* people repented of their sins, believed in, and devoted themselves to Jesus as their Lord and Savior, they *immediately* got baptized (Matthew 3:2-6; Acts 2:38-44; 8:36-37; 16:30-34), which involved <u>full-bodily immersion</u> like our sinless Lord did as an example to identify with us, and as the Ethiopian eunuch did, when they were baptized (Matthew 3:16; cf. Acts 8:39). I also learned that when someone 'truly' commits *themselves* to Christ, they only 'need' to declare their faith and be baptized <u>once</u>. You never hear of a 'truly' converted Christian in the New Testament 'recommitting themselves' and being 'rebaptized.'

Years later, I was sitting behind the nursing station of the Psych ICU with two nurses. The nurse on my left had just converted to the Jehovah's Witnesses, and the nurse to my right, Jeanette, was a 'mainstream' Protestant Christian. The patients were asleep in their rooms at that time, and somehow the subject of Christianity came up. I remember the Jehovah's Witness telling me that her husband was a Jehovah's Witness before they met and prior to her conversion. I had told her that I was raised Catholic and believed Jesus was the Son of God. She mentioned that she also believed that Jesus was the Son of God. I asked her since we believed the same thing about Jesus, 'why' she called herself a 'Jehovah's Witness.' She told me that she didn't believe that Jesus *was* God, because she didn't believe the Bible taught that. She also didn't believe that Christians should celebrate Christmas and other holidays, as well as birthdays for the same reason. She also stated that she didn't believe in receiving blood transfusions, because 'the life of the flesh is in the blood' (Leviticus 17:11). In fact, I remember her <u>stating</u> that the Bible didn't support these things. I remember not really knowing how to respond to her, because I honestly didn't know if the Bible denied the Deity of Christ, prohibited the celebration of holidays and birthdays, or forbade reception of blood transfusions. It wasn't until several years later after I became a believer in the inerrancy and Inspiration of the Bible, and when I began to study it, I found out that Scripture actually *supports* the Deity of Christ (John 1:1,14; 8:58-59, cf. Exodus 3:14-15; John 10:30-33), as well as the 'traditional' concept of the Trinity (One God, but Three distinct 'Persons')(Matthew 28:19, c.f. Matthew 3:16-17; 2 Corinthians 13:14), that Jesus Himself celebrated Jewish 'holidays' like Passover and the Feast of Unleavened Bread (Matthew 26:17), and that when the LORD told Moses that the 'life of the flesh was in the blood' (Leviticus 17:11) that He was forbidding the *eating* of the blood (v.12-14) – but He wasn't saying anything about forbidding the *transfusion* of blood from one person to another 'intravenously' for life-saving purposes. But, because of my lack of Biblical knowledge on these subjects, I didn't know how to respond – so I didn't. Instead, I could feel the blood inside me starting to boil, because, in a sense, she was telling me that what I believed was 'wrong,' and since I couldn't defend my beliefs, my gut reaction was to get angry, but I didn't immediately show it. I just remained silent. Jeannette – the 'mainstream' Protestant to my right – obviously didn't agree with her, and I remember her basically disputing with her, stating that the Bible doesn't say anything about 'forbidding' blood transfusions, because God was all about saving and *preserving* life, not ending it. And then I remember the Jehovah's Witness saying "well, that's just your 'interpretation'" – something that I have come to hear years later, whenever I disagree on a doctrinal issue with another Christian, and whenever I would back up that disagreement with Scriptural support, and the person I'd disagree with couldn't. I also remember asking Jeannette that if she believed the same things I did about Christianity, then why she wasn't Catholic like me. I remember the look on her face. She didn't want to say anything to offend me. She desired to be as empathetic as she possibly could and chose her words carefully. She basically told me that she wasn't a Catholic because there were things that the Catholic church teaches that aren't Biblical, and she believed in the sufficiency of Jesus' death on the cross to atone for her sin. All I could remember from my upbringing was the carved golden image of Jesus dying on the cross behind the altar in my old church, so I told her that I believed that too. She then compassionately said that the Catholic church also believes that you're saved when you're baptized. However, as I found out years later, a person isn't saved when they're baptized, but rather when they place their faith and trust in Jesus as their Savior, repent of their sins, and then *after* they are saved, <u>then</u> they get baptized (Acts 2:38-47, cf. Matthew 3:2-6 and Luke 3:3; Acts 3:19; 8:36-38;10:43-48; 16:14-15, 30-34; etc).

At this point, the blood inside my body was boiling like water inside a pressure cooker ready to burst! My face was probably as red as a lobster, and if steam could come out of my ears, it probably would have. I felt like I was 'getting it' from both sides, and I remember saying to both of them, "Look, you can believe whatever you want, but I'm Catholic, I've always *been* Catholic, and I'll always *be* Catholic, and what I believe is what I believe, and no one is going to persuade me any different! Everyone is entitled to their own '**<u>truth</u>!**'" When you ask someone why they believe differently about Christianity than you do, and they tell you that what you believe isn't

Biblical, in your mind it's the same as saying *'you're wrong!'* – even if they don't use the actual word 'wrong.' Implying that you're wrong sort of 'stings' and almost instinctively, you get defensive, because you're assuming that that person is attacking your very core – your beliefs, which is what *identifies* who you are. The problem was that I didn't really know 'why' I believed 'what' I believed – just that I believed it. I just knew that hearing 'it's not Biblical' angered me – even though I didn't actually 'believe' in the inerrancy nor the Inspiration of the Bible, nor knowing whether my beliefs were Biblical or not. And yet, if you were to ask me back then 'why did I get so *angry* over something I didn't believe in anyway?' looking back, I don't know if I could have given you an honest answer 'why' that would make me <u>angry</u>, because anger is usually a reaction you give when you acknowledge that there may be an element of truth from the source of that anger – something I didn't come to realize until years later after my conversion. Nor did I realize that I was equating 'opinion' with 'truth,' which isn't the same thing. In fact, I wasn't really certain 'what' I believed, because I didn't know the <u>*source*</u> of my beliefs, other than from my childhood. The sad part was that the anger that I projected – particularly towards Jeanette – wasn't really justified, because *she* wasn't pressuring *me* with questions, but rather *I* was pressuring *her* with questions, and her objective, empathetic replies (which I found out years later were indeed Biblical) were in response to me probing *her*. So, in reality, my anger was the result of me being ill-equipped 'to make a defense to everyone who asks you to give an account for the hope that is in you, yet with gentleness and reverence' (1 Peter 3:15), just as she had. Once again, I had failed to be 'open-minded' to the beliefs of other people, who disagreed with my *personal* beliefs, even though I had been taught to do otherwise in my childhood, and I definitely wasn't being 'gentle' nor 'reverent' towards Jeanette. Although I was an adult, I still hadn't learned the wisdom taught to me from my childhood by those who raised me. Years later, after I 'truly' accepted Jesus into my heart as my Savior <u>and</u> Lord, and *genuinely* repented of my sin against God, I reminded Jeanette (the 'mainstream Protestant' who I am still friends with to this day) of that conversation that the three of us had, and I apologized for my behavior and attitude towards her, because I now know that all she was trying to do was share the Truth of the Gospel with me. She said she remembered that conversation, and that no apology was necessary, because the important thing was that I am saved and have accepted the Truth, <u>now</u>. What a wonderful and humble example of 'how' a *genuine* Christian is to react in the face of bitter opposition!

YOUNG ADULTHOOD – RETURN TO COLLEGE

It wasn't until I had returned to college in my early thirties when I started to think about my faith again. I had just ended a serious relationship with a young lady, and I began to think about my religious beliefs and worldview. I was beginning to return to the church of my youth, but I had also remembered the treasure of experiences I had accumulated with people from other denominations of Christianity, religions, and worldviews, and I began to realize that 'opinion' doesn't necessarily equal 'Truth.' I learned this when the terrorists bombed the World Trade Center on September 11, 2001. Most of the civilized world didn't believe that what they did honored God, but the cowards who committed that horrific crime to humanity on <u>MY</u> American soil *did* believe it honored God. So, unless God believes that two completely opposite beliefs and opinions can be true at the same time, then either those criminals are right in believing that they honored God, or most everyone else, who didn't believe their cowardice assault against our nation honored God, are right. Now, I'm not attempting to 'diminish' the value of personal opinion. Rather, reflecting on this made me realize that there's a <u>difference</u> between 'Truth' and 'opinion,' and I didn't want to live my life based on a *personal* opinion that 'might' be wrong, no matter how strongly I believed in 'my' opinion that I couldn't support any further than my 'own' *belief.*

Around this time, my mother began attending Bible studies where she worked. I remember her asking me to 'watch her,' and if she started 'acting or talking funny' to let her know. So, even though we had both been brought up in a religion that professed to base its beliefs in the Bible, and we had not one but TWO Bibles in our house, we still didn't know what 'Bible study' was really about. I remember thinking (incorrectly) that it involved something similar to the Jehovah's Witnesses who periodically knocked on my front door, when in reality, Bible study is <u>nothing</u> like that.

Over time, I began to see positive changes in my mom – how she spoke, how she interacted and reacted with her boss, coworkers, friends, family, and with me. Mom has always been a very loving, patient, and caring person, even when it's not always reciprocated by others – including me. We have always had a healthy and mature mother-son relationship. However, I noticed these changes occurred at a 'spiritual' level. She became more concerned about not only how her words, actions, and attitudes affected other people, but also how they affected <u>God</u>. Growing up, I had been taught 'the Golden Rule' (*'love your neighbor as yourself'*), which I would like to believe everyone has a desire to follow, unless you're either an antisocial sociopath or just plain self-centered and care about no one except yourself. However, the difference was that Mom's 'reason' for desiring to not purposefully offend others wasn't merely because she didn't want to offend them, but primarily because she didn't want to offend <u>God</u>. It is wrong to sin against others because <u>God</u> doesn't want us to sin, and that when we sin, ALL sin is against God (Psalm 51:4). I was always taught not to offend others, but I never realized that when we offend others, indirectly, we are offending God as well, because *He* doesn't want us to sin against others. So, when we do sin against others, we are sinning against God too, because we are disobeying Him, which is something I don't ever remember being taught as a child, and when I learned this, it began to change my whole outlook and attitude for the better when I would interact with others. I started to be more concerned about what *God* thought about my speech and actions, more so than what people thought. I slowly went from desiring to be a 'people-pleaser' to desiring to be a 'God-pleaser.' I later realized this is what Jesus meant when He said that 'if' you *truly* love God 'with all your heart, and with all your soul, and with all your mind' that you'll also 'love your neighbor as yourself' (Matthew 22:37-39).

On Ash Wednesday 2004, Mom and I went to see 'The Passion of the Christ.' I remember feeling tired when we went, and when the lights turned down in the theater, my eyes began to drop, but they opened quickly when the first scene came on the screen with a verse from the Old Testament:

"He was wounded for our transgressions, crushed for our iniquities; by His wounds we are healed." – Isaiah 53:5 700 B.C.[1]

That got my attention, and throughout the remainder of the movie, I don't think I blinked once. In fact, when the movie ended, and the people around me began to leave, I don't remember anyone saying a word. It was so quiet that you could literally hear a pin drop. Almost simultaneously, my Mom and I wiped the tears away from our eyes, because for the first time, I think we both truly understood 'what' Jesus did *for us*, and the incredible Personal agony and torture He had to endure – physically, emotionally, and, especially, *spiritually* – in order to accomplish that. Essentially, Jesus experienced the eternal agony, suffering, and pain of Hell *for us* on the cross, simply out of **love** for us, and because there was no other way for us to pay the eternal wrath of God for willfully sinning against Him. It also made me realize something else. The reality or myth of those events would profoundly affect what I *personally* believed. The belief (or disbelief) in the crucifixion and resurrection of Jesus isn't about 'religion,' but about whether or not they were 'real' events. If they weren't real events, then Christianity is nothing more than one of

---

[1]   *"The Passion of the Christ"* (February 25, 2004). Gibson, M. ("Director"). Icon Productions. [Film].

the thousands of religions in the world. But if they <u>were</u> real events, then Christianity isn't about 'religion,' but about *reality*. At that moment, I <u>needed</u> to know whether or not Christianity was true or not. It wasn't enough for me anymore to be satisfied with 'MY' *personal* 'opinion,' because I didn't want to believe in something false – while denying something that is true – merely for the sake of maintaining my opinion. I needed to know if it *was* true, because if it was true, then I wanted to live my life based on <u>Truth</u> from that point on and no longer on 'opinion' – even if that opinion was *mine*. And Truth (as well as faith) is based on evidence (Hebrews 11:1), not opinion [see Appendix A].

Later that year, after being 'open-minded' to the views of others that differed from my own, and objectively examining the evidence for Christianity, I came to the conclusion that historically, logically, theologically, intellectually, and most important, <u>Biblically</u>, Christianity – including the Resurrection of Jesus – *was* true, and that it wasn't 'just a bunch of stories' that contained some 'moral teachings' [see Appendix B]. I accepted the reality that the Bible and Christianity, including the Resurrection of Christ, aren't about 'religious opinion,' but about historical <u>Truth</u>. It wasn't something that anyone, including my mom, Mary Ann, Campus Crusade for Christ, or Jeannette – that 'mainstream' Protestant nurse – would be able to 'talk me into' or convince me of. It was <u>evidence</u> that only the Holy Spirit could convince and convict me of (John 16:7-8,13; cf. Hebrews 11:1), which I had to be 'willing' to be open-minded to accept, which meant acknowledging that 'my' *personal* worldview that was based on 'my' *personal* opinion 'might' not be '100% true.' Today, I realize and have accepted that my faith in the Bible and Christianity isn't based on 'my' *personal* opinion or religious worldview, nor anyone else's, but rather on the willingness to discern between 'Truth' and 'opinion.'

Needless to say, from that point on my great-grandmother's Bible in that shiny, wooden-like box was no longer protected from dust anymore, because the box was opened and it was being *used*.

Chapter One

The 'Wayside' Child

Not every child is brought up with the same experiences or exposure to the Bible and Christianity. In fact, even in Biblically-based homes, not every child has the same experiences or exposure, even *within* the same family. Some children have parents who attempt to the best of their ability to share the Gospel with all their children equally and in the same way. Others have parents who share the Gospel with their children, but for one reason or another, these parents don't 'invest' as much time with one child or another. Whatever the reason (intellectual differences between children and/or parents, motivational differences, desire or lack thereof, other parental responsibilities resulting in a lack of available time, etc), parents don't necessarily do this because they 'love one child more than the other' or desire for one child to be 'saved' over another. Christian parents <u>love</u> their children not only by feeding and protecting them *physically*, but also feeding and protecting them *spiritually*. I think this is something children who are born to Christian parents don't

1

really fully appreciate until they become parents themselves. Also, every child is different and unique, because God made them that way, because God has a unique and special purpose for each one of us. That's how involved He wants to be in our lives, which is something children of Christian parents need to really realize and appreciate how much God loves them and *wants* to be such an intimate and special part of their lives!

Why are children, in general, close to their parents when they are young? Because their parents protect them, provide for them, nurture them, and make them feel loved: they make sure they have enough to eat, they provide them shelter, they clothe them, they make them feel safe, they make them feel loved, and much more – all the necessary *physical* and *emotional* needs of a child. Now, I realize that not 'every' parent does all these things, but I'm referring to loving parents, who provides for, protects, and loves their children. However, the loving, Christian parent does all these things as well, but they do something else in addition to all this, which is extremely more important: they provide and protect their children *spiritually* as well, by sharing the Truth of the Gospel of Jesus Christ with their children, because they know that as important as providing for their child's physical and emotional needs are, their children's spiritual needs are actually *more* important. The apostle Paul writes to Timothy that physical fitness and needs are 'only of little profit, but godliness is profitable for *all* things' (emphasis added)(1 Timothy 4:8). This is because life will eventually end, as well as one's physically and emotionally fulfilled needs, but only *spiritual*, godly 'fitness' will benefit in both this world *and* the next one. Likewise, Jesus tells us 'For what does it profit a man to gain the whole world, and forfeit his soul?' (Mark 8:36). By Jesus saying that, He's not implying that physical and emotional needs aren't important and vital to life – because they *are!* However, when each of us takes our last breath and closes our eyes for the last time, even if we have received all the necessary physical and emotional needs necessary for life, none of those *earthly* needs will help us when we're standing before God, if we haven't had our *spiritual* needs met – i.e., the saving knowledge that Jesus Christ is our Lord and Savior, as well as the need to repent of our sin against God, which includes changing our desire to live for ourselves to a desire to live for Him. Christian parents are the only parents who are aware of this spiritual *need*, because they themselves accepted this need and Truth of the Gospel of Jesus Christ and the need of a Savior for <u>their</u> sin against God. So, they love their children enough to share this 'need' – the Gospel – with them.

Unfortunately, many children of Christian parents make the mistake of thinking that their parents simply want their children to "believe what *'they'* believe." However, that isn't the case at all. Christian parents want their children to accept the *Truth* of the Christian faith, because a Christian parent's faith is based on <u>evidence</u> (Hebrews 11:1), not a personal or religious opinion [see Appendices A and B]. The apostle Peter tells us that Jesus' disciples didn't just 'make up' what they were preaching about Jesus, but rather they were '<u>eyewitnesses</u> to His majesty' (2 Peter 1:16). The apostle John was also an 'eyewitness' (John 19:35; 1 John 1:1-3), as was the *unbelieving* Saul of Tarsus who later became the apostle Paul after seeing the risen Christ on the road to Damascus (Acts 9:5; 22:8; 1 Corinthians 15:8), as was James the half-brother of Jesus (1

Corinthians 15:7), and 'more than five-hundred eyewitnesses' (1 Corinthians 15:6). In addition, the entire Gospel of Luke is based on reliable and verifiable eye-witness accounts (Luke 1:1-4). In fact, Luke's account of the details in his gospel is *so* historically accurate that renowned archaeologist and historian Sir William Ramsay (1851-1939) wrote:

> "Luke's historical accuracy, supported by archaeological evidence, provides credibility to his depiction of Jesus Christ and the accuracy of his writings. Luke is a historian of the first rank; not merely are his statements of fact trustworthy, this author should be placed along with the very greatest of historians. The book of Luke is unsurpassed in respect of its trustworthiness."[1]

Considering the book of Acts, which details the history of the early first century Church, including the conversion of Saul of Tarsus who was an eyewitnesses of the resurrected Jesus on the road to Damascus (Acts 9:1-19), Ramsay went on to write:

> "Further study . . . showed that the book [Acts] could bear the most minute scrutiny as an authority for the facts of the Aegean world, and that it was written with such judgment, skill, art and perception of truth as to be a model of historical statement."[2]

---

[1] Ramsay, W. M. *The Bearing of Recent Discovery on the Trustworthiness of the New Testament,* Grand Rapids: Baker Book House, 1953

[2] Ibid, 85

"I set out to look for truth on the borderland where Greece and Asia meet, and found it there [in Acts]. You may press the words of Luke in a degree beyond any other historian's and they stand the keenest scrutiny and the hardest treatment..."[3]

To quote an excerpt from the pamphlet, 'Evidence for the Resurrection': 'If Luke was so particular about the minor details, he most likely would be just as particular about the important ones.'[4] So, a Christian parent's faith about the events of the Bible isn't based on their *personal* and religious 'beliefs,' but rather on the fact that they are *historically true* – not just 'a bunch of stories,' but *historically true* stories.

So, even though these verifiable facts and historical stories are taught to children of Christian parents, why do they suddenly decide one day to stop believing in these historical facts? Jesus tells us why, by explaining the Parable of the Four Soils (or Parable of the Sower). In Matthew 13:1-23, Jesus explains four different types of 'soils' that the 'Sower' spreads 'seeds' on. Jesus tells His disciples that the 'seed' is the 'Word of the Kingdom' (ie: the Gospel)(v.19). After He leaves the large crowds who were following Him 'superficially' (v.36), He explains that the 'Sower' is the 'Son of Man' (ie: Jesus) 'Who sows the good seed' (v.38). However, He also explains that the 'seed' falls on four different kinds of 'soil.' Just as four children can be brought up in the same home and all be taught the

---

[3] Ibid, 89

[4] *Evidence for the Resurrection,* Torrance, California: Rose Publishing, 2004

same Christian and Biblical Truth, they may also have four <u>different</u> earthly *internal* experiences when they are exposed to worldly influences.

The first 'soil,' or worldly influence that affects a child internally, involve the 'seeds' (the Gospel) that 'fell by the road, and the birds came and ate them up' (v.4). Jesus goes on later to explain that the 'birds' represent 'the enemy' (v.19), 'the enemy...the devil' (v.39), who 'snatches away what has been *sown in his heart*' (emphasis added). Another wards, these are people who not only *heard* the Gospel at one time, but also took it to *heart*. However, it was merely a 'scattering' of the Gospel that they only believed at a *superficial* level. They may have had an 'intellectual' belief in the Gospel, because they simply believed what they heard, but it was never 'sown' *permanently* in their hearts. When children are young, they tend to believe whatever they are taught by people they trust, regardless of whether it's true or false. When I was growing up, I believed what my family and religious leaders taught me about God, Jesus, and Christianity, because I had no reason to believe otherwise. I had no reason to think that what they were teaching me was anything else but the truth. It never occurred to me that they 'might' not actually know *why* they believed what they believed, which explains why when I questioned something, I was simply told, 'You just have to have faith.' Unfortunately, that sort of 'non-answer' is what actually leads children away from the Truth of the Gospel when they grow up and begin to be influenced by worldly beliefs that contradict Truth. However, as previously mentioned not 'all' children raised in the same Christian family have the same experiences, even *internal* experiences. When children begin to grow, they begin to think for themselves and develop their own beliefs about the world around them. This is actually a **good** thing, because a child's belief about anything should not be based simply on what their parents believe. A child brought up in a Muslim or atheistic family is being taught a false worldview, because it's not based on <u>Truth</u>. Likewise, even in Christian families, many times parents don't teach the Gospel accurately to their children. Sometimes they 'add' things to the Gospel, like salvation through faith in Jesus Christ AND participating in something else. This is because Christian parents are HUMAN too and are capable of being wrong, which is something their children sometimes forget or don't even realize. So, even in Christian families it's good for children to ask questions, and even doubt what they've been taught, because that demonstrates that they are desiring to learn <u>Truth</u>, not just automatically believe what they've been taught.

However, in the process of questioning what they've been taught, sometimes children go too far and are merely questioning their parents simply for the sake of questioning them. This is no longer the child pursing Truth, but rather the child willfully rebelling against their parents, which can occur at an early age, even when the child is still living at home and attending a Christian church and even a Christian school. This can happen for many reasons, even in loving Christian homes, but the primary reason is because even Christian children are *conceived* in sin (Psalm 51:5). Therefore, they have 'inherited' what's commonly known as 'original sin' from Adam, which has been passed down through their parents (Romans 5:12). Even the most fundamentally, Bible-obeying Christian child occasionally disobeys their parents, because they've inherited this 'original sin.' However, when it gets to the point that this disobedience to their parents is the result of not believing in the reality and Truth of the Gospel, then this disobedience is actually the result of not believing in <u>God</u> through His Word. Jesus stated that this *internal* disbelief is the result of 'the enemy...the devil' (Matthew 13:39) coming along and 'snatching away' the Truth of what's been taught to them (v.19). Before any *person* can negatively influence them, children have an *internal* struggle going on inside themselves, which is being influenced by the devil. I had a conversation with a friend who was raised in the same 'denomination' of Christianity that I was, but he didn't believe what I now believe about Christianity and the Bible. When I asked him what made him so sure that what he believed about God was true, he stated that he believed what his heart told him. Jeremiah 17:9 states, 'The heart is deceitful above all things, And desperately wicked; Who can know it?' (NKJV). The problem with simply 'trusting in your heart' is two-fold: First, you're trusting in something that is *internal*, which is subjective. This is called 'circular reasoning' (*"I believe that I'm right, because I believe that I can't be wrong."*) This is not being objective. Objectivity is the result of believing in something reliable that is *external* and based on verifiable evidence. Children who 'believe their heart' are basically saying that the source of truth is *themselves*. This is normal for very, young children, because they have not learned the difference between 'Truth' (which is objective) and 'opinion' (which is subjective). However, this lack of discernment should begin to fade as the child ages and begins to learn the difference. Unfortunately, for many children, this lack of discernment never fades, and their understanding between the difference between 'Truth' and 'opinion' never matures.

Also, by a child making themselves the source of all truth, they're making themselves out to be their own 'god,' because they are believing in a form of 'omniscience' (being a 'know-it-all'), which leads to believing that anyone who disagrees with them is automatically wrong, and not accepting correction – even from their parents – when they are shown that what they are believing is wrong. Unfortunately, this prideful refusal to accept correction is the result of their *temporary, intellectual* belief in the Gospel not resulting in a *permanent, spiritual* <u>acceptance</u> of the Truth of the Gospel. This type of 'hardness of heart' is what Jesus experienced from the Pharisees who refused to believe in Him and His Gospel message, by 'invalidated the word of God for the sake of *your* tradition' (emphasis added)(Matthew 15:6). We don't think of personal, internal beliefs that contradict Scripture as being 'tradition.' However, all 'tradition' is defined as is a belief or practice that isn't supported by, or contradicts, Scripture, because it's a *willful rejection and refusal to believe* in what's been taught to them. Children who refuse to believe in the Gospel taught by their Christian parents, pastors, and/or teachers are actually rebelling against God <u>Himself</u>, because "<u>ALL</u> Scripture is Inspired [*God*-breathed] by God and profitable for teaching, for *reproof,* for *correction*, for *training in righteousness*; so that the man of God may be adequate, *equipped for every good work*' (emphasis added)(2 Timothy 3:16-17). Without using Scripture as the moral guide of God to 'reprove' and 'correct' bad behavior, the child has the 'freedom' to decide what is and what is not moral, which begins by refusing to obey their parents which is a direct violation of God-breathed Scripture (Ephesians 6:1), and specifically the fifth commandment of <u>God</u> to 'honor your father and mother' (Exodus 20:12; Ephesians 6:2).

Once again, when Jesus emphasizes that when the 'seed' of the Gospel is 'scattered' on a person's heart, albeit not *permanently*, the 'source' of the Gospel being 'snatched away' is the devil (Matthew 13:19). This is because Jesus states that they didn't *truly* 'understand' what they were being taught. If they did, they wouldn't have had a reason to disbelieve it and disobey God, nor their parents. It's like someone *hearing* about gravity verses someone *understanding* what gravity is. Once you *truly* understand it, there is absolutely nothing that anyone can convince you of to make you disbelieve in gravity. The same is true with *truly understanding and believing* in the Gospel. As previously mentioned, their 'understanding' was a *temporary, intellectual* belief in the Gospel, but not a *permanent, spiritual* belief in it, which is why they rejected it later, and it is this lack of *spiritual* discernment that allows the devil to 'snatch away' the Gospel from their heart. Jesus even says about those who *truly* believe in Him, 'they will never perish; and no one will *snatch* them out of My hand' (emphasis added) (John 10:28). This is an early sign to parents that their child is not really 'in Christ,' despite being exposed to the Gospel Truth. Later in Chapter Five, we'll explain what parents can lovingly do when confronted by their children's disbelief and disobedience. The point Jesus is making, is that the reason why that 'Wayside child' didn't accept the 'seed' of the Gospel into their heart was because the child *allowed* Satan to deceive them and 'snatch away' the Gospel from them, before it was able to become a permanent part of their spiritual mindset. And this has been happening since the garden of Eden, when Satan deceived Eve into disbelieving and disobeying what God commanded her and Adam not to do (Genesis 3:1-6). So, although Adam *heard* what God had commanded him not to do, which Eve was fully *aware* of (v.2), their *willful* disbelief and disobedience to God resulted in their lack of a *spiritual, permanent* <u>understanding</u> and <u>acceptance</u> of God's command, just as the 'seeds' were 'snatched away' when 'the birds came and ate them up' (Matthew 13:4). After all, you can't truly accept and understand something you *willfully* gave away. However, Adam and Eve were still responsible for their actions, because they *heard* what God commanded them not to do, so they couldn't plead ignorance. Likewise, a child who hears the Truth of the Gospel and allows Satan – or someone else – to convince them that it isn't true, also can't plead ignorance with God, but rather is responsible to God for their disbelief and disobedience, because they heard the Truth but *chose* not to take the initiative to learn if what they were taught was indeed true. So, instead they made a choice to remain spiritually 'blind' like Pharaoh did, who *chose* to disbelieve the miracles performed by God through Moses (Exodus 7:8-11:10), because God had 'hardened his heart' (Exodus 11:10). Another wards, God doesn't 'force' His will on us, but merely makes us blatantly aware of it, so we are 'without excuse' (Romans 1:20). Likewise, when a child *chooses* to not allow the Truth of the Gospel to become a permanent part of their heart, God hardens their heart too, and allows them to remain in the 'spiritual darkness' that they love (John 3:19).

So, why do children of Christian parents choose spiritual darkness, or spiritual blindness, over spiritual Truth? As we mentioned previously and as we'll cover in another chapter, it has absolutely nothing to do with the amount of evidence available to them, but rather their spiritual *inability*, or lack of spiritual discernment, to escape their spiritual blindness. Spiritual blindness is really no different than physical blindness. When it comes to the physical world, people who are physically blind tend to believe and understand the explanations of other blind people, because they share the same experience that those without sight have – blindness. However, just because the blind share this same experience, that doesn't mean that the blind can adequately explain sight to another blind person – in fact, they can't – because they themselves don't understand sight. Therefore, they can't explain nor believe in a true understanding of sight, because they haven't ever experienced true sight themselves. Furthermore, since the blind can't understand sight, they are unable to believe something visually explained to them by those who can see, because they can't believe something they can't understand. And even if a blind person suddenly receives sight, and finally understands and believes what 'seers' have tried to explain to them when they were blind, *they* are then unable to explain sight to the blind, even though they were once blind, because even the 'former blind' can't explain true sight to those who are still blind. The same is true for those who are in spiritual blindness. They might 'think' they understand Truth, but because they are spiritually blind, they are only going to accept explanations of reality by other spiritually blind people, even though none of them can actually 'see' spiritual Truth, because they are all spiritually blind. And even when someone who was once spiritually blind can suddenly 'see,' that previously spiritually blind person is unable to explain true spiritual 'sight' to someone else who is still spiritually blind, because that person still clouded in darkness is no more capable of understanding spiritual 'sight' anymore than the person, who can now spiritually 'see,' was able to when *they* were spiritually blind. I remember when the 'veil' of spiritual blindness was removed from my eyes. I imagine that it was similar to the post-Damascus road experience that Saul of Tarsus had when he was filled with the Holy Spirit and 'immediately there fell from his eyes something like scales, and he regained his sight' (Acts 9:17-18). The 'scales' that fell, or the 'peeling away,'[5] from his physical blindness allowing him to see again, I believe is similar to what happens when someone's spiritual blindness gets 'peeled away,' and they can truly spiritually 'see' for the very first time, much like Saul. However, before that 'peeling away' occurs, it is impossible for anyone to really be able to believe in and accept the Truth of the Gospel, regardless of how much evidence or information they have access to, because only the Holy Spirit can 'peel away' those 'scales' of spiritual blindness, in much the same way that He did with Saul.

Nothing is more frustrating for a Christian parent who *knows* the Truth and intensely tries to share that Truth with their children who they love, only for them to prefer to remain in spiritual blindness by not even willing to *listen* to their parents. It's one thing to hear and reject the Truth – but it's quite another thing to not even take the time to *listen* to the

---

[5] Vine, W. E. "Scale", *Vine's Expository Dictionary of New Testament Words*. Blue Letter Bible. 24 Jun, 1996 23 Mar 2014. http://www.blbclassic.org/search/Dictionary/viewtopic.cfm?topic=VT0002486

argument. Have you ever found something out to be true and tried to tell someone about it, only for that person to reject it by not even listening to you and instead choose to believe the exact opposite? That's what I did when I refused to even *listen* to the people from Campus Crusade for Christ in the Student Union, or to Jeanette back when I was working in that Psych ICU. It wasn't just a matter of me not believing, but rather, I refused to even take the time to *listen* to what they had to say, but rather I kept my mind closed, and instead responded with anger and disbelief <u>before</u> I even heard their side of the story. This is a growing problem I've noticed with not only adult children of Christian parents who have drifted away from Christ, but also with non-christians in general. That's because when people have established a particular belief about something – regardless of whether or not that belief has any solid evidence to back it up – once that belief has 'established roots' in their mind, they begin to believe that any other belief 'must' be wrong. So they won't take the time to learn if an opposing belief has any merit, because that belief is not the belief which has already been established in their minds. When I was a child, my mom used to tell me, 'Just because you want to believe it will happen that doesn't mean it will.' Good advice, Mom! If we're honest with ourselves, all of us have had experiences and thinking like that at one time or another.

As a child, I remember I was balancing a broom between the front door and the living room of my grandparents' house, and my baby cousin was in her walking stroller, and my mom warned me that my cousin was nearby and that if I didn't stop, I was going to drop the broom, and it might hit my cousin.

However, I didn't believe her and kept doing it. Well, I dropped it, and it started falling towards my cousin. Fortunately, she moved out of the way just inches before it fell on her. Needless to say, I received a spanking, and I was sent to my room. Now, my mom had no way of knowing for certain that was going to happen, but having more common sense than I did at that time, she 'knew' what was going to happen, as opposed to my 'wishful thinking' that it wouldn't. So, why didn't I listen to my mom? Because "I" didn't believe it was going to happen, because "I" knew better, because "I" was in control of how things were going to turn out – or so I thought. It was actually an early form of rebellion that children naturally go through when they begin to exercise independence from their parents, which, again exercising independent thinking 'can' be a **good** thing. However, in this situation, that rebelliousness towards my mom could have resulted in the broom hitting my baby cousin and hurting her, which, fortunately, it didn't. Another example is a parent warning their child about looking both ways before crossing a busy intersection. Technically, there is no way of a parent knowing that their child is definitely going to get hit by a car if they don't look, but the likelihood that they won't is slim to none. And if a child doesn't listen to the wisdom of their parent, they have an extremely high risk of getting hit – or worse. However, the consequence of a child not even *listening* to their parents about the Truth of the Gospel, but instead being 'hard-hearted' like Pharaoh and the Pharisees and 'doing their own thing' is far worse than receiving a spanking for disobeying and eternally more fatal than getting hit by a car. But, just as I 'knew' that I wouldn't drop that broom and that my mom was wrong, and the child who 'knows' that they won't get hit by a car crossing a busy intersection and not believing their parent, likewise, the child who refuses to listen to the Truth of the Gospel from their Christian parent, because they 'know' it's not true is basing their disbelieve and disobedience on nothing more than their *personal* opinion, rather than on evidence. But, just as not believing in my mom about the broom and the child not believing in their parent and crossing the busy intersection anyway wasn't worth it, is 'exchanging the truth of God for a lie' (Romans 1:25) and 'suppressing the truth' (v.18) for simply the prideful sake of holding onto 'my' beliefs, really worth it in terms of eternity?

One last related point to bring up in this chapter is that another reason why children of Christian parents have abandoned the faith is because many of them really don't seem to care. And they don't care, because if their rejection of the Truth of the Gospel doesn't have immediate consequences, they don't think their disobedience, disbelief, and rebellion actually affects them, because they can't 'see' the consequences in the *present*. And even if they think it 'might' affect them, they think that if their disbelief doesn't affect other people, then 'what harm is it doing?' And if it's not doing any harm, then they perceive that their parent and others are just trying to 'interfere' in their lives, that they are trying to 'control' what they believe, and that they should just 'mind their own business.' However, as previously mentioned their disbelief *does* affect them and <u>will</u> have enormous, negative, and eternal consequences that will never end. Also, as mentioned in the Prologue, their disbelief *does* affect other people, like their parents, their relationship with their Christian friends, and most importantly their relationship with God, which is the most important relationship they will ever have. I have personally witnessed the intense and deep sorrow of Christian parents dealing with the reality of their children, who they have nurtured, loved, and shared the Truth of the Gospel with them, only for their children to abandon the faith.

I was talking with my beloved Lucia ("Pusa") the other day about children of Christian parents who abandon the faith despite being exposed to all the evidences that God and Christianity are true, and she pointed out that when they claim to not believe in them anymore, they aren't truly convinced and confident in their disbelief. Essentially, Pusa was saying that, in reality, their 'disbelief' is actually the result of them reacting emotionally and subjectively, rather than intellectually and objectively. Another wards, after being exposed to all the evidence for the Truth for the existence of God and the reality of Christianity, logically, they honestly shouldn't come to the conclusion that God and Christianity are false or 'just a bunch of stories,' *if* they were truly basing their decision from an intellectual and objective point of view. This will be covered in more depth in Chapter Three, when I give an example of a child of a well-known Christian parent, who abandoned the faith – not because of a lack of evidence, but because for emotional reasons, which is clear from her 'deconversion testimony,' even if she didn't realize it when she deconverted or when she wrote it. Basically, these children have what Pusa calls an 'insincere atheism' towards the Biblical God, because although they claim to not believe in Him for intellectual and objective reasons, the actual reasons that they give for their deconversion is actually based on either a lack of understanding of the evidence that was never truly rooted in

17

their heart (which we'll cover more in Chapter Two), or their deconversion is more likely influenced by their self-perceived, unfulfilled desires or 'wants' not being met from their Christian upbringing which they attempt (unsuccessfully) to try to 'fill' with temporary, worldly desires and wants (which we'll cover more in Chapter Three). So, it's not that they suddenly discovered and embraced a worldview that is more 'real' or more 'true' than Christianity, but rather they embrace an 'insincere atheism' towards Christianity that is based on nothing more than unfulfilled wants and desires. And what makes it 'insincere' is when they are questioned about 'why' they abandoned the faith, the reasons they give aren't really intellectual, objective reasons, but rather emotionally-based and subjective. This is why the apostle Paul said they *'suppress the truth'* (emphasis added)(Romans 1:18). So, it's not a matter of them not being *exposed* to the Truth, but rather they flat out *reject* it, no matter how much evidence they have been exposed to from their Christian upbringing. This happened once when I spoke with a woman who claimed to have a Christian upbringing, but is now a professed atheist. But when I asked her how the universe came into existence without God (the same question I pondered on when I was in college, before becoming a Christian), and when she gave the common atheist answer – a black hole 'created' the universe – after I explained the logical problems with that 'theory' (which the scope of this book doesn't allow me to go into), she had no answer for me, and quickly backed down on her accusation that Christians like me are 'anti-science' – which we're not. So, rather than accept that the Bible and Christianity have a much, more logical explanation for the existence of the universe, which King David describes 'the heavens are telling of the glory of God,' which 'night to night reveals knowledge' (Psalm 19:1-2), and the apostle Paul states 'His invisible attributes, His eternal power and divine nature, have been clearly seen, being understood through what has been made, so that they are without excuse' (Romans 1:20), she willfully chose to 'suppress the truth' (v.18) and 'exchanged the truth of God for a lie' (v.25) – the lie of atheism (as well as other non-christian worldviews), which their emotional, subjective decision affects not only them, but also others who have raised, nurtured, and loved them in the Truth. We'll cover this conversation with my co-worker in more depth in 'Point Seven' of Chapter Six.

Unfortunately, even if they realize their disbelief does affect other people, once they have abandoned the faith, then they have accepted that they aren't 'bound' to it anymore, so they are free to abandon the conviction of being concerned about how their actions and disbelief affect other people as well – including their parents. They simply don't care anymore, because they don't have a *reason* to, because, now, life is "all about *'me.'*" Now, I'm not implying that they have necessarily become heartless, antisocial narcissists. Rather, they no longer have any moral boundaries *outside* their own that they've established for themselves, which can – and will – result in enormous consequences not only to themselves, but also other people, which we will explore in more depth in Chapter Three. They become so focused on themselves and fulfilling their own needs and wants – including acquiring them from other people, if necessary – that they don't feel that they have the responsibility to do the same for others *unless* it will somehow benefit them. This is called manipulation, which a child learns at a very early age, which they 'should' grow out of. Unfortunately, for this 'soil' of child they don't, and this childish way of manipulating others extends into adulthood and into their adult relationships, which can cause serious and even permanent, life-long problems, even with *their* own children. The problem that they don't 'see' is that most of the time, their actions, which is the result of their rejection of Christian Truth, don't have *immediate* consequences, and if they don't see it, they won't accept that it'll happen to them. 'It won't happen to *me*.' I remember talking to a lady in her early twenties who had been smoking cigarettes since her mid- to late teens, who was aware of the dangers of long-term smoking, including the extreme addicting power it has, especially after numerous years of use. Her response was that those dangers would never happen to her, because she doesn't intend on smoking that long, and that she can quit at any time. I responded to her by saying, 'If that's true, than why can't you quit right now?' She said she could if she wanted to. I responded with, 'Okay, then since you can, then quit right now.' In the middle of the puff on her drag, she attempted to respond, but nothing came out of her mouth except smoke. She realized that at that moment, she didn't want to, but what she may not have accepted (or maybe realized) was that the real reason was because she *couldn't*. She has already become addicted to a substance that she didn't think could control *her*. That was a few years ago, and at the writing of this book, she is still smoking. This same lack of seeing the *immediate* consequences of rejecting the Truth of the Gospel is also true. Since they can't 'see' the long-term and permanent negative effects it has on their relationship with God, then they don't believe that they have anything to worry about. However, consequences aren't always immediate, such as the consequences of smoking.

And when the consequences do begin to surface, such as lung cancer, by then, it's too late to reverse the damage. Likewise, when the consequences of rejecting the Truth of the Gospel surface, it's too late. Just as the time to stop smoking is 'now,' the time to accept the Truth of the Gospel is <u>now</u>, which is why the apostle Paul said, *"Now* is the day of salvation" (emphasis added)(2 Corinthians 6:2), because we have no guarantee in life of anything beyond our next breath. 'Tomorrow' may never come.

Chapter Two

The 'Rocky' Child

E ven if children initially embrace the Truth of the Gospel, that doesn't mean they will continue to embrace it. I have had the benefit and privilege of attending numerous different 'denominations' of Christian churches and services (Catholic, Greek Orthodox, Lutheran, Baptist, Presbyterian, Pentecostal, Evangelical, Messianic-Judaism, 'non-denominational,' etc) – I even attended a wedding once between a Christian man and a Jewish woman. And what I have learned by attending ALL of them, is that no matter how doctrinally sound the teaching of the Gospel is in a church or service, and no matter how 'involved' a child is in that church, the child still has to realize three things: one, their *need* of a Savior and 'why' they need Him; two, their 'need' for this Savior to also be their <u>Lord</u>; and three, that becoming a *genuine* Christian is accompanied by hardships.

When I first accepted the Truth of the Gospel in August 2004 and accepted Jesus Christ as my Savior and Lord, it felt like

I was suddenly able to 'see' in a much more clearer way that seemed like I had just had 'spiritual blindness' removed from my soul. The only way I can describe it, is that all the things about God, Jesus, and the Bible, as well as all the doctrinal and social issues related to them that I didn't agree with when I wasn't a Christian, it all suddenly made sense and was clear as a bell. It was like a light turned on inside my soul. I could 'see' clearer now, and couldn't understand why I didn't 'get it' before. And for the first time, I was really willing and able to understand the difference between 'opinion' and 'Truth,' which so many Christians over the years had attempted to explain to me which, at that time, I neither wanted to, nor was able to, accept it. The apostle Paul describes that when a person *truly* accepts Christ as their Savior AND Lord, that Christ lifts a 'veil' from their heart (2 Corinthians 3:14-15). A 'veil,' in this sense, is a 'covering' which prevents something from being 'seen' and understood. One of the things that is understood when Christ removes this 'veil,' is when a person accepts Him as Savior AND Lord, is that the Christian life isn't going to be necessarily easy. In reality, our new-found faith will be tested to see if it's genuine, and, unfortunately, what I've witnessed is that many times, Christians – including children of Christian parents – have no problem accepting Jesus as *Savior*, but have difficulty in accepting Him as *Lord*. By 'Lord,' that actually means 'Master' over every aspect of our lives – our actions, speech, thoughts, *and* attitudes. The writer of Hebrews states that God is 'able to judge the thoughts and intentions of the heart' (Hebrews 4:12). So, it isn't enough to just '*act* Christian,' but also to '*think* Christian.' Scripture states that God is 'all-knowing' (1 John 3:20) and that Jesus 'knew all men' (John 2:24). So, a child who thinks they can somehow 'trick' God into believing that their heart is right with Him by 'acting good' is only fooling themselves. There is a level of commitment that God, through His written word, expects out of those who *truly* commit themselves to Him. Obviously, God doesn't expect perfection, because that is impossible for anyone, except Jesus who never sinned (2 Corinthians 5:21), which is 'why' we need a Savior. However, God expects us to 'desire' to be committed to Him, even under the most excruciating of trials, and unfortunately this is where the faith of many children of Christian parents waver and grow cold.

During my first experience in a Biblically-based Christian church [and by 'Biblically-based,' that means they believe and preach in the 'sufficiency' of the Bible for the teaching of Christian doctrine (2 Timothy 3:16), including salvation (John 3:16; Ephesians 2:8-9)], there was a LOT that you could get involved in. In fact, it was encouraged, and missions were an important theme and part of church life and exposure to the congregation. After only attending the church for a little over a year, I became a member of the Missions Committee, and after another year, I became the Chairman (of course, I believe this mainly occurred because there were only THREE of us on the committee at that point). It was a tremendous responsibility, a humbling privilege and honor, and I learned invaluable information about what happens in the missions field, including how missionaries are chosen and what kind of experiences they have – both good and bad. Unfortunately, what I began to see was that some children who were brought up in Christian families had a somewhat 'overly glorified' and 'romantic' impression of what missions was about. Missionary work is '<u>rock</u>'-<u>hard</u> <u>work</u>. It's more than just 'witnessing' to people and 'leading others to Christ' in the missions field. There is a lot of preparatory work that's involved before even stepping foot into it, and once there, there's a lot of 'culture shocks,' as well as other unforeseen and unplanned experiences that you don't always expect. And most of these 'Christian kids' were no older than thirteen or fourteen years old (in some extraordinary cases, even younger!), so to this day, I have a tremendous amount of admiration and respect for them, and I am indebted to that church for allowing me to be a part of that godly experience in serving our Lord in missions. I was never personally a missionary myself, but I can tell you that when missionaries came back, they were often ecstatic about their experience, especially if they led someone to the Lord, but they also explained the hardships they went through being in a completely different country and culture for the first time in their lives, and for many of them, away from their families for the first time. Some of them even began to doubt their own faith being away from the comforts from their home and church life. Now, I'm not saying this to minimize the joy or necessity of missionary work, because it IS joyful when you realize that everything you are doing on the mission field is for the Lord and is glorifying Him (1 Corinthians 10:31). However, for many Christian children who have grown up in a sort of 'Christian worldview bubble,' the hardships experienced on the mission field for the first time, can test the faith of children who haven't *legitimately* and *genuinely* accepted Jesus as Lord.

The second 'soil' that Jesus taught about was the 'seed' that 'fell on rocky places, where they did not have much soil' (Matthew 13:5). This kind of 'soil' is very shallow, atop a layer of bedrock, where a seed is able to spring up quickly, but it 'has no depth of soil.' And when the sun comes out, it scorches it and it 'withers away' (v.6). Jesus explained later that people who hear the Gospel 'immediately receives it with joy' (v.20), but because their faith has no 'firm root,' it is only 'temporary' when 'affliction or persecution arises' and they 'immediately fall away' (v.21). I've personally seen in Christian churches, children who get excited about the 'life' of missionaries, being a pastor, elder, or deacon in the church, a pastor's or deacon's wife, or other 'church life.' Now, it's a wonderful thing to be 'fired up for the Lord.' After all, God wants us to be that way towards Him. However, the reality about 'church life' isn't all a bed of roses. It also comes with the enemy attacking us at every corner, attempting to make our commitment to the Lord as difficult as possible. Satan does this, because he knows that when a person *truly* accepts Christ, they have just been released from the 'domain of darkness' (Colossians 1:13), and Satan has just lost another soul from the pits of eternal Hell and damnation. Therefore, Satan works overtime to prevent any other souls from making that 'escape.' So, for children who haven't *truly* accepted Jesus as their Savior AND Lord yet, they are tested with trials to see if their commitment to Christ is real or not.

The 'large crowds' who followed Jesus never really believed <u>in Him</u> (Matthew 13:2), which is why He 'left them' (v.36), and why even many of His Own disciples 'withdrew and were not walking with Him anymore' (John 6:66). They had no problem following Jesus when it was beneficial for them and for Him to be their <u>Savior</u>, but the moment He taught something they couldn't really understand or accept, they abandoned Him, because accepting Him as their <u>Lord</u> meant changing their lifestyle or mindset, which was too 'difficult' for them (v.60). Likewise, children of Christian parents who make a *temporary* emotional, 'surface-level,' superficial 'commitment' to the Lord, when 'afflictions and persecutions arise' they 'fall away' from the faith, because the 'true' Gospel never took 'firm root' in their souls, and never transformed their lives. When this happens, this demonstrates that they only understood 'half' of the Gospel message – the 'accepting Jesus as *Savior*' part, but not the 'accepting Jesus as *Lord*' part. This includes the reality that a child is going to experience, which they perceive as 'disappointments' from God, when they experience something bad, and then pray to God for 'fix' it, but don't feel that God has heard them and didn't answer their prayer *on 'their' terms.* However, this 'genie-like-god' mentality of the One True God Who 'fixes' things just because we pray to Him, is a false form of Christianity. When Jesus was on earth, although He performed many miracles, His *primary* purpose and will was to **preach** (Mark 1:34-39) and 'seek and save that which is lost' (Luke 19:10) – *spiritually* – not 'fix' and 'heal' people *physically* or *mentally*. Likewise, God's will isn't necessarily to 'fix' the evil injustices and ailments in the world 'now,' but rather to 'cleanse us from all unrighteousness,' through our ONLY 'Advocate with the Father, Jesus Christ the <u>righteous</u>' (1 John 1:7-2:22). So, when children experience what they consider an 'injustice' that has occurred to them, and their prayers aren't answered, they feel God has abandoned them, become 'angry with God,' and feel that since He's abandoned them, in retaliation, they have decided to abandon Him, by no longer obeying, or even believing in, Him. However, the God of the Bible **never** 'abandons' anyone. He is with us even in our most darkest hours, God has promised us that He 'will never leave you nor forsake you' (Hebrews 13:5)(NKJV). However, because children can't 'see' God experiencing their personal strife and trials that they're experiencing, they don't believe He is actually there, so then one day they just decide to stop obeying, and even stop believing in, Him. Unfortunately, this is something that is very common in the Christian church. Ray Comfort and Kirk Cameron on their television program 'Way of the Master' had a segment called 'Hell's Best Kept Secret,' where they talked about the 'Fall Away Rate' of Christians who 'make a decision for Christ,' 'say a sinner's prayer,' or 'make an altar call,' only later to completely walk away from the faith. This is somewhat of a paraphrase of one of the facts that were made in the program:

> "80-90% of those who are making 'decisions' for Christ are now 'falling-away' from the faith…. A major denomination in the U.S. was able to obtain 294,000 'decisions' for Christ…unfortunately they could only find 14,000 in fellowship, which means they couldn't account for 280,000 of their decisions."[1]

The apostle John tells us that, unlike the predestined 'elect,' they were never *truly* converted, because they were 'not really of us' (1 John 2:19). This is because false converts are normally attracted to the 'saving part' of the Gospel, but aren't initially told about the 'dying-to-self part' of the Gospel and becoming a 'new creature,' who 'no longer lives for themselves' (Romans

---

[1] Ray Comfort and Kirk Cameron, *Way of the Master: Hell's Best Kept Secret*, Living Waters Publication, (television program). http://www.livingwaters.com/outreach/the-way-of-the-master

6:1-8; 2 Corinthians 5:15-17). As a result, they eventually 'fall-away' from the faith. As Mom has always said, it appears easy to 'become' a Christian, but it's a lot harder to 'live' as a Christian. The problem lies with a false understanding of what it truly means to be a Christian. Being *truly* devoted to Christ means that you're going to give up some things like false self-beliefs in 'Who' God is, and even experience losing some things, including possibly friendships. The apostle Paul stated 'For to me, to live is Christ and to die is gain' (Philippians 1:21). He understood the eternal benefit and wondrous joy of trusting in Christ and putting Him FIRST above all other things and relationships. Jesus even stated, 'They will be divided, father against son and son against father, mother against daughter and daughter against mother, mother-in-law against daughter-in-law and daughter-in-law against mother-in-law' (Luke 12:53). Jesus even said He came to bring '<u>division</u>' (v.51), but a division which results in the unification of the *true* family of God, which will last for all eternity. However, when it comes to 'giving up' something, unfortunately, that's not a very popular concept to accept, especially if it involves 'giving up' one's personal belief system. But, that's because children of Christian parents don't truly understand the eternal 'gain' that Paul was talking about. They can't fully comprehend that 'momentary, light affliction is producing for us an eternal weight of glory far beyond all comparison' (2 Corinthians 4:17), because they desire to only 'see' the things that are 'temporal' that won't last (v.18). So, when persecution comes – whether literal persecution or in the form of someone verbally 'persecuting' us for our faith – the uncommitted child many times will 'give in' to peer pressure, because 'everyone is doing it' (which in reality not 'everyone' is), rather than obey God and their Christian parents. Anything worthwhile involves sacrifice, including true commitment and conversion, because when we sacrifice something eternally worth<u>less</u>, we gain something eternally worth<u>while</u> – 'citizenship in Heaven' (Philippians 3:20).

Still, this is hard to accept, because children can't 'see' the end result, and they value their lifestyle, friendships, and mindset so much, they don't want to give them up – even for something they <u>know</u> is true. It's 'too much' to give up. Since becoming a Christian, I have experienced loss in many ways, including friendships I've had for over twenty-five-plus years, *because* of my faith. And even 'some' of my family have even 'distanced' themselves from me, because they don't share my desire for the Truth of the Gospel and the Bible (or perhaps because I don't share 'their' *personal, subjective* 'opinions' about God and Heaven). However, what I have 'gained' are such enriching and rewarding friendships and relationships with my 'heavenly family' – those who have also accepted Jesus as their Savior AND Lord – that I wouldn't want any other kind of intimate relationship that doesn't involve Christ at the center of that relationship. And in terms of eternity, I'd much rather have fellowship with them, than to reject Christ and have fellowship with those particular friends and family from my 'old life,' because when I take my last breath and close my eyes for the last time, all that will matter is 'who' (and more importantly '**W**ho') I'll be spending eternity with. Now, I'm not implying that a Christian shouldn't be friends, nor associate, with non-christians. All I'm saying is that Christian relationships are exponentially more fulfilling – spiritually – in the long run in sharing the same faith with other Christians, because that faith has eternal rewards, both presently and in the future, that are completely void in non-christian beliefs found in non-christian relationships. So, I'm experiencing a little 'piece of Heaven' on earth right now through those relationships that I never experienced in my former ones, albeit not a perfect experience, since I still have to experience trials and tribulations every single day. But when I put into perspective what I have to look forward to, those trials and tribulations are more than tolerable. If the apostles could endure *literal* persecution, imprisonment, torture, and even death like James (Acts 12:2) and Paul (2 Corinthians 11:23-27) did for something they <u>knew</u> to be true, I think we can endure those daily 'momentary, light afflictions' for Christ's sake – and, ultimately, for our own sakes.

When I was reading about the 'seeds' that fell on the rocky places in Matthew's Gospel, I thought about a friend of mine (out of respect for him, he'll remain nameless) who I shared the Gospel with several years ago, when my faith was still in its infancy. His only 'religious' background that I knew of at the time was Mormonism on his mother's side and practically atheism on his father's side. Beyond that, I really didn't know anything about his personal religious or worldviews – that wasn't something we really discussed. At that time, he was going through some real personal trials in his life, and it was the first time I had ever seen him cry, because in one particular area in his life, he had felt like a complete failure. We have all had those kind of moments – some more serious than others. I knew my friend needed my love and support, so I took him out for lunch one day and sat there and just listened (Mom used to tell me, 'you have two ears for listening and only one mouth for talking, and there's a reason God made us that way').

Even if a friend can't solve your problems for you, sometimes all you need is just for them to listen to you unload and rant about whatever is going on. After he unloaded, I felt that God had given me a window to witness to him, because he *needed* the best Friend anyone could ever ask for. Just prior to His crucifixion, Jesus referred to His disciples as 'friends' (John 15:15). However, just one verse before that, Jesus 'defined' the kind of friendship <u>He</u> had established with them – one that involved doing 'what I command you' (v.14). Now, on the surface, that doesn't sound like such a great friendship. However, Jesus was acknowledging that friendship with Him is a two-way street that involves sacrifice for each other. Jesus' sacrificed *Himself* – the 'greater love' - to atone for the sins of His 'friends' (v.13), while He expected His disciples to sacrifice anything (and everything) for Him – including their own livelihood and putting up with ridicule and persecution for His sake. (Personally, I think His disciples got the better end of the deal!)

After I shared the Gospel with my friend, he started going to the church I was attending, the weekly Bible study that I still attend, and he even got a shave and cleaned up his act. For the first time, literally in years, since I had known him, he was filled with real joy – joy that could have only come from our Lord. He really seemed to enjoy his 'new found faith.' He was meeting new people – people who loved Christ, and welcomed him at church with a sincere smile and a genuine outstretched hand of friendship. He really seemed to embrace it, and he and I were having deep theological discussions about Christianity that we had never had before in the history of our friendship. And I know that it was God working in his heart. He had even gotten a new job – a better job, in terms of income. Jesus told His disciples, 'that whatever you ask of the Father in My name He may give to you' (John 15:16). Of course, I was quick to point out to him that that doesn't mean that you can treat God like some sort of 'grant-me-three-wishes genie.' That's <u>not</u> the God of the Bible. Rather, God does answer our prayers, provided that those prayers are <u>God</u>-centered and will glorify <u>Him</u> and that we continue to obey Him (John 14:13-15). Looking back, maybe the 'newness' of his Christian 'experience' and the new job made Christianity appear thrilling. I think about the 'fall-away rate' that Ray Comfort and Kirk Cameron talked about on their show that was mentioned earlier. Not only was he experiencing something new, God had also provided a new, better-paying career for him, simply out of love for him, and so that <u>He</u> could be glorified. However, as Jesus warned with the 'seeds' that fell on rocky soil, although 'immediately they sprang up, because they had no depth of soil,' because 'they had no root, they withered away' (Matthew 13:5-6). Unfortunately, slowly over time, my friend's new-found faith began to 'wither away.' I began to see him coming to church less and less, until he completely stopped coming altogether. I even stopped hearing from him for awhile, until he lost his job, and he started coming to church – sporadically – and them tapered off completely again. A couple of years later, he told me that, truthfully, he didn't really believe everything in the Bible, but when I asked him, 'what' he didn't believe in, like most skeptics, it involved specific things about Scripture that contradicted his lifestyle and personal beliefs. He also admitted it was a faith issue (or lack thereof). Like the 'large crowds' who had 'superficially' followed Jesus, and simply had a surface-level 'commitment' which is why He 'left them' (v.36), despite initially 'springing up' with joy, my friend had not planted 'firm roots' in his soul (v.20-21), and like some of Jesus' disciples 'withdrew and were not walking with Him anymore' (John 6:66), so did my friend.

I think sometimes when 'immediate' results come from praying to God for what a person 'thinks' they need, sometimes that gives a person an initial false first impression of what being a 'follower' of Christ really means. There is actually quite a bit of heartache, sacrifice, ridicule, and persecution in being a *genuine* believer in Christ. And I think when God allowed some of what He gave my friend to be taken away, he may not have known how to handle that 'affliction.' His family weren't Biblically-based Christians either, so I don't know how much 'persecution' he was receiving from them. In some ways, he also falls under the 'seed' that fell among thorns (Matthew 13:7) - which will be covered in the next chapter - because he also got 'choked out' by the cares, riches, pleasures, and 'worry of the world and deceitfulness of wealth' (v.22). I hear from him every now and then, and when I do, he shares stories with me about the direction of his life, which deep down, I know he realizes those things aren't things that are God-honoring, but he does them anyway. Unfortunately, he has drifted back into his old lifestyle and mindset. However, he has never stopped being my friend, and I love him like a brother, and I pray <u>constantly</u> for him, because he is piling up mounds of spiritual 'debt,' that he will one day have to account for when he stands before God – just as we all will. The only difference is that he doesn't have an 'Advocate' standing in his place *for him* – 'Jesus Christ the righteous' (1 John 2:1), because he never *truly* repented for his sin against God that eternally separates us from Him. And because he had been exposed to the Truth, he won't be able to plead ignorance before God (Romans 1:20), but rather, God's wrath will be even more intense and carry a heavier burden (v.18). I can't help thinking about the words of warning from our Lord to the hypocritical scribes and Pharisees, regarding the fact that because they had *access* to the Truth – which Paul and Stephen described as them being 'entrusted with the oracles of God' (Romans 3:1-2; cf. Acts 7:38)(and were supposed to be accurately teaching and practicing it, but weren't), their 'condemnation' in Hell would be 'greater' (Matthew 23:14)[2] – even moreso than 'for the land of Sodom and Gomorrah in the day of judgment' (Matthew 10:15), which will occur at the 'Great White Throne' Judgment, when they will be 'judged from the things written in the books, according to their deeds' (Revelation 20:12). And that's because <u>ALL</u> sins – including sins against other people - are sins against <u>God</u> (Psalm 51:4; cf. Roman 3:23), and sin <u>needs</u> to be dealt with by a Just God.

So, did my friend actually believe about Jesus, the crucifixion, and His atonement for our sins? At an intellectual, superficial, 'surface-level' understanding, yes. However, believing in something *intellectually* is quite different from believing in something that is 'sown' *in your heart*, because believing in something in your heart requires a *change of your heart* (emphasis added)(Romans 6:1-8). Just because someone has intellect and believes in the 'facts' that are in Scripture

---

[2] Matthew 23:14 – although this verse is not found in the earliest Greek manuscripts, and probably not part of the original text, what Jesus taught about 'greater condemnation' in Hell is a true teaching found elsewhere in Scripture (Matthew 10:15; Revelation 20:12; etc.)

doesn't automatically make them a Christian or that that will prevent them from going to Hell *when* they die. As Pastor Craig Groeschel point out, "Belief isn't the same as personal knowledge."[3] In fact, Paul warns us that 'professing to be wise, they became fools' (Romans 1:22). Rather, a change of heart as the result of *genuine* repentance and faith in Christ (Acts 3:19; 10:43) – not an 'intellectual, superficial acceptance' of the words in Scripture – will lead to salvation from eternal damnation. And the sign to others, and most importantly to God, that repentance and faith in Christ is genuine, is evidenced **BY** a person's outward actions, or 'works' (emphasis added)(James 2:18), albeit not the *means* of salvation, which is the shed blood of Christ on the cross. Unfortunately, my friend's outwards works, especially as of late, aren't evidence to others nor to God that his 'faith' is genuine. I pray that my friend *truly* repents and gives His life over to Christ, so his 'load' will be placed on Jesus' shoulders, instead of his. Eternity is long time to be wrong.

God also doesn't want a relationship with us on '*our* terms' or 'in *our* own way,' but on His. It's commonly said that the 'god' that people tend to believe in and worship is a god who condones their thoughts, speech, behavior, and attitude, rather than those of the 'One *True* God.' That is one of the many areas where Christianity is unique to every other religion. Most other religions base 'right' and 'wrong' and acceptance into Heaven, or a better 'reincarnated' life, based on the person following a certain set of 'rules' that the

---

[3] Craig Groeschel, *"The Christian atheist: believing in God but living as if he doesn't exist,"* p. 33. Grand Rapids, MI: Zondervan, 2010

individual shares and agrees with. Another wards, one of the main reasons a person is attracted to a 'god' of a particular religion is because they *already* believe in the same 'rules' of that religion and that 'god' – including the 'non-organized' religion of *self* - even if those rules contradict the rules of another religion and another 'god' that their family or friends believe in. Where Christianity is unique is that becoming 'righteous,' attaining salvation, and entering Heaven <u>when</u> we die, has nothing to do with sharing a mutual belief in the 'rules' of Christianity or the Christian God. Rather, we don't become *self*-righteous, but instead, *God makes us righteous.* For example, God *declared* that Noah was righteous (Genesis 7:1), and that he had 'found favor in the eyes of God' (Genesis 6:9). But Scripture doesn't specify what particular 'criteria' that God used to declare Noah righteous, nor what strict 'rules' that Noah followed in order to find favor with Him. However, verse nine does say that Noah 'walked with God.' This phrase 'walked with God' was also used in the previous chapter to describe Enoch's relationship with God (Genesis 5:24). In that genealogy from Adam to Noah and his three sons, Enoch is the *only* person who 'God took' without experiencing death. The writer of Hebrews states that before Enoch was 'taken up he was pleasing to God' (Hebrews 11:5).

What had Enoch done to please God? The very next verse tells us: 'without *faith* it is impossible to please Him' (emphasis added)(v.6). So, the reason both Enoch and Noah 'walked with God' and were declared righteous, isn't because of what they *did*, but because of 'Who' they *believed* in. They <u>trusted</u> what *God* said was true, rather than trust in their *own* beliefs about their *own* 'version' of a personal god. In Proverbs 3:5,

King Solomon writes, 'Trust in the LORD with all your heart and do not lean on your own understanding.' It wasn't because they followed a set of 'rules' that God laid out, but because they *believed* God in the way <u>He</u> wanted them to trust and believe in Him. That is also why God 'credited' Abraham 'as righteousness,' because Abraham *believed* God (Romans 4:3). I was at a funeral once, and the daughter (who was a Christian) was giving a very sweet, humble, and heart-felt eulogy for her lovingly and dearly departed mother. However, she stated that her mother 'worshiped God in her *own* way.' The reason this is so disheartening is because, as mentioned previously, that isn't the kind of relationship God wants – nor expects – from us. God desires a relationship in '<u>His</u> *own* way.' Unfortunately, many times this is how people – including people who refer to themselves as 'Christian' – view their relationship with God the Father and Jesus. They 'set the ground rules' with God exactly 'how' their relationship with Him is going to go. A husband who tells his wife, 'I'm going to love you, but only on *my* terms' isn't truly demonstrating unconditional love. Rather, it's demonstrating that his affection towards her is going to be based on a set of 'rules' that the spouse must either meet or accept, and if she doesn't, she just has to live with it. Marriages like that don't last very long, because either the spouse who was given the conditions leaves, or they remain and live a loveless marriage. So regarding Christ and His Church, why would 'His bride' (Revelation 19:7) even begin to think that God would accept a relationship with Him based on '*our* terms' or 'in *our* own way' instead of on <u>His</u>? Unfortunately, I've witnessed many people – even in the Church – 'accept' God, but only on the 'condition' that it doesn't involve having to admit to others that they are specifically worshipers of the

Jesus of the Bible, because they are afraid of the 'persecution,' in the form of ridicule and even distancing of family and close friends, that they'll receive from others.

Sadly, I've even seen people in the Church begin to pick up worldly bad habits from their secular friends, including using God the Father and Jesus' Names as four-letter filth words, and not feel any remorse, in order to 'fit in.' Instead of them being a 'light of the world' (Matthew 5:14) to lead others towards Christ, they are allowing others to lead *them away* from Him. Yet, they still consider themselves to be a committed follower of Jesus, but as Pastor Craig Groeschel correctly points out, 'The way you address him or refer to him just might reveal the depth of your intimacy. Or lack of it.'[4] This is a major problem that I have witnessed with children in the Church lately. They claim to have a 'personal relationship' with Christ, as well as use other 'Christian lingo,' but still feel the need to go along with the crowd in order to avoid 'affliction and persecution' from their friends – including, oddly, with other children in the Church! However, if they actually have a 'personal relationship' with Christ, that would be reflected in their speech and testimony for Christ to their friends as well. And as Pastor Craig also points out, "If you know God, you are likely to be far more specific with him, and the words you use will reflect your accurate understanding of him.... What do you call God? Your answer may be a clue to how well you know him. Or don't."[5]

---

[4] Ibid, p.40

[5] Ibid, p.42

Sometimes persecution and personal affliction can be perceived from coming from the child's spiritual leaders and even from the child's own Christian parents themselves. I realize this is a sensitive and controversial subject, but it is a reality that I have heard many children bring up. I heard and saw this a lot when I worked in psychiatry. Many of the inpatient children there didn't always have the best relationship with their parents, and I don't recall very many of them expressing any real relationship with Jesus Christ, or even God in general, even if their parents did. So, I don't think it's reasonable to assume that children raised in a Christian family automatically have a wonderful relationship with their spiritual leaders or parents. One thing I learned is that when you hear a complaint about someone from someone, to remember that there are two sides to every story…and in-between those two stories, the truth is in the middle there somewhere. In a child's mind, sometimes affliction and persecution can be perceived as a parent being 'too strict' from the child's point of view. And sometimes, when the child prays to God for help, and He doesn't seem to be listening, or caring, the child begins to lose the faith that their parents and spiritual leaders have taught them to be true. And when the very people who are teaching you something that *they* believe to be true (even if it is true), and then they are perceived by the child as being 'un-christlike' in their speech, actions, or attitude towards their child, that can lose credibility in not only their relationship with their child, but also lose credibility for their witness for Christ to the child as well. Now, I'm not implying that problems between Christian parents and children are <u>always</u> the parent's fault. Rather, I'm trying to get across that parents need to be aware of the *perception* that the child is having towards the parent's reactions, and for the parent to inquire and clarify any misperceptions – or even real perceptions – that the child is experiencing. In Chapter Five, we'll be exploring some solid Biblical ideas and commands from our Lord, and how to implement them in order to establish, or reestablish, the relationship between the Christian parent and their unbelieving child.

Lastly, children of Christian parents may not always be 'well-equipped' to deal with the persecutions and ridicule of the world, when they experience them. This can sometimes be the result of Christian parents keeping their children in what, again, my mom calls a 'Christian bubble,' which will be explored more in the next chapter. When a child is 'safe' in a tight-knit Christian community, they aren't exposed to the ridicule and persecution of society that's run by 'the god of this world' (ie: Satan)(2 Corinthians 4:4), as other children are. However, when they get out in the 'real world,' they may know everything they have learned about Christianity and the Bible, but they may not now how to handle the everyday verbal, and other types of, attacks by non-christians on Christians, simply because they *are* Christians, and hold to Biblically-supported social issues that society might find 'offensive,' 'bigoted,' or simply 'ignorant.' As a result, children may feel so overwhelmed and a loss for words to defend their faith under this spiritual onslaught, that the more their faith is tested, if they haven't established a solid foundation in their Christian faith that can stand up to any adversity or attack, they're exposed to serious risk of abandoning the faith.

The apostle Paul reminds Timothy that it was 'from childhood you have known the sacred writings which are able to give you wisdom that leads to salvation' (2 Timothy 3:15). And Paul reminds Timothy of 'who' it was who taught him (v.14) – his 'grandmother Lois' and his 'mother Eunice' (2 Timothy 1:5). Paul also reminds us that fathers too are to 'bring them up in the discipline and instruction of the Lord' (Ephesians 6:4). And part of that 'bringing up' is what Scripture instructs us to 'always being ready to make a defense to everyone who asks you to give an account for the hope that is in you' (1 Peter 3:15). Unfortunately, I've noticed more times than I'd like to admit, that many parents of Christian children, don't really know any more 'why' they believe what the believe, than their children do. There are pros and cons to being brought up Christian. One big pro is prolonged exposure to the Truth of the Gospel and service to Christ. One disadvantage is the doubt that resides in most, if not nearly all, children who are raised Christian, about whether or not the Truth they believe in is actually 'their' independent faith, or simply a matter of them believing in the same faith as their parents, because they grew up in that environment. Christian parents *really* need to be aware of this, and if they see their child struggling or having doubts, not to just 'shrug it off.' I was once told by a Christian parent, whose adult child was doubting whether or not they were really a Christian, that their doubt was actually proof that they *were* a Christian, because a non-christian wouldn't be worried about that. Personally, I think that's a very dangerous philosophy, because you're gambling with your child's salvation, rather than addressing that child's doubt, which if left unchecked, may fester to unbelief later in life, when the child may not be able to effectively address the persecutions and verbal challenges to the faith. Plus, that parent's philosophy actually contradicts the writing of the apostle John, which essentially says 'These things I have <u>written</u> you' pertaining to believing in Jesus Christ, and *believing in Him*, that 'you may *know* that you have eternal life' (emphasis added)(1 John 5:13). So, that idea (that actually doubting that you're a Christian is actually proof that you are one) is contrary to Scripture. Although we should check ourselves in our daily walk with Christ and obedience to Him, an unchecked doubt, fueled by persecution and affliction from the outside world, can lead to real doubt and possibly abandonment of the faith by the child.

Our children are the future of the Church. We <u>need</u> to pay attention to not only what children are telling their parents about their beliefs, but also what they are *not* talking about, or possibly holding back, out of embarrassment, fear, or ridicule from their Christian parents, spiritual leaders, or others in the church, before someone from the world confuses them about the Truth they were taught.

Chapter Three

The 'Thorny' Child

Not all children who grow up in Christian families can so easily resist the worldly pleasures that are so easily attainable and available to them. When I was younger, it was harder for adolescents to obtain the 'naughty eye-candy' that is so easy to access today with the world of the Internet, as well as what's permitted on television, radio, and especially in the movies. Don't get me wrong, if we wanted to find it, we *would* find it. However, it took more than just the simple click of a mouse on the computer or pushing a button on the remote control. It took 'effort,' for lack of a better term, to access that 'eye-candy.' Today's world is much, more ungodly than I remember from my youth. So much more is 'allowed' today than even thirty years ago, and it's much, more easy to obtain. Since Mom and I embraced the Truth of Christianity, the Bible, and Jesus, we have noticed how 'some' Christian families almost 'shelter' their kids from these evils. Now, I'm not saying that Christian parents shouldn't 'filter' and monitor what their children see on social media, and even 'who' they hang out with. I think it would be irresponsible parenting if they didn't. However, sheltering a child *too* much, may lead to temptations later when they are forced into the real world when they are older, and when they may have real difficulty resisting these temptations. Another wards, sheltering a child *too* much from the world when they are young may actually make those later temptations too easy for children to accept, without the proper guidance 'why' they should be rejected beyond "because God (or the Bible) 'says so.'"

I have noticed that many children of Christian parents who experience some form of 'trouble' as they get older, is because their 'Christian bubble' is on such a short leash, that when they finally get out into the world, like Mom says sometimes, 'It's like a kid in the candy store, and they just go nuts!' Now, I realize that not <u>every</u> child who is sheltered by their Christian parents become 'troubled children' as they get older. But, just as Jesus talked about four different 'soils' that His 'seed' of the Gospel fell on, likewise, not all children are necessarily going to turn out the same in terms of their spiritual walk with Jesus and commitment to Him, either. Furthermore, Jesus also points out that out of the four soils that He spreads His Gospel on, only one out of the four soils produces actual spiritual 'good' fruit (Matthew 13:23). On the Sermon on Mount, Jesus warns us about false prophets who disguise themselves in 'sheep's clothing, but inwardly are ravenous wolves' (Matthew 7:15). Jesus goes on to identify them by our ability to 'know them by their fruits' (v.16a), that 'grapes are not gathered by *thorn* bushes' (emphasis added)(v.16b). Jesus explicitly uses the same term – thorn – in Matthew 7:16 that He uses later when He describes the 'seeds' that 'fell among *thorns*, and the thorns came up and choked them out' (emphasis added) (Matthew 13:7). Jesus later explains the 'seed' that was 'sown among thorns' is someone who 'hears the word, and the worry of the world and the deceitfulness of wealth choke the word, and it becomes unfruitful' (v.22). Unfortunately, that is what happens to many children of Christian parents who abandon the Christian faith – they get 'choked out' by the 'deceitfulness' of the acceptance from their secular relationships which provide temporary approval, which they don't realize *won't* last. This is what I believe happened to my friend in Chapter Two, who embraced Christianity for awhile, but once God began to bless him spiritually as well as in other ways, after awhile he began to serve those *blessings* rather than the One Who *gave* him those blessings, in the same way the apostle Paul wrote that people in his day 'worshiped and served the *creature* rather than the Creator' (emphasis added)(Romans 1:25). Likewise, many children of Christian parents do indeed 'hear the word' of the Truth of the Gospel from the time they are very young, either from their parents, from church, and/or from a Christian education. However, just because someone has *listened* to the Truth of the Gospel, that doesn't necessarily mean that they truly *hear* the Gospel, which is why Jesus states 'He who has ears, let him *hear*' (emphasis added)(v.9). Now, obviously, we all have ears, and most of us have the ability to hear – *physically*. However, the kind of 'hearing' Jesus is talking about is *spiritual* 'hearing,' that can only occur when a person is willing and able to accept what is being told to them.

In Chapter One, we discussed that physical blindness is no different than spiritual blindness, in that the only way that someone can really believe in and understand true 'seeing' is for their blindness to be 'peeled' away, just as Saul of Tarsus' spiritual blindness 'fell something like scales, and he regained his sight' (Acts 9:18), when he was 'filled with the Holy Spirit' (v.17). Likewise, people are also 'spiritually deaf' until God gives them spiritual 'ears [to] let him hear' (Matthew 13:9). Children of Christian parents who hear the Truth of the Gospel through their Christian upbringing, usually know Scripture, and can even quote it, better than most children their own age. In fact, many of them can even quote more Scripture than most adults can. However, the 'amount' of Scripture they can quote doesn't necessarily equate to the depth of their spiritual 'hearing.' It may only mean that they have the intellectual ability to memorize and recite large amounts of Scripture, much like children born to Muslim parents have the intellectual ability to memorize and recite large amounts of passages from the Qur'an. Another wards, 'quantity' does not necessarily equate to 'quality,' or another way to put it, just because your child is able to memorize a large percentage of Scripture doesn't mean that they have repented and are genuine Christians. It may just mean they have the ability to memorize.

Growing up, I remember that memorizing was a key part of my religious upbringing. At my school and parish, students were required to memorize various prayers, and we were <u>expected</u> to memorize these prayers word-for-word, until we memorized them perfectly. We learned the 'Our Father' (aka: 'The Lord's Prayer'), the 'Hail! Mary,' the 'Apostles Creed,' the 'Nicene Creed,' the 'Act of Contrition,' the 'Mealtime Blessing' ('Bless us our Lord, and these thy gifts…'), and various other prayers that I have long forgotten. There were also countless prayers and responses that we were expected to recite during Mass in response to the pastor's prayers. Memorization was a 'big deal' in my church. However, even with all the memorizing I did, I can't tell you for certain, if you would have asked me the context of what I memorized, if I could tell you – without reciting it – what it was that I supposedly believed about those prayers. Although I 'believed in God the Father Almighty' and 'Jesus Christ, His only Son our Lord,' if you asked me to explain to you what it meant – Biblically – for Jesus to be the Son of God, while at the same time, be God Himself, I don't believe I could even begin to attempt to explain it. I never remember thinking about Jesus in that way. I just looked at Him as being the Son of God, Who died on the cross for our sins, but I didn't really understand the eternal significance of what my 'sin' did to my relationship with God. And as a result, I viewed 'sin' as something that I did towards another person, rather than what 'sin' does towards God.

While still an adolescent, I remember going to my best friend's house, because he told me that he found a copy of his father's Playboy magazine in the garbage, and that he hid it in his underwear drawer. (How ironic that it was in a filthy garbage can that he retrieved a filthy magazine filled with pornography.) He told me that after school, he and a neighborhood friend were going to look at it, and he invited me over, but not to tell anyone. As a curious, young adolescent 'red-blooded,' American boy I decided to come over and view it with them. Although it was exciting seeing an adult woman without any clothes on, there was a part of me that felt extremely guilty for looking at it, because deep down, I knew that what we were doing was wrong. I remember thinking, 'What if his parents catch us?'

'What if they tell my mom and my grandparents?' 'What if my teachers and priests at school find out?' 'How am I going to be able to look them in the eye and explain my actions?' I had the reputation of being the 'good kid' at school. I was one of the few kids who didn't swear or even lie. What kind of reputation would I have if it got around that I was spending my free time reading Playboy magazines with my friends? However, it never occurred to me, 'What did *GOD* think about what I was doing?' Even though I memorized all those prayers in school and all those responses in church, I didn't actually understand 'what' I had memorized nor the significance of those prayers. Parents just assume that because their children are 'good' and don't get into trouble at school or at home that they naturally assume that their children are Christian, because they are a 'good student' and stay out of trouble. A similar question was raised in an independent video that I saw, which was recorded and uploaded on YouTube, which doesn't seem to be online anymore, nor have I been able to find a 'mirror video' of it on the Internet. A woman had asked Pastor John MacArthur in a 'Question and Answer' session, which was either at an undisclosed church or auditorium:

> "If a Christian child who is brought up in a Christian family and goes to a Christian school, just because

they don't want to talk about who is and who isn't saved, that doesn't mean they aren't a Christian?"[1]

Pastor MacArthur's response was:

"It pulls up an issue of Christian parents assuming because their children are not rebellious, they go to church, they go to a Christian school, that they have really been regenerated. If they were really truly Christ's, they would want to talk about it. We've got to assume this folks, we all know the stories of second generation, third generation, fourth generation Christian kids who grow cold to the things of Christ. Your first responsibility as a parent is the salvation of your children. That's your 'mission field.' They are coming into your house unconverted reprobates. The Devil's in your house. They ARE the children of the Devil – they ARE! They are the children of the one who was a killer and the liar from the beginning. He's their father, and once they've reached the 'age of accountability,' then they transition from under the protective care of God, into the 'domain of darkness,' and your task is not to make 'good hypocrites' out of them. Your task is to unmask the reality of their hearts. People ask, 'how do you do that?' Well, first of

---

[1] This was an independent video made by someone in an unspecified auditorium, who recorded and uploaded a "Q and A session" with Pastor John MacArthur on YouTube, which was in the public domain. However, at the time of the writing of this book, this video does not appear to be present any longer on YouTube, nor have I been able to find a 'mirror video' of it anywhere else on the Internet. John MacArthur is the senior pastor-teacher of Grace Community Church in Sun Valley, California.

all, you pray continually for them, and secondly, you live that life before them."[2]

Unfortunately, that was all of the video, but it brought up some very important and significant points. Just because a child of a Christian parent doesn't 'get into trouble' doesn't automatically make them a Christian, anymore than I was a Christian when I was viewing that Playboy magazine with my buddies as an adolescent, despite having memorized all those religious prayers and responses in church and school, because any guilt that I experienced was related to worrying about 'getting in trouble' with parental or school authorities, rather than the guilt of offending God. As previously mentioned, my fear and understanding of sin was related to how it would affect my relationship with *other people*, but it never really occurred to me how it affected my relationship with *God*. The most that I understood how it affected my relationship with God was that if God didn't want me to do it, it was because it would negatively affect my relationship with others, 'if' I got caught. And that was my real motivation for taking the risk – I figured, 'Hey, if nobody finds out, then no one is the wiser, so no harm done.' If my mom, grandparents, teachers, and classmates didn't find out what I was doing, my relationship with them remained the same, and my reputation as a 'good kid' remained intact. Therefore, the only risk is getting caught, and if I don't get caught, no relational damage or embarrassment occurs.

What I didn't realize is that relational damage *did* occur at a much more important level – my relationship with <u>God</u>.

---

[2] Ibid.

Although other people were none the wiser, God was, because God knows everything (1 John 3:20), which includes Jesus Who knows our very thoughts (Matthew 12:25; John 2:24). And since He knew what I was doing, it was negatively affecting my relationship with Him, which really explains why I felt guilty, because <u>ALL</u> sin is against God (Psalm 51:4). It wasn't until later in my life when I *truly* accepted the God of the Bible, repented of my sin against God, and *genuinely* accepted Jesus as my Savior <u>AND</u> Lord, that I realized that when a person sins, they don't just sin against another person, but, primarily, they are sinning against *God*. So, even if no one ever found out, *God* knew. He was right there observing what we were doing, because not only is God 'all-knowing' ('Omniscient'), but He's also 'ever-present' ('Omnipresent')(Jeremiah 23:23-24). Children of Christian parents may believe that God doesn't know what they are doing in isolation from everyone else, but not only does God <u>always</u> know what we're *doing*, but He also <u>always</u> knows what we're *thinking* too, which even our deepest thoughts are judged by God (Hebrews 4:12). Also, what I didn't realize was that my relationship with other people *was* being negatively affected, even though they didn't know what I was doing, because their impression of me was false. Who a person is, is defined based on what they actually do and think. So, since their impression of me was of an innocent kid who didn't do anything wrong, and I led them to believe that, despite doing the opposite by looking at that Playboy magazine with my buddies, I was being willfully deceptive, and the 'perceived' relationship between other people and myself had changed. "I" had changed that relationship, because that perception of me was no longer mutually believed.

Now, I'm not trying to be a religious extremist or legalistic prude, but I'm trying to point out that relationships negatively change when people do something to change their *perception* of themselves, even when other people don't know it. It's similar to when a man cheats on his wife, but she doesn't know about it. Is his relationship with his wife changed, even though she's not aware of his infidelity? Of course it is. It doesn't matter that she is 'none the wiser.' Their perception that he is a faithful man is no longer mutual. Their relationship has been negatively changed, because of what *he* did and now knows differently about his perception of himself, which is no longer mutually shared with his wife. This is why God commanded married couples, 'You shall not commit adultery' (Exodus 20:14), which 'adultery' is defined Biblically as one 'who has unlawful intercourse with the spouse of another.'[3] However, adultery is not just *limited* to sexual intercourse with another person (which that would definitely apply), but it also includes a married person having sexual *thoughts* of someone other than their spouse. Jesus explicitly equated lust with adultery (Matthew 5:27-28), but He wasn't actually adding anything to the Old Testament, but rather reinforcing it. As Pastor John MacArthur points out in his book, *The Jesus You Can't Ignore*:

> "...when Jesus said lust is a violation of the moral principle underlying the seventh commandment, he wasn't adding anything to the law. Lust was *expressly*

---

[3] *Vine's concise dictionary of the Bible. Strong's concise concordance omnibus*, p. 7. Nashville, Tennessee: Thomas Nelson, Inc., Copyright © 1997, 1999

forbidden by the tenth commandment, and it was identified with the sin of adultery in Proverbs 6:25."[4]

So whether someone commits adultery either *physically* or *mentally*, they are not only violating their marriage vows with their spouse, but they are also violating the law of God, which is why I felt guilty looking at that Playboy. I had no idea if I was lusting after other men's wives, and even if I wasn't, I was still lusting after a woman who wasn't *my* wife, which as Pastor MacArthur previously pointed out 'Lust was *expressly* forbidden by the tenth commandment' (Exodus 20:17).

Although I never admitted this to my mom, grandparents, or teachers when I was an adolescent, it still made me feel guilty. I actually held onto that guilt for quite sometime, and finally confessed it to a priest in my church during confession, even though now I know that Scripture says that when we 'hold fast to our confession' that we 'do not have a high priest who cannot sympathize with our weaknesses... yet without sin. Therefore let us draw near with confidence to the throne of grace' (Hebrews: 4:14-16). However, that didn't change the fact that my relationship with others had changed, because our mutual perception of me had changed, which included my relationship with God, even though He forgave me, when I genuinely repented of my sins against God in August 2004, and truly accepted Jesus Christ as my Savior <u>and</u> Lord.

---

[4] John MacArthur, *"The Jesus you can't ignore: what you must learn from the bold confrontations of Christ,"* p. 138 (italics in the original text). Nashville, Tennessee: Thomas Nelson, Inc., 2008

When children of Christian parents abandon the faith, they do the same thing. They don't believe that their disbelief is harming anyone, including themselves or God – but it is. It's harming their relationship with their Christian parents, Christian friends and other peers, and most importantly, their relationship with God. It's also harming their relationship with *themselves*, because they have just traded the Truth for a belief system that is false. And for the 'thorny' child, this happens for numerous reasons.

One reason that Jesus mentioned previously is that they get 'choked out' by the cares, riches, pleasures, and 'worry of the world and deceitfulness of wealth' (Matthew 13:22), by allowing themselves to be seduced by the lustful distractions that the world promises them, but never fully delivers. The real deception of worldly pleasures and desires that contradict the Word of God is that they are *immediate* pleasures that provide *temporary* wants and desires, but in the long run (and especially in terms of eternity), don't fulfill a person's needs *permanently*. Everything that is available to us – food, shelter, clothing, money, transportation, traveling, recognition, shopping, technology (like gaming, Facebook, etc), gambling, alcohol, drugs, pornography, sex, etc – all have two things in common: one, the feeling received from these experiences are temporary, and two, in order to retain the feeling we had when we first received it, it needs to be *continually* replenished or reinforced. Everything gets old, wears out, or fades. Even cars and houses get 'old.' They begin to break down, things need fixed, they aren't as solid or as reliable as when we first got them, so we can either fix them, or eventually, we have to get rid of them, and 'replace' them with something 'new.' And that's what happens when children of Christian parents abandon the faith. At a certain age, the Christian faith gets 'old' after awhile, especially when they are exposed to 'new' worldly experiences, people, and things that appear 'exciting' and 'fun' at first, but like anything else, even those worldly experiences, people, and things get 'old' after awhile, and need to be 'replaced.' That's why even worldly relationships with non-christians break up or result in adultery or fornication, because there are no objective moral boundaries in their relationship, because the Christian boundaries set by God had already been rejected and replaced with their 'own' *subjective* boundaries set by the unbelieving adult child, which can be broken at will, because there is no *objective* moral code that needs to be lived by. This constant 'want' to replace or reinforce worldly pleasures is similar to someone who's addicted to heroin trying to 'relive' their first emotional experience on it, which is called 'chasing the dragon.' However, from what I've read and witnessed from working on a detox unit, they are never able to experience it to the same 'level' they were able to experience the first time. They will never be able to experience the same 'rush' they had during their first experience, which is why it's called 'chasing the dragon,' because they never actually 'catch' that first experience again. Yet, they keep relentlessly trying over and over again, but to no avail, only to sink deeper and deeper into addiction, until the addiction either enslaves them or kills them. They are no longer in control of their drug habit, but rather their drug habit is in control of *them*.

However, this dependency on reinforcement to satisfy a temporary, worldly 'want' isn't just limited to drugs, but any worldly desire that is in direct contradiction to the Word of

God. Even romantic relationships and sex with non-christians needs to be reinforced or replaced, because it doesn't provide the same *permanent* closeness and intimacy, like when a person is in a Christian relationship or marriage (in terms of sex, Biblically, it is restricted to marriage), because what is lacking in non-christian relationships and marriages, which prevents them from the kind of deep, permanent closeness and intimacy that's found in Christian ones, is the presence of the Holy Spirit. That's because the Holy Spirit is God – the third 'Person' of the Trinity – and when both people in a relationship are committed Christians, they <u>know</u> that the other person's Authority is Jesus Christ – God the Son – the second 'Person' of the Trinity, and submits their desires and will to *Him*, rather than to *themselves*. This gives both people the assurance and evidence that their faith is genuine (Hebrews 11:1), and they can each trust the other person with anything, because they are submitting themselves to the will of God, Who Himself is trustworthy and commands both people in the relationship to be faithful. And a committed Christian desires to be faithful and obedient to God. However, that level of assurance and evidence is not found in non-christian relationships and marriages, because the only 'authority' that either person has is themself. Neither one of them can ever provide any definite assurance to the other person that they will always remain faithful to them. All they have is their word, but since they abandoned God's guidelines for fidelity and trust, they have no boundaries they have to obey – including their own. God doesn't change (Malachi 3:6) and neither does his commandments regarding relationships and marriage, which is why Christian couples can completely trust each other. However, that doesn't apply for the non-christian couple, because mankind – and its rules – *can* and *do* change. Now, I'm not saying that a non-christian couple will 'always' lead to infidelity or breakup, or that Christian couples are 100% immune to infidelity. I have personally know non-christian couples who have been faithful and committed to each other for years, and I have also seen Christian couples (unfortunately) suffer the physical, emotional, and spiritual consequences of a Christian spouse willfully disobeying our Lord's commands of marital fidelity. But the point is that there are no 'non-christian guidelines' that must be followed that will convince or can assure that the other person in the non-christian relationship or marriage will remain faithful or committed to the other person. This is why Scripture warns Christians to not be 'unequally yoked' with a unbeliever (2 Corinthians 6:14)(NKJV), because the authority, beliefs, and guidelines about fidelity from the non-christian in the relationship begins and ends with *them*, rather than with God, which includes the ability to *change* the rules about fidelity in the relationship. Since God can't change, neither can His rules about fidelity. The same can't be guaranteed in a non-christian relationship or marriage.

This 'unequal yoking' can even be found between a Christian, whose sole Authority is the Bible, and someone who belongs to another Christian denomination whose sole Authority is not. By 'sole Authority is not the Bible,' this refers to people who belong to denominations of Christianity whose rules about marriage are not limited to Scripture. Many times children of Christian parents who abandon strict, Biblically-based teachings about marriage and 'yoke' themselves with someone who belongs to a Christian denomination who don't follow these strict, Biblically-based teachings, also can't be assured about the fidelity and trust in their relationship or marriage. For example, there are churches that don't believe in the permanency of marriage, accept 'non-traditional' marriages (ie: marriages that are not limited to only one husband and one wife), or they allow for the couple to 'redefine' the rules of marriage for themselves. This is especially troublesome when one person in the relationship considers themselves to be 'non-practicing' in their particular denomination, because then they are no different than the non-christian, whose authority is *himself*. Although they identify themselves as a 'self-proclaimed' Christian, they are only a nominal 'Christian' – that is, when someone asks what religion they are, their particular denomination is what they identify their religion as. But, there's no real commitment to that denomination, let alone God, and neither is their commitment in their relationship guaranteed either. This is also why Christians should take some 'real' time to find out if the person they are in a relationship with has a deep, committed, *genuine* relationship with Jesus Christ, because if they have no desire to be committed to God and His rules about relationships and marriage, Who they 'claim' to worship, how is that any assurance that they will always be committed to another human being?

But it's not just relationships with their Christian parents and peers that children abandon and replace with non-christian relationships, but it's also the Christian faith altogether that they abandon. And that's because they were never truly saved to begin with. If you noticed, the title of this book is "Why do children of Christian parents abandon **THE** faith?" rather than "<u>their</u> faith." That's because, Scripturally, even if a child is brought up in a Christian home, attends a Christian church, and even has a Christian education, that doesn't automatically mean that they *are* Christian. As the late, Christian evangelist, Billy Sunday, once said, "Going to church doesn't make you a Christian any more than going to a garage makes you an automobile."[5] And one of the key signs whether a child with a Christian upbringing is a true Christian or not is whether they *remain* in the faith. The apostle John wrote in 1 John 2:19:

"They went out from us, but they were *not* really *of us*; for if they had been of us, they *would have remained with us*; but they went out, so that it would be shown that *they all are not of us*" (emphasis added).

Another wards, the reason they left was because they were never Christians to begin with, because, Scripturally, there is no such thing as an 'ex-Christian,' since a *genuine*, committed Christian can't lose their salvation (John 3:16; 10:27-29; Romans 8:38-39; etc), which includes loss of salvation due to disbelief. They may have had a Christian upbringing and had a lot of exposure to the Christian faith, Christian surroundings, people, events, and even the ability to memorize large amounts of Scripture, but exposure and the ability to memorize aren't proof that a person is a Christian, anymore than someone who is brought up in Islam and has claimed to have memorized the Qur'an, automatically means they are a Muslim. I knew someone who had memorized an entire chapter in the New Testament, and she often questioned whether or not she was really a Christian, and when asked what the chapter was about,

---

[5] Billy Sunday, *"Billy" Sunday, the Man and His Message: With His Own Words Which Have Won Thousands for Christ*. Original Publisher: John C. Winston Co.; Publication date: 1917

she had difficulty explaining it. Having the ability to memorize doesn't automatically mean that what you've memorized has rooted a permanent place in your heart and that you actually believe it, or even understand it. An example of this is the unfortunate 'deconversion' story of the daughter of a well-known Christian apologist[6] – Rachael Slick.

Pusa and I read an article on the Internet about the daughter of a notable Christian apologist, who after years of being taught the Truth about the Christian faith, one day she decided to abandon it and she is now a self-professed atheist.[7] She described many events in her life that she explains led up to her 'deconversion,' but there are a few significant points that really stood out that are worth mentioning from her story, which begins with a conversation and question that she had with a friend of hers:

> "If God was absolutely moral, because morality was absolute, and if the nature of "right" and "wrong" surpassed space, time, and existence, and if it was as much a fundamental property of reality as math, then why were some things a sin in the Old Testament but not a sin in the New Testament?

---

[6] Rachel Slick is the daughter of the President and Founder of the Christian Apologetics and Research Ministry (www.carm.org/matt-slick)

[7] Hemant Mehta, *"The Atheist Daughter of a Notable Christian Apologist Shares Her Story,"* The Friendly Atheist. (July 15, 2013). http://www.patheos.com/blogs/friendlyatheist/2013/07/15/the-atheist-daughter-of-a-notable-christian-apologist-shares-her-story/

> Everyone had always explained this problem away
> using the principle that Jesus' sacrifice meant we
> wouldn't have to follow those ancient laws…. In fact,
> by the very nature of the problem, *there was no possible
> answer that would align with Christianity.*
>
> I still remember sitting there in my dorm room bunk
> bed, staring at the cheap plywood desk, and feeling
> something horrible shift inside me, a vast chasm
> opening up beneath my identity, and I could only sit
> there and watch it fall away into darkness."[8]

There is much more to this part of the article, but the part
that really surprised me that made her doubt her faith, and
eventually led to her abandoning of it, was her question to her
friend, 'why were some things a sin in the Old Testament but
not a sin in the New Testament?' I can understand why she
felt the usual answer she heard ("…that Jesus' sacrifice meant
we wouldn't have to follow those ancient laws") didn't really
satisfy her question. But that's because both her question and
the answer aren't completely accurate.

First, sin doesn't stop being sin – ever. But particular
commands from God have not always necessarily applied
to everyone throughout human history, and this is why one
person can do something and it's a sin, while someone else
can do the exact same thing, but it's not a sin. For example,
if a heterosexual married woman is having sex with a man

---

[8]   Ibid. The use of italics are in the original article, while the words in the
article that are underscored were added by me to focus on those particular
points of her story.

who is her husband, she's not committing any sins, but if a homosexual man is also having sex with a man who he's in a civil union with, he's committing a sin - actually, it's two sins: homosexuality and fornication. Both people are having sex with only one man, but the homosexual man is committing sins because he's violating the commands of God, while the heterosexual woman is not committing a sin because she is not violating the commands of God. That's because the commands to 'be fruitful and multiply' to married couples applies to one <u>man</u> and one <u>woman</u> to obey. However, if the man violates this command and engages in a sexual relationship with another man, it's a sin, because not only did God not command him to engage in that type of relationship, but God also <u>specifically</u> commanded him *not* to engage in it (Leviticus 20:13), which the apostle Paul reinforces as 'committing indecent acts' (Romans 1:27). This also applies to other laws that only applied to **Old Testament <u>Israel</u>** and not the **New Testament <u>Church</u>**.

For example, God explicitly stated that observing the Sabbath (which began at six o'clock in the evening on Friday and ended at six o'clock in the evening on Saturday) was specifically a sign between God and the sons of **<u>Israel</u>** (Exodus 31:16-17). In fact, Moses specifically told Israel that the covenant God made with them, 'The LORD *did not make this covenant with our fathers*, but *with us*, with all those of us alive here today' (emphasis added)(Exodus 5:3). Another wards, these *specific* commands were given to *Israel*, not their forefathers, like Abraham, Isaac, and Jacob. Therefore, their forefathers could not be held accountable by not following them – and therefore not being sinful, because God didn't make this covenant with *them* nor gave them these commands to follow. The same thing applies to the Church, which is why Peter declared during the Jerusalem Council, 'why do you put God to the test by placing upon the neck of the disciples a yoke which neither our fathers nor we have been able to bear?' (Acts 15:10), and also explains why God commanded Peter that he could now eat with Gentiles (Acts 10:13-15), because God was making a distinction between **Old Testament <u>Israel</u>** and the **New Testament <u>Church</u>**. So, those Jews who had not accepted Christ as their promised Messiah were still bound to the Old Testament Law, while Peter and other believing Jews were part of the New Testament Covenant, because they 'are saved through the grace of the Lord Jesus, in the same way as they [the believing Gentiles] also are' (Acts 15:11). This also applied to specific dietary laws and wearing certain garments in the Old Testament, such as not eating pork and wearing mixed fabrics, because God had made Israel 'holy' (or 'different, set apart') from the pagan nations, whose practices, clothing, and eating customs reflected their worship and idolatry to false gods. So, in order to help keep Israel from falling into idolatry, as well as remain strong and healthy, God gave specific commands like these to protect **<u>Israel</u>**, and any violation of these commands was sinful, and would result in punishment. However, some sins, like murder and homosexuality, were universally applied to everyone, because sins like these applied to ALL people groups from EVERY generation, such as murder in pre-Flood times (Genesis 9:6), which extended even into the New Testament Church era (Romans 13:9). So, it wasn't a matter of some things being a sin in the Old Testament but not a sin in the New Testament, but that when God gave a command to a particular group of people but not others, the group who willfully and purposely disobeyed God's commands committed sin, which is why the apostle Paul stated, 'whatever the Law says, it speaks to those who are under the Law' (Romans 3:19) and 'For when Gentiles who do not have the Law do instinctively the things of the Law, these, not having the Law, are a law to themselves, in that they show the work of the Law written in their hearts' (Romans 2:14-15).

Another comment in the article was her assumption that Christians don't acknowledge science, which she attributed that to their environment.[9] This statement really surprised me, because I've been on her father's Christian apologetics Web site many, many times, and it's just filled with pages and pages of how science actually *supports* God, the Bible, and the Christian faith. So, there's not a dichotomy between '*science* and Christianity,' but between '*atheism* and Christianity,' or more specifically 'atheism and *theism*.' Her assumption based on her statement is that 'a rational Christian' doesn't take science into consideration for their faith. Personally, I don't know one Christian who does not recognize that science and Christianity are supportive of one another. It's true that the Christian faith isn't *dependent* on science, since not everything in the Bible can be *proven* with science, like miracles and the existence of God, angels, and demons. However, scientific *claims* in the Bible have never been disproven with science, which many Christians are more than eager to point out. In fact, many scientific claims in the Bible weren't able to be proven using science until hundreds – even thousands – of

---

[9] Ibid.

years after they were penned in the Bible. So, I'm not sure where she got the idea that science is somehow 'avoided' by Christians, because of their 'environment.'

A third comment at the end of her 'testimony' declared not only how she felt about her life since her 'deconversion,' but also how she felt – and feels – about God, including barely fearing Hell, only praying occasionally, and loving the 'God of Freedom' more now than the God of the Bible.[10] These comments speak volumes. First, as a professed atheist, I'm not sure why she's continuing to spell 'God' with a capital 'G,' especially the abstract 'god' of freedom. Atheists generally spell it in the lower case, especially when referring to *the* God of the Bible as a way of not acknowledging His existence. It also describes that her impression of God was a God of binding, like the feeling of being bound in prison and enslaved with restrictions. It is true that historically, many Christians have viewed God as a dictator that barked out orders with nothing more than a bunch of "thou shalt's" and "thou shalt not's," and preached a 'god' who was looking down on humanity just waiting to condemn them. However, that's not actually the God of the Bible, Who is really a balance of a righteous Judge, as well as a merciful and loving Savior (Isaiah 43:3). And as a Savior, God actually leads people to 'real' freedom through faith in the shed blood of His Son, Jesus Christ, Who shed His blood *for* us, 'freeing' us from the bondage and slavery of sin. However, because of her inaccurate and unbiblical impression of 'Who' God actually is, based on her alleged childhood experiences, Rachael fell

---

[10] Ibid.

into the 'acceptance trap' of the false worldview of atheism – the worldview of 'accepting you just as you are – not judging you.' What parents – even Christian parents – don't realize is that all their children want is to be *accepted* and loved by their parents for 'who' they are and who *God* wants them to be – not what *their parents* would 'like' them to be. Our children are not meant to be "mini-me's" of their parents, including 'mini-Christian apologists' – unless of course that is what *God* calls them to be. As C. S. Lewis put it:

> "When you find yourself wanting to turn your children, or pupils, or even your neighbours, into people exactly like yourself, remember that God probably never meant them to be that."[11]

So, when Rachael received this 'acceptance' from her new atheistic relationships which – based on the implications of her 'deconversion' testimony she didn't feel she received as a child from being 'obedient' to her father - this must have seemed like a breath of fresh air, but as we'll see, this is only a temporary and false illusion. Second, if she's 'truly' an atheist, then why does she '*barely* fear Hell now' and her 'instinct to *pray* only turns up on rare occasions'? As an atheist, 'Who' is she praying? 'Who' would send her to Hell? Like most atheists I have encountered, they don't truly disbelieve that God exists, because they make similar statements like this.

---

[11] C.S. Lewis, "Mere Christianity: a revised and amplified edition, with a new introduction, of the three books, Broadcast talks, Christian behavior, and Beyond personality," p. 185. Copyright 1952, C.S. Lewis Pte. Ltd. Copyright renewed 1980, C.S. Lewis Pte. Ltd. HarperCollins Publishers: New York, NY.

That's because Scripture tells us that <u>everyone</u> acknowledges at some level that the God of the Bible exists, even if they won't outright admit it: "…because that which is known about God is *evident within them*; for God made it evident to them. For even though *they knew God*, they did not honor Him as God or give thanks, but they became futile in their speculations, and their foolish heart was *darkened*" (emphasis added)(Romans 1:19,21). 'Darkened' – just like the way Rachael described her 'deconversion' experience ('I could only sit there and watch it fall away into *darkness*'). So, 'atheists' like Rachael aren't actually 'true' atheists, but rather they willfully reject what is 'evident' about God, and because for whatever subjective reason, they choose to repress what is evident and embrace the bondage of slavery.

How can sin be slavery? Unlike a servant, a slave is owned. But ownership is not limited just to purchasing a product (or people) and owning it (or them). A person can be a slave to something that controls *them*, rather than the person controlling *it*. We already covered addiction to foreign substances that people willfully place in their bodies in Chapter One. Someone who says 'I can quit anytime I want,' but then doesn't quit when asked if they can quit right now, is a slave to it. I've heard many people over the course of my life say, 'I just don't want to quit right now, but I can later when I'm ready,' however, today most of them are still engaging in that addictive behavior or 'hooked' on that addictive substance. Sex, overeating, spending, profanity, and many other things can also make a slave out of a person, because they can become so addicted to and dependent on those things, that they either can't control themselves, or if they are taken away for a certain amount time, after awhile they begin to crave them, and even experience some physical and emotional withdrawal symptoms from them, such as irritability and other uncontrolled (and even irrational) emotions and behavior. When a person gets to that point, they have become a slave to those things because they are unable to refrain from those types of activities, and those things become their 'god,' instead of the God Whose desire is to convict us of those sins that enslave us, and to protect us from them and love us. In Rachael Slick's 'testimony,' she went on to define the kinds of things she had 'freedom' from.[12] If you take the time to read them it's an interesting list, because Pusa and I noticed what the actual 'freedom' she is embracing from: freedom from <u>authority</u>. Authority from God, authority from the 'rules' from her upbringing, authority from consequences to her actions, and authority to maintain 'pure' thoughts are all things she suddenly feels relieved to be rid of. However, are those things necessarily 'good' to be rid of, or can the result of ridding those things from our lives, potentially place us in a state of 'slavery'? If we examine the opposite of the things that she feels 'free' from and is now feeling 'free' to embrace – disobedience and resistance; freedom to think *anything* impure, corrupt, dishonest, or fraudulent; arrogance; pride; lack of remorse, shame, commitment, and responsibility – she's actually embracing *rebellion*. So, someone who refuses to be obedient to an Omnipotent God will have difficulty being obedient to anyone else, because as previously mentioned, their only moral standard for their behavior and thoughts are those established by *them*. And since 'they' were the ones

---

[12] Ibid. Mehta, *"The Atheist Daughter of a Notable Christian Apologist Shares Her Story."* (2013)

who established these 'standards of behavior,' since they are no longer bound by God's standards, they have the 'freedom' to change their own. So, how can they ever truly be trusted by anyone about anything? Plus, once a pattern of immoral behavior and impure thoughts becomes 'mainstream' to a person, like any other addiction, if the individual attempts to stop it, it can become extremely difficult to stop, because the experience of those actions and their thoughts have become permanently etched in that person's mind, which are nearly impossible to forget. They are powerless to forget them, and can even hinder one's intellectual, moral, and spiritual growth and relationships with others, which is a form of enslavement – those memories and thoughts have 'enslaved' *them*.

Now, you might ask, "How is having freedom to think, 'immoral' or 'wrong,' and how does it affect anyone other than that person?' But as we discussed earlier in this chapter, just as me having lustful thoughts by looking at that Playboy magazine when I was an adolescent changed my relationship between my mother, grandparents, teachers, spiritual leaders and myself, by no longer sharing the mutual belief that I was pure of mind (even though they weren't aware of it at the time), likewise, the 'freedom' to think other things that God calls immoral will eventually lead to enslavement of that sinful thinking. Now, I'm not asserting that *all* males who look at Playboys will *always* engage in physical fornication or cheat on their wives. However, not only do those risks increase, since the experience of those lustful thoughts becomes a permanent memory etched in their brains, but also, because of that experience, the inability to not think of those lustful thoughts actually *enslaves* them. Remember, a person can be a slave to something that controls *them*, rather than the person controlling *it*, and that includes ones thoughts. For many people, they may not think that this a big deal, because – like Rachael – they don't think the 'freedom from the perpetual heavy obligation to keep every thought pure' isn't that big of a deal. However, by saying that, they aren't really seeing the forest for the trees, for the reasons listed above. Plus, when they begin to *think* immoral thoughts, then that can also lead to thinking that *acting* on those thoughts aren't wrong either, especially if other people don't find out, since they have abandoned God's 'moral compass' for their own. Morality suddenly becomes a matter of being *subjective*, rather than being *objective*, because there is no godly moral 'boundaries' to abide by. Now, this may seem like 'real freedom' on the surface, but it's actually enslavement, because their desire to think and do what they 'want' can become so strong, that they eventually become unable to refrain from even thinking about it. In this way, it's no different from any other drug. Even when people someday *need* to stop a particular addiction, they find that they can't, because their prolonged use has made them enslaved to it. Likewise, even the 'freedom' to willfully think ungodly, immoral thoughts can lead to enslavement, because it too can become an addiction. For example, if all a husband has been doing is lusting after the centerfolds in Playboys, and his wife finds out and asks him to stop, if he's been doing it for decades and believes he's 'not doing anything wrong, because no ones knows nor is getting hurt,' it's going to be extremely difficult to stop his addiction, and impossible to remove those thoughts in his brain. So, even if he does stop looking at them, he's become enslaved to the years of memories of those centerfolds that he *can't* blot out of his head, which he would have never had if he had been obedient to God, rather than allowing himself to become enslaved to his own thoughts.

Getting back to Rachael's 'deconversion' testimony, Pusa and I noticed that her memories from her upbringing were mostly feelings of satisfaction from pleasing her father during her 'daily challenge' of him asking her theological questions and her answering him correctly.[13] Now, I'm not trying to place 'blame' on her father for her becoming an atheist. That was *her* choice to reject the Truth of Christianity that her father taught her, and instead to embrace the falsehood of atheism. However, my point is to illustrate 'how' she 'exchanged the truth of God for a lie' (Romans 1:25). She described her 'daily challenge' with him as 'mind twisting,' as well as other negative terms and phrases to describe her alleged childhood experiences.[14] Other uses of this kind of 'demand and expectation for obedience' is used subtly, but noticeably, throughout her testimony, as well as rewards and punishment for particular behavior. For example, there's a photo of her in the article smiling and receiving an award from Awana for her exemplary academic status, which goes on to mention her memorization of over 800 Bible passages, as well as a photo of her with other home-school children holding letters that spell out "OBEY."[15] As Pusa and I discussed, 'there are two sides to every story.' Now, I'm not insinuating that many of those experiences aren't true – I have no reason to. However, common sense tells you that when you hear only one side of a story, only one side is being told, and as

---

[13] Ibid.

[14] Ibid.

[15] Ibid.

my mother always used to tell me, 'There's his side, there's her side, and somewhere in the middle is the whole truth.' I noticed that the two themes that seemed to keep surfacing in her article were 'obedience' and 'freedom.' Whether this was deliberate or not, Rachael seemed to be implying that because of her desire to be 'obedient' during her upbringing that she equated 'obedience' with 'lack of freedom.' And this is something that is universal with all children – their obedience to their parents is an attempt to receive acceptance from them, but when it goes unfulfilled, they seek that acceptance elsewhere – even if that 'acceptance' isn't good for them long-term. However, even if the consequences of a lack of obedience from our childhood doesn't always seem 'fair,' especially when we look back at them when we're older and compare them to the consequences (or lack thereof) in non-christian families, that doesn't mean that those consequences were necessarily 'unfair.' It also doesn't mean the people who are 'enforcing obedience' are necessarily enforcing it *Biblically*.

I remember a Christian parent, who when he read Proverbs 13:24 – "He who withholds his rod hates his son, But he who loves him disciplines him diligently" – he took it literally about the rod. He stated that when he felt his children's disobedience was bad enough to warrant punishment, that he used a small wooden rod to spank them on their 'derrière,' instead of using his hand. He argued that children should have fear towards the *object*, rather than the parent spanking them, because they should begin to not like the *object* that is source of their discipline, rather than begin to not like the parent's *hand* – and, thus, not like the *parent*. Therefore, to avoid the *source* of discipline, they will begin to avoid the disobedient behavior as well, but not their parent. I'm not going to attempt to defend which 'mode' of physical discipline is 'better,' since it's beyond the scope of this book. However, the point of physical discipline is to teach the rebellious child that willful disobedience to parents is disrespectful not only to the parent, but also to Jesus Who died for their sin on the cross *for them*. So, before a child can begin to obey a loving, merciful God Who exists but they *can't* see, they need to learn to be obedient to their parents who they *can* see. And without learning this obedience, how can they learn to be obedient or faithful to anyone else, such as the 'mutual' submission and faithfulness between husband and wife (Ephesians 5:21-33)? Unfortunately, I realize that many parents go beyond Biblical discipline and become abusive towards their children. However, child abuse (physical or mental) – even in the name of Christ – is unbiblical and is actually being *disobedient* to Christ, Who said, 'but whoever causes one of these little ones who believe in Me to stumble, it would be better for him to have a heavy millstone hung around his neck, and to be drowned in the depth of the sea' (Matthew 18:6). Plus, this kind of treatment can actually lead a child, who was brought up in a Christian family, *away* from Christ, and embrace a false theology or worldview. So, although this type of Christian parent may believe that the 'discipline' that they use on their children is to keep them submissive and prevent them from abandoning the faith, in reality this kind of 'discipline' (which in reality is abuse) may actually backfire.

Jesus had (and has) a special place in His heart for children. The apostle Paul reaffirms *loving* discipline of disobedient children by their parents that doesn't involve 'provoking your children to anger' (Ephesians 6:4), as well as children obeying their godly parents (v.1). So, even if parents don't *lovingly* discipline their children in the way Jesus commands them to, it's unreasonable and unjustifiable for children to equate the actions of their parents, with what God's actual commands them regarding discipline in His Word. Unfortunately, for many children of Christian parents, like Rachael, because of their perceived negative childhood experiences, which 'seem' to greatly outweigh the earthly – and more importantly the eternal – benefits of being brought up Christian, they reject *ALL* of what they've been taught, because of those 'bad' experiences. They abandon the 'entire' Truth, because 'part' of the Truth wasn't being obeyed by their parents. But is that really being objective – judging and abandoning an entire faith, based on the disobedient actions of individuals who belong to that faith? Is it really justifiable to throw the baby out with the bathwater, rather than judge a faith on the merits of its founder – which, in the case of Christianity, is Jesus Christ, Who loves and protects children, but also *lovingly* disciplines them when they are wrong? That's like equating the negative treatment of someone from a particular race, and then attributing that behavior towards their entire race, which we would rightly call 'racism.'

I remember the first time as a kid when I went to see the fireworks with my mom. We decided to take the bus downtown in order to avoid the heavy traffic on the way back home. After the fireworks were over, and we were standing on the corner in the downtown waiting for the bus to take us back home, I remember a cherry bomb went off by my feet. I must have jumped a foot it was so loud! My ears continued to ring which seemed at the time to last forever. When we looked around, we were the only people of our race in our line of sight. As far as I could see, everyone else was of a same minority race. I hadn't done anything in order to provoke anyone to warrant a cherry bomb going off by my feet which nearly deafened me, so I didn't understand 'why' whoever set it off singled me out. After we got on the bus, the vast majority of people on the bus were of that same race that had surrounded us on that corner, verses just a handful of people who were of the same race as Mom and me. Whenever the bus stopped, I noticed numerous people jumping out the window without paying the fare. (This was back when you paid for your bus ride *after* you got off the bus.) I also remember whenever we stopped, this one guy reached over the side of the bus, grabbed a garbage bag on the side of the road (it was garbage pickup the next day), and hit the side of the bus as hard as he could. When the bus driver found out, he stopped the bus, walked to the back of the bus, and just stared at the guy without saying anything. The guy he was looking at just stared back at him, and neither of them exchanged a word. After the last individual, who was of that minority race, got off the bus, then the real 'action' happened. Suddenly, bags and bags of garbage started flying through the window. My mom instinctively covered my body with a blanket. However, some of the garbage made contact with my mom's hand that was covering me and it got cut – not enough to need stitches, but it was still bleeding. Another gentleman on the bus wasn't so lucky. He actually got his head partly cut open by the flying debris, and he was bleeding pretty profusely. We ended up having to make a stop at the bus station, because they had to change buses, since the bus we were on – which was a *brand new* bus - had a huge dent in the side of it. By God's grace, we made it safely back home. Now, would it be fair of me to judge those individuals' entire race, based on the actions of a few people, simply because they were of that particular race? Absolutely not! That's called racism – something Jesus (Who, as a Jew – ethnically - was a minority Himself) would be vigorously against. Yet, so many people will make the exact same negative accusations and false stereotypes towards Christianity in general, because of the actions of individuals, who call themselves 'Christians,' who are actually *disobeying* the founder of their faith – Jesus Christ. So, how is that any different or justifiable?

This same kind of 'equating negative treatment from someone from a particular religion, and then attributing that behavior towards their entire religion,' is a form of religious bigotry, that some term 'religism' which is defined as *'the expression of fear towards, hatred towards, or discrimination against, persons of a specific religion affiliation, usually a minority faith.'*[16] However, 'religism' isn't just limited to a 'minority faith.' It can also be expressed towards a 'majority faith,' like Christianity as well, from the result of the treatment from a few 'bad apples,' who affiliate themselves with that faith and are disobeying Christ. So, 'how' can children condemn their own parents' disobedience towards Christ as being 'wrong' or 'immoral,' and then in the next breath become disobedient towards Christ

---

[16] B.A. Robinson, "Religiously motivated fear, hatred, animosity, intolerance, conflict, oppression, etc. A new English word: 'Religism,' which means bigotry towards other religions/belief systems." Originally published on: 2009-JUL-12. Last update: 2013-MAY-20. Copyright 2009 to 2013 by Ontario Consultants on Religious Tolerance. http://www.religioustolerance.org/religism.htm

themselves by abandoning the faith, including abandoning 'obedience, submission, and pure thinking'?

Unfortunately, that's what a lot of children of Christian parents do. Because of perceived 'bad' experiences from their childhood, they forget about all the 'good' that was the result of being raised with the Truth, including the love and opportunity that Christ showed them by placing them in an environment, where they had first-hand knowledge and access to the Truth, so that way they won't be able to 'plead ignorance' before God, because they *know* the Truth. However, being exposed to the Truth and memorizing hundreds of verses from the Bible doesn't guarantee that a child is going to *remain* in the faith as demonstrated earlier. So, although becoming familiar with what the Bible says and even being able to quote Scripture to help in our Christian growth is a good thing, it's more important to *understand* the Gospel message, including 'what' Jesus saved us *from*, and as a result of understanding that, also understanding 'what' it means to be a follower of Christ, and the importance of obeying God. However, because that is so often missed in upbringing, even the most 'Scripturally-familiar' child may not actually understand the Gospel, even if they can quote passages like John 3:16. Just like the child who was able to quote an entire chapter from the Bible, but had difficulty explaining what it meant without reciting it, likewise, the most 'Scripturally-familiar' child isn't a guarantee that they understand - or even believe in - the Gospel, beyond the explanation they have memorized. We'll cover more of what parents and religious leaders can do in Chapter Five, in order to aid children who are brought up in the faith, including those who are being to doubt it, as well as those who abandon it.

However, even if all these 'precautions' are done, sadly, many children still abandon the faith, because as Jesus said, they get 'choked out' by the worry of the world and the deceitfulness of wealth' (Matthew 13:22). Yet, that is what so many children of Christian parents end up doing. That *temporary* 'wealth of the world' is so enticing on the surface, that they begin to crave the temporary 'here-and-now wants' of the world, more than they desire their eternal needs and *permanent* rewards awaiting them in Heaven that even when the apostle Paul caught a glimpse of 'Paradise and heard inexpressible words, which a man is not permitted to speak' (2 Corinthians 12:4), he wasn't able to describe using human language the awesomeness of what he saw and heard! But, because they can't 'see' or 'hear' those promises of God in the 'here-and-now,' they would rather experience the temporary 'here-and-now' and abandon the permanent. However, as Jesus warns us, 'For what does it profit a man to gain the whole world, and forfeit his soul? For what will a man give in exchange for his soul? For whoever is ashamed of Me and My words in this adulterous and sinful generation, the Son of Man will also be ashamed of him when He comes in the glory of His Father with the holy angels' (Mark 8:36-38). Is exchanging the Truth of God for the 'deceitfulness' of a lie really worth it in terms of eternity and experiencing the 'shame' of Jesus when we finally stand before Him, face-to-face? Jesus further warns us, 'No one can serve two masters; for either he will hate the one and love the other, or he will be devoted to one and despise the other. You cannot serve

God *and wealth'* (emphasis added)(Mark 6:24). Obviously, this doesn't mean a believer can't be rich. God gave King Solomon riches, as well as wisdom. So, money itself, and the acquisition of money isn't evil. However, as the apostle Paul points out, 'For the *love of money* is a root of all sorts of evil, and some by longing for it have wandered away from the faith and pierced themselves with many griefs' (emphasis added) (1 Timothy 6:10), which is why Paul goes on to tell us to 'flee from these things' (v.11). So, children with this 'thorny soil' don't actually abandon the faith because they *truly* believe that there isn't any evidence for the Christian faith, but rather, they become so drunk with worldly pleasures, which will eventually fade away, that they reject the Truth and create a 'god' in their mind that doesn't actually exist, in order to continue to indulge in the pleasures of this world that don't promise any eternal rewards – only temporary pleasures that will eventually wither away.

I was at a funeral in the last couple of years, and the adult child of the deceased stated that her parent "had a relationship with God in '*her* own way.'" I don't claim to know what was in her parent's heart before she died, but I had known her for several years. Although she was brought up in the exact same 'denomination' of Christianity as I was, her commitment to Christ wasn't much different than mine was in my twenties, when I still believed in 'a' god, but didn't embrace Jesus being the ONLY Way to God (John 14:6). My memories of her 'relationship' with God, was using God's and Jesus' Names as curse words without conviction, her lack of desire to attend the church she professed to belong to, and her explicit lack of belief in the Bible – much like I used to. When I ran into her a couple of years before she passed, the subject of faith came up, and I told her that the reason I didn't believe some of the things I was raised with, was because they weren't supported by the Bible, which her reply was "PFFF! The Bible!" To my knowledge, I don't think she every embraced the Jesus of Scripture, Who stated "I am the way, the *Truth*, and the life; no one comes to the Father but by Me' (emphasis added)(John 14:6). If you notice throughout this book, I purposely spell the word 'Truth' with a capital '**T**,' because Jesus explicitly states that **'He'** is the Truth, not merely that He told the truth (which He did that as well). That's because throughout Scripture, Jesus and Scripture are described as 'Truth,' such as in John 17:17: 'Sanctify them in the truth; *Your word is truth'* (emphasis added). So, Jesus wants us to believe in God and 'have a relationship' with Him based on *His* standards, not 'in *our* own way.'

However, this is a decision that children of Christian parents – as well as all of us – have to make for ourselves. What 'kind' of reality and relationship with God are we going to embrace – a 'reality' and relationship based on nothing other than our own *personal* desires in order to justify our worldly lifestyles that are willfully disobedient to God, or 'the' reality based on the Truth of the Gospel of Jesus Christ, based on the evidence of His bodily resurrection that proved Who He was – the *only* Truth and relationship that we can ever have with God? Unfortunately, most people are going to choose the former, including the 'god' of their imagination that doesn't exist, because believing in *that* 'god' allows them to continue to engage in their lifestyle that is in opposition to the *real* God of Truth – Jesus Christ. Otherwise, if they acknowledge the God that *actually* exists but continue believing in a false worldview and refusing to be obedient to Him, then they must also acknowledge the Hell that Jesus originally 'prepared for the devil and his angels' (Matthew 25:41), which is also the eternal destiny of those who reject Him and are willfully disobedient to Him (v.46; cf. Revelation 20:14-15). This is why believing in the *real* Truth – rather than a fantasy that has been created in an individual's mind – is critical, because without objective, godly standards for us to guide us to the Truth, as the late Dr. Walter Martin wrote in his book, 'Kingdom of the Cults':

> "It has been wisely observed by someone that 'a man who will not stand for something is quite likely to fall for almost anything.'"[17]

So, although opinion is valuable, Truth is necessary.

---

[17] Walter Martin, "The Kingdom of the Cults," p.18. Revised, Updated, and Expanded Edition, October 2003. Bethany House Publishers: Grand Rapids, MI

Chapter Four

The 'Good' Child

I t might be surprising to know that contrary
to popular belief, there is no such thing as a
'self-righteous Christian.' I realize and understand
that many times Christians can *act* 'self-righteous,' however,
the *behavior* that 'some' Christians display is a far different
thing than the way 'genuine' Christians view themselves.
Unfortunately, the 'Christians' and churches that make the
news who yell 'fire and brimstone' to anyone who doesn't
agree with 'their' view of Christianity is usually the impression
that people have and think of when they refer to Christians
as being 'self-righteous.' However, 'these' individuals aren't
an accurate representation of *Biblically*-based Christians,
who <u>don't</u> consider themselves 'righteous' in the eyes of God
by anything that they have done to 'merit' God's grace and
acceptance of salvation and entrance into Heaven at death.
Rather, *genuine* Christians understand that it is GOD Who
'makes' us righteous through the saving work of Jesus' shed
blood on the cross *for* us, which Christians refer to as 'the

Atonement.' Just as God told Noah before he entered the ark that 'you alone I have seen to be righteous before Me in this time' (Genesis 7:1), because 'Noah found favor in the eyes of the LORD' and 'walked *with* God' (emphasis added)(Genesis 6:8-9) and 'did according to all that the LORD commanded him' (Genesis 7:5), it is <u>only</u> by the grace and mercy of a loving God that we are 'made' righteous – not because Christians somehow believe that they are more 'worthy' or 'holier than thou' than everyone else. Jesus even warns us about 'self-righteously' exalting ourselves, because if we do we WILL be humbled (Luke 14:11), which He explains in the parable of the two men who went up to the Temple to pray (Luke 18:9-14) – a self-righteous Pharisee who praised himself before God, and a tax-collector who asked God for mercy. And it was the humble tax collector who Jesus exalted and 'justified,' while the self-righteous Pharisee who exalted himself was humbled (v.14). Unfortunately, most people – including children of Christian parents, as well many of the parents themselves - 'think' they are like the humble tax collector, but in reality, they are more like the self-righteous Pharisee. Part of the problem is that even Christians believe they are 'good.' But by saying that, they are defining 'goodness' based on the standards of their *own* view like the Pharisee, rather than on *God's* standards like the way the tax collector understood his own sinfulness and UNrighteousness before God, because they don't have an accurate understanding of what <u>God</u> defines as 'good' or what a 'Christian' is.

First, we need to understand what the Bible defines as 'good' verses how people in general define 'good,' and then what Jesus refers to as the 'good soil.' Anyone who has read the New

Testament is familiar with the story of Jesus and the rich young ruler who referred to Jesus as 'Good Teacher' (Mark 10:17), which Jesus responds with 'Why do you call Me good? No one is good except God alone' (v.18). By saying this, Jesus wasn't denying His Deity, since elsewhere in Scripture Jesus affirms it (Matthew 28:19; John 8:58, cf. Exodus 3:14-15; John 10:30-33; etc). Rather, His reply was in response to how this ruler, as well as people today, liberally defines 'good.' We tend to say "he is a 'good' person" and ask "why do bad things happen to 'good' people?" However, the problem with this loose definition of 'good' is that it's too subjective. There are no parameters, so one person may view another person as being 'good,' while someone else may find that same person as being 'not good.' So, who is right, and how do you determine that? Some people may argue, 'It's just a matter of opinion.' However, as we covered previously, opinion does not always equal Truth. So, while an opinion of someone 'might' be true, it might also be 'not true,' especially when two opinions conflict with each other. Therefore, Truth – not opinion – needs to be the objective criteria in determining if someone is 'good' or not. The apostle Paul goes so far as to quote Psalms 14:1-3 and Psalm 53:1-3 stating, 'THERE IS NONE RIGHTEOUS, NOT EVEN ONE...THERE IS NONE WHO DOES GOOD, THERE IS NOT EVEN ONE' (Romans 3:10-12). The type of 'good' that Paul is referring to is *moral* goodness, which he says no one 'does.' That's because 'this' kind of 'good' can only be done by God Himself, because 'He' is the only objective, moral Lawgiver. Three characteristics of God (among others) is that He's 'Omnipotent' ('all-powerful')(Job 42:4), 'Omniscient' ('all-knowing')(1 John 3:20), and 'unchanging' (Malachi 3:6), so since He can *do* anything, *knows* everything, and is incapable of change, which are not characteristics of human beings, that makes God objective in terms of morality, so He alone has the right to define what 'good' is.

Now on the surface, God being 'unchanging' might be viewed as being 'inflexible.' However, the inability to change is not actually being inflexible, but rather demonstrates objectivity to Truth, because Truth can't change. So a Being Who is unable to change actually demonstrates that *His* morality is based on Truth, because Truth can't change either. If God could change, then so could His morality, and if His morality changed, then His morality wouldn't be based on Truth that does not change, but would merely be based on opinion that may or may not be true. So, although we all know of stubborn people who *refuse* to change 'certain' aspects of their behavior, that's because of their *choice* not to change. You may ask, 'If God is all-powerful, then 'why' doesn't He have the power to change?' That's because in order to be God, He can't do anything to violate His perfect, eternal nature, otherwise, He'd cease to be God. And again, even 'if' He could change, then mankind would have no objective moral standard to live by, outside of *their* opinion which may conflict with someone else's opinion, and then no one could objectively claim if an action or thought is 'moral or immoral,' 'good or bad,' or 'holy or evil.' And it is ONLY the God of Scripture Who is all-powerful, all-knowing, unchanging, and is *always* moral and *always* does 'good.'

So, what is meant by the 'good soil,' and who does it apply to, since 'no one does good'?

In Chapter Two, I mentioned Ray Comfort and Kirk Cameron from the television series "Way of the Master," which is put out by "Living Waters Publication."[1] One of their outreach programs has been going out on the street and going up to individuals and asking them "Do you think you're a good person?" They then cover some of the Ten Commandments from the Bible, and ALL of the people they've interviewed have admitted to breaking at least a couple of them (some of them had the courage to admit to breaking them all!) They then go on to ask that if a person commits a crime, such as murder, rape, or theft, and stands before a judge in court, would that judge be 'just' if he let that person go scot-free? Most of them say 'no,' because the crime goes unpunished. The same thing is true when we sin against God, because God views sin – even sins we consider 'not that serious' – as a 'crime' against Him. King David confessed to God, 'Against You, You only, I have sinned… So that You are justified when You speak And blameless when You judge' because 'in sin my mother conceived me' (Psalm 51:4-5). Most people think that we're 'born good,' and 'become sinful' later. However, in reality, we're actually *conceived* in sin. Another wards, we don't 'become' sinners because we've sinned, but rather we sin *because* we were conceived *in sin*. Our *conception* in sin is what makes us sinners, not because we choose to sin latter in life. So, that's why 'No one is good except God alone' (Mark 10:18). However, a person can be 'innocent,' while at the same time not being capable to be, or do, 'good' by God's standards. One of the Hebrew words used in the Old

---

[1] Ibid. *Way of the Master*, "Living Waters Publication." http://www.livingwaters.com/outreach/the-way-of-the-master

Testament for 'innocent' ('naqiy') literally means 'clean, free from guilt or punishment, exempt from obligations,'[2] such as babies and young children (Psalm 106-37-38), as well as those who are mentally handicapped. Jesus even states 'Let the children alone, and do not hinder them from coming to Me; for the kingdom of heaven belongs to such as these' (Matthew 19:14). So, although they, too, are conceived in sin, what makes them all 'innocent' or 'free from judgment' before God, is because none of these people have the mental capability of *willfully* sinning against God like older children and adults can. Both Judas Iscariot and Pontius Pilate used a similar word for 'innocent' in reference to Jesus (Matthew 27:3-4,24), Who is both 'good' <u>and</u> 'innocent.' However, although babies are innocent, since they are conceived in sin, they aren't 'good' by God's objective moral standards. So, since even babies aren't 'good,' despite being innocent, because they were conceived in sin, then who are the people of the 'good soil' that Jesus talked about?

At the beginning of this chapter, I used the term 'self-righteous Christian,' which, Biblically, is an oxymoron, like 'icy hot,' a 'little big,' or 'pure evil.' That's because a genuine Christian doesn't believe that they can make themselves 'right' with God on their own. In a sense, Christians are actually less 'religious' than most other people in terms of salvation, because most non-christians who believe in God and an afterlife, honestly believe they are 'good enough' to merit Heaven on their own 'good efforts,' while not taking into account all their 'bad

---

[2] "Innocent" (Hebrew: 'naqiy') – transliteration and definition: http://www.blbclassic.org/lang/lexicon/lexicon.cfm?Strongs=H5355&t=NASB

efforts' and how those affected their relationship with God. It is <u>only</u> the Christian who believes that GOD is the One Who has to *make* a person 'righteous,' first, before they have any chance of entering Heaven. And it's through faith in Christ's 'finished' work on the cross that 'justifies' – or 'declares' a person 'righteous' – before God (Romans 5:1), and not because of a person's 'works' (Ephesians 2:8-9). Now, a word of caution here: I'm not implying an 'easy-believism' salvation here, because true genuine faith involves repentance, or a 'turning away' from a willful sinful lifestyle against God and turning *towards* God, which Paul describes as a 'walk in newness of life' being '*freed* from sin' (emphasis added)(Romans 6:1-7), as well as James who warns us that only 'true' salvific faith is demonstrated 'BY works' (emphasis added)(James 2:18) which is the visible RESULT of salvation (v.22) – but not the MEANS of salvation. That would be 'works-based' salvation, which is unscriptural and a false salvation plan, because it involves the efforts on the part of the 'not good' sinner trying to merit salvation from God, like the criminal who tries to 'merit' a not-guilty verdict from the judge in court and be let go scot-free. Both individuals (the 'self-righteous' sinner who believes in a works-based salvation plan and the criminal who wants off scot-free) are not part of the 'good soil,' because they aren't acknowledging 'who' they really are in the eyes of God, and that there is nothing they can 'offer' God, because God doesn't 'need' anything, nor will He accept anything from us, because 'all our righteous deeds are like a filthy garment' (Isaiah 64:6). Rather, it is what a person genuinely chooses to believe, which is evident in the results of what their belief 'produces' before others and to God.

Jesus stated that the 'seeds' that fall on good soil yields up a crop (Matthew 13:8). This is because unlike the 'rocky places, where they did not have much soil' which meant 'they had no root' (v.5-6), this 'good soil' has more than enough to plant a deep 'root.' As a result of having enough 'good soil' for the 'seed' to plant a deep enough root in, the seed that 'springs up' doesn't get 'scorched out' by the sun (v.6), but rather 'yields a crop, some hundredfold, some sixty, and some thirty' (v.8). In the Old Testament, a 'hundredfold' represented a 10,000% percent return on a crop, or an 'exceptional' or an 'inconceivable abundance' (Genesis 26:12). Last spring when Pusa and I were planting flowers and plants in the front of my house, in one of the particular flowerbeds, the Dusty Millers grew a lot higher than any of the other flowers and plants in the flowerbeds. However, even though they were planted in the same soil, they didn't all grow to the same height. Some grew twice as high as others and one particular Dusty Miller grew three to four times as high (about three feet!), despite being planted in the same soil. So, although the soil produced the same 'crop' from the same kind of seed we planted (v.8), they produced different 'heights' of the same crop. Likewise, when a person truly 'hears' the Gospel message (because God allows them to), and truly 'understands' the Gospel (that is, they accept the Gospel and allow it to penetrate their heart), the result will be that that person 'bears fruit' (ie: produces good works)(v.23). Another words, the person who doesn't just superficially 'listen' to the Gospel (v.14-15), but truly 'hears' the Gospel clearly (v.9) will demonstrate that the Gospel has truly penetrated their heart by willfully doing things to advance the kingdom of God on earth that God would approve of (ie: evangelizing; a change in a person's thoughts, speech, attitude;

a godly change in relationships with family, friends, and co-workers; a desire to have a more intimate relationship with and knowledge of God through studying His Word; etc). However, not everyone who accepts the same Truth of the Gospel is going to produce the exact same results, any more than the same seed that was planted in my flowerbed in the same soil last spring produced the exact same height of the same Dusty Millers, but they *will* be fruitful. As Pastor John MacArthur states in the footnotes of his NKJV Study Bible regarding Matthew 13:23:

> **"13:23 the good ground.** As there were 3 soils with no fruit, thus no salvation, there are 3 kinds of good soil with fruit. Not all believers are equally fruitful, but all are fruitful (cf. 7:16; John 15:8)"[3]

As Jesus points out there is a difference between *truly* 'hearing,' verses 'hearing, but will not understand' and 'seeing, but will not perceive' (v.14), because the latter 'scarcely hear, and they have closed their eyes' (v.15). Another wards, unlike someone who hears the Gospel message, accepts it, and demonstrates this by allowing the Gospel to accomplish results in their lives, the other three types of 'soils' don't allow that to occur. This is because they never took the Gospel seriously. They may have had a superficial knowledge of the Gospel, which they may have heard repeatedly from childhood, and even been able to quote hundreds of Scripture passages by heart,

---

[3] John MacArthur, "The MacArthur Study Bible," (footnotes, p.1418). Copyright 1997 by Word Publishing. *The Holy Bible, New King James Version* Copyright 1979, 1980, 1982 by Thomas Nelson, Inc., Nashville, TN. Used by permission. All rights reserved. (boldface in original)

but as previously mentioned in my example of Rachael Slick, superficial knowledge and intellectual ability to memorize isn't the same as that knowledge and memorized verses penetrating a person's heart to the point of an actual, *permanent* faith. In fact, earlier in Matthew's Gospel, Jesus states that 'Grapes are not gathered from *thorn* bushes nor figs from thistles, are they? So every good tree bears good fruit, but the bad tree bears bad fruit. A good tree cannot produce bad fruit, nor can a bad tree produce good fruit. Every tree that does not bear good fruit is cut down and thrown into the fire. So then, you will know them by their fruits' (emphasis added)(Matthew 7:16-20). This is a warning that just because a child may grow up in a Christian family, that doesn't automatically mean that *they themselves* are Christian (Matthew 7:21-23). And the warning signs to parents are the 'fruit' ('grapes' verses 'thistles') that they bear in their lives. During a Bible study I had at my home earlier this year, I referenced from a previous Bible study I had last year that out of the approximately 2+ billion self-professed 'Christians' in the world, approximately 75% (or three out of four) of them believe in a false salvation plan, and during the Bible study we discovered that it's even higher than that for non-christians who believe in a false religion or worldview (around 92%). And these figures include children of Christian parents who abandon the faith. As mentioned in the Prologue, two-thirds of children who are brought up in Christian homes stop attending church in their twenties. I felt it was relevant to bring up, because when a child that a parent loves and teaches them the Truth of the Christian faith, only for them to abandon it when they get older, it can cause the parent severe feelings of embarrassment, especially around other Christian parents whose children have not abandoned the faith. Feelings of 'what did I do wrong!' begin to surface. However, I thought it would be helpful and somewhat therapeutic to show that these parents are not alone, because the <u>majority</u> of children raised in a Christian household abandon the faith at one point or another – including children of pastors. So, if you are a parent whose child has abandoned the Christian faith, you're <u>not</u> alone – and there 'is' *real* hope, as we'll cover in Chapter Five. Similarly, Jesus mentions four different kinds of soils, and three of them (or 75%) represent individuals who have heard the Gospel, but are not saved, because the Holy Spirit has not convicted them of the Truth, and their hearts have not been regenerated, because of their willful rejection of the Gospel when it's heard. So, even though the Holy Spirit is the One Who actually convicts and regenerates a person's heart (John 16:8; Titus 3:5), we'll cover in Chapter Five the things that a Christian parent can do proactively before these warning signs come up, and even after they begin to surface.

Now, you might ask yourself, "How can two children who have the same Christian upbringing end up believing opposite things in terms of salvation, Jesus, and the Bible? Why is the Gospel 'sown' in the heart of the 'soil' of one child, but not another?" Jesus' disciples wondered something similar when they asked Him, 'Why do You speak to them [the 'large crowds' (v.2)] in parables?' (Matthew 13:10). Jesus' reply was 'To you it has been granted to know the mysteries of the kingdom of heaven, but to them it has not been granted... because while seeing they do not see, and while hearing they do not hear, nor do they understand.' (v.11,13).

But 'why' hasn't Jesus 'granted' them 'to know and understand the mysteries of the kingdom of heaven'? As mentioned in previous chapters, the other 'soils' represent the hearts of the three other types of children. Although God is a loving and merciful God, He also doesn't force His will on others, especially those whose hearts are so hardened, like the Pharaoh before Moses and the Pharisees, Sadducees, and scribes before Jesus, even though they all heard the Truth. Unlike the 'good soil' child who Jesus has 'granted' the knowledge of the Gospel Truth, the children represented by the other three 'soils' willfully rejected the Gospel because either: 1) it never penetrated their heart because they *refused* to even 'hear' and accept it (the 'Wayside' child – Chapter One); 2) their 'commitment' is superficial, surface-level, and temporary which is why they 'fall away' under 'afflictions and persecution' (the 'Rocky' child – Chapter Two); or 3) they allow themselves to be seduced by the temporary and deceitful cares, riches, and pleasures of the world that won't last, and they trade the Truth for lies (the 'Thorny' child – Chapter Three). What all these three kinds of children have in common is that the Gospel Truth was never able to penetrate their hearts, because they were both unable AND unwilling to accept it. For the purpose of space, and since it's beyond the scope of this book, I'm not going to go into the whole 'Calvinism' verses 'Arminianism' debate. However, it's worth repeating that God is the One Who regenerates the heart of an individual, and it's through His eternal Sovereign election process, which I don't have the intellectual or spiritual ability to comprehend completely, how a person is saved through predestination (Matthew 22:1-14; Romans 8:28-33; Ephesians 1:4-5,11; etc.), and that *none* of Jesus' 'sheep' Who 'hear My voice' will ever be 'snatched' away (Matthew 10:27-29), because Jesus states 'all that He [the Father] has given to Me I lose nothing' (John 6:39). Another wards, <u>everyone</u> Who God the Father has promised to Jesus to save, *will* be saved. However, since we don't know 'who' that is, that is why we are to 'preach the Gospel to all creation' (Mark 16:15).

So, a child who grows up in a Christian family who truly 'hears' and 'accepts' the Gospel Truth, and never 'falls away from the faith,' isn't because they are somehow 'better,' 'more good,' or 'more worthy' than children who do fall away, because people by themselves can't make themselves worthy before God because they are sinful (Matthew 22:8), but like Noah, GOD is the One Who *makes* us worthy, or 'righteous' through regeneration, conviction, repentance, and faith in Christ's shed blood on the cross for our sins. But, because these children of Christian parents who received the 'seed' in 'good soil' were both willing and able to truly 'hear' the Gospel Truth, and not just ignore it and simply dismiss Scripture as 'just a bunch of stories' – and going on to believe in something false – is 'why' unlike the other three kinds of 'soils' who will 'go away into eternal punishment,' these 'good' children will go away 'into eternal life' (Matthew 25:46). That is a decision that every child (and every adult, for that matter) has to decide for themselves: accept the Truth that their Christian parents taught them from their youth and benefit from that acceptance *eternally*...or reject the Truth for whatever emotional, afflicting, or worldly reason, and accept the consequences for buying into that lie *eternally*.

Eternity is long time to be right, but it's equally a long time to be wrong. I encourage you to choose wisely – not emotionally.

Me as an altar boy at Blessed Sacrament
Parish in Toledo, Ohio where I served as the
Treasurer of "The Knights of the Altar"

Family church photo (beginning clockwise from
upper left) - Mom (Darlene Christie), me, Grandpa
(Donald Murphy), Grandma (Florence Murphy). They
all played a big role in my early religious life.

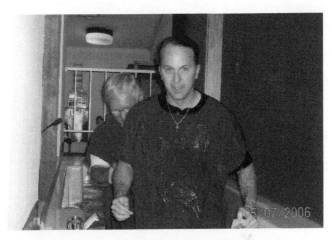

My baptism at Bethany Community Fellowship in Sylvania, Ohio. Unfortunately, the heater in the baptismal pool wasn't working, so it was a very cold, but memorable, event! (May 7, 2006)

As you can see EVERYONE is welcome to our Bible studies, including my mom's late poodle - Cerise. (I miss you nipping at my heels, "Boo-Boo!")

Photo of me at the "empty tomb" of Jesus at the Holy
Land Experience in Orlando, Florida (July 19, 2011)

Celebrating our 5th Anniversary AND 50th Bible study
that I lead out of my basement, which Lucia ("Pusa")
affectionately nicknamed "Toledo Underground
Church." [From right to left – Rachel, Olivia, Michael,
Tom, Kimberly, Mom, Lucia ("Pusa"), Mary, Laura,
John, Sharon, Sonny] (November 10, 2012)

Photo of the Dusty Millers that Pusa and I planted
last summer that "yielded a crop, some a hundredfold,
some sixty, some thirty" (Matthew 13:8)

Me, Pastor John MacArthur, and Lucia ("Pusa"), as Pastor
MacArthur signs Pusa's "MacArthur Study Bible," while
we were visiting Grace Community Church in Sun Valley,
California to listen to him preach (August 4, 2013)

Photo from Bethany Romanian Pentecostal Church in Niles, Illinois. (From right to left) - Me, Lucia ("Pusa"), and a Romanian couple we met there on June 1, 2014 where I asked Pusa to be my wife (she said "Yes!"), which just happened to fall on my late Grandma Florence's birthday. (I miss you and Grandpa!)

Photo of me at the ProclaimFM 102.3 radio station in Holland, Ohio being interviewed by Mark Howington to promote my book "Not Really 'Of' Us."

Chapter Five

What can "I" do?

I f you're a concerned parent, or even a concerned Christian in general, for the future and eternal, spiritual well-being of our youth, like most people I wouldn't be surprised if you are reading this chapter first. There's nothing wrong if you are doing that, and there is certainly no 'law' saying that you can't, especially if you are the concerned parent of a child who has drifted away from the faith, or if you have some other family member, friend, or acquaintance who is close to you who has wandered away from the faith. Naturally, you want to get some 'answers.' So, if this is all the time you have to read, then by all means, begin reading here. However, it might be more helpful if you start at the beginning of the book, because I attempt to explain my own mindset when I was younger and 'why' I didn't embrace the Christian faith, and then continue to explain in each chapter the different *reasons* why children of Christian parents abandon the faith. Just like any other problem, it's more helpful to understand 'why' a problem occurs, rather than just 'jumping' to the solution, because it's beneficial to understand the 'root' (no pun intended) of the problem. It also helps to understand the specific reason(s) for the problem, so when you approach your child, you can be at least somewhat equipped with some background knowledge, before attempting to 'fix it.' Remember, your child did have exposure to the Gospel (some more detailed and involved than others), yet they abandoned the faith anyways. So, at this point, you're asking yourself 'why?' Therefore, attempting to find a solution, before answering that 'why' question, might be putting the cart before the horse. Also, please keep in mind, this chapter isn't a 'guarantee' that your child will come to Christ. This isn't a 'follow steps one through ten' and your child will automatically accept Christ by 'step ten.' As we've already covered in this book, and what we'll go over in more detail in this chapter, is that we have to remind ourselves that the *Holy Spirit* is the One Who convicts and regenerates hearts (John 16:8; Titus 3:5), not us. However, as previously mentioned, there are things, Scripturally, that God wants you to do when raising your Christian child, in addition to sharing the Gospel (after all, any child who abandoned the faith knew the Gospel already, but they walked away from it anyways), as well as things that you can do if they do abandon the faith.

1. **Pray** – This might seem like a 'no-brainer.' But, you'd be surprised the people, including Christians, who forget to do this very simple task, as well as not realize (or perhaps, not believe) how effective it can be. After all, Scripture is filled with examples of answered prayers. James even reminds us, 'But if any of you lacks wisdom, let him ask

of God, who gives to all generously and without reproach, and it will be given to him. But he must ask in faith without any doubting, for the one who doubts is like the surf of the sea, driven and tossed by the wind' (James 1:5-6). Of course, a word of caution is necessary, because that doesn't mean that <u>every</u> time we pray to God for something, He's going to answer it in the way or timing that we expect – including prayers related to our children's salvation. Like Mom has always said, 'God isn't like our personal genie, where we rub a lamp and He grants us three wishes.' Unfortunately, many Christians think of God that way when they engage Him in prayer. They expect 'instant results,' or at least *specific* results that they expect will be 'granted.' In fact, this false impression of God is what leads many children of Christian parents to abandon the faith in the first place. Many times children are told by their Christian parents to simply "pray for anything in Jesus' Name, and He will grant it, because you are His child, and God is 'in control.'" Unfortunately, they base their view of God on passages like Matthew 7:8, where Jesus says 'For everyone who asks receives, and he who seeks finds, and to him who knocks it will be opened' (Matthew 7:8) and 'Whatever you ask in My name, that will I do... If you ask Me anything in My name, I will do it' (John 14:13-14). However, there is much more to those passages than this 'unidirectional' type of prayer request. We have to remember that we are praying to the <u>GOD</u> Who created the universe and everything in it (Genesis 1:1), including <u>us</u>! We also need to remember to respect and revere God, by reminding ourselves 'Who' we are actually talking *to*, rather than approach Him as

Someone we go to when we 'need' something. As Pastor
Craig Groeshel points out:

> "But when you remember who you're talking to –
> when you acknowledge that the God of the universe
> is honestly, truly excited to hear from you – that truth
> alone will change your attitude towards prayer."[1]

However, the psalmist also reminds us about the God of
the universe that 'The fear of the LORD is the beginning
of wisdom; A good understanding have all those who do
His commandments; His praise endures forever' (Psalm
111:10). So, although the God of the universe is indeed
'excited' to hear from us, the psalmist is also pointing out
that we are to have a reverential and respectful 'fear' of
God of the universe, just as we should towards our parents
who created us and reared us. Parents must be a model
for their children by respecting God in the way that He
deserves, so that their children can see the importance
of respecting Him, as well as their parents, which the
apostle Paul commands children to obey and honor their
parents (Ephesians 6:1-2; Colossians 3:20), because the
same God Who created them, also had them be conceived
and born to their parents. And as mentioned in Chapter
Three, just because a parent may disobey God themselves,
and not necessarily discipline a child Biblically, that's no
excuse for disobeying *them*. Two wrongs don't make a
right. However, it is imperative for Christian parents to be

---

[1] Craig Groeschel, *"The Christian atheist: believing in God but living as if he
doesn't exist,"* p. 78. Grand Rapids, MI: Zondervan, 2010.

obedient to God, and obey Him *themselves*, and don't be hypocritical ('Don't do what I do; do what I say'), because that will send a conflicting message, and even risk their children drifting *away* from God.

Getting back to proper praying. Rather than the 'genie praying' that Christian parents so often teach their children, we have to remember that although God *does* answer prayers, God does have certain conditions:

a. <u>Prayer that glories *Him*</u> – when Christians read Scripture passages about praying like John 14:13-14, they tend to forget about the part in verse thirteen that says, 'so that the Father may be glorified in the Son' and the following verse 'If you love Me, you will keep My commandments' (v.15). As previously stated, prayer is not 'unidirectional,' but rather a TWO-way street. When we pray, we should not pray selfishly, but pray with the intent that the prayer will glorify *God* - not ourselves, or what 'we want.' Now, praying for your children's salvation is by no means selfish. However, when you pray for that, it should be in a manner that you're not just asking for it to make *you* feel better, but that the prayer will bring glory to God – even if that specific prayer request isn't ever answered with a 'yes.' Another wards, the prayer request of Christian parents for the salvation of their children should be just as 'God-centered' as any other prayer request, rather than 'me-centered.' Our intent shouldn't be anymore 'in need,' than if we were praying for the salvation of someone not related, or unknown, to us, or for any other kind of prayer request. God is to be the <u>focus</u> of every prayer request, regardless of 'what' we are praying about or 'who' we are praying for. God deserves that much from us... and more.

b. <u>Prayer that doesn't harm but is good</u> (Matthew 7:9-11) – you might think "in what way would praying for the salvation of our children 'harm' them? Isn't the alternative – our children not ever coming to Christ and suffering eternity in Hell – far more 'harmful'?" Of course that would definitely be more harmful than anything else. However, the 'harm' I'm referring to is the parent's *intent* of their prayers to bring their child to Christ. As mentioned in Chapter Three, sometimes parents only want 'mini-me' versions of themselves in order that their children 'obey and do their bidding.' However, that is not the type of relationship that God wants between Christian parents and their children. In the same passages where the apostle Paul commands children to obey and honor their parents, he also commands Christian fathers '*do not provoke your children to anger*, but bring them up in the discipline and instruction of the Lord' (emphasis added)(Ephesians 6:4) and 'do not exasperate your children, *so that they will not lose heart*' (emphasis added)(Colossians 3:21). Unfortunately, many Christian parents do 'provoke' and 'exasperate' their children, which actually lead them *away* from Christ when they get older and accept the temporary, false 'acceptance' from their non-christian relationships and peers mentioned in Chapter Three. And many of these same kind of Christian parents who pray for the salvation of their adult children, who abandoned the faith, pray only for their children to return to that same unbiblical 'provoking' and 'exasperation' they received from their parents that led them away from Christ in the first place. So it is this kind of 'harm' to children of Christian parents that God does <u>not</u> want their parents to pray for them to return to. As mentioned in 'point a,' the prayer request of Christian parents for the salvation of their children should be just as 'God-centered' as any other prayer request, rather than 'me-centered.'

c. <u>Prayer that is according to God's will</u> – when Jesus was praying in the garden of Gethsemane (Matthew 26:36), He said to His Heavenly Father, 'if you are willing, remove this cup from Me; yet *not My will, but Yours be done*' (emphasis added)(Luke 22:42). In fact, in Mark and Luke's account it doesn't say that Jesus *prayed* for His 'cup' to be removed, but merely that Jesus *said* that if God were 'willing,' that it would be removed (Mark 14:36; Luke 22:42). And in Matthew's account when Jesus fell on His face and prayed, again, He merely *said* 'if it is possible, let this cup pass from Me; yet not as I will, but as You will' (Matthew 26:39). Jesus wasn't actually expecting His Father to prevent the crucifixion since dying on the cross for our sins is what He came to do, but rather He was verbally expressing His explicit lack of desire to endure the torture of the crucifixion that He knew He had to endure, which is evident in Luke's account of Jesus' agony in the garden when 'His sweat became like great drops of blood falling down upon the ground' (Luke 22:44)(NKJV), which Pastor John MacArthur expands on in his footnotes of this verse in his study Bible:

> **"22:44 like great drops of blood.** This suggests a dangerous condition known as *hematidrosis*, the effusion of blood in one's perspiration. It can be caused by extreme anguish or physical strain. Subcutaneous capillaries dilate and burst, mingling blood with sweat. Christ Himself stated that His distress had brought Him to the threshold of death (*see notes on Matt. 26:38; Mark 14:34;* cf. *Heb. 12:3,4*)."[2]

Jesus being 'all-knowing' was well aware that the crucifixion was the will of God, which is why He didn't explicitly *pray* for the crucifixion not to happen, but rather prayed that the *Father's will* be done, not His. When we pray – even for the salvation of our children – we need to pray that the *Father's will* – not necessarily *our will* – be done, just as Jesus did, even when making specific prayer requests. And because we don't know what the Father's will is regarding the

---

[2] John MacArthur, "The MacArthur Study Bible," (footnotes, p.1561). Copyright 1997 by Word Publishing. *The Holy Bible, New King James Version* Copyright 1979, 1980, 1982 by Thomas Nelson, Inc., Nashville, TN. Used by permission. All rights reserved. (boldface and italics in original)

salvation of our children, when we pray for them, we need to pray in the same way Jesus prayed in the garden. Jesus stated 'For I have come down from heaven, *not to do My own will*, but the will of Him who sent Me. This is the will of Him who sent Me, that of *all that He has given Me I lose nothing*, but raise it up on the last day. For *this is the will of My Father*, that *everyone who beholds the Son and believes in Him will have eternal life*, and I Myself will raise him up on the last day' (emphasis added)(John 6:40). So, the 'will of the Father' is that only those who the Father 'has given' to Jesus, who 'believes in Him will have eternal life.' However, since we don't explicitly know whether or not that includes our children (since only God is 'Omniscient'), we still need to pray that if it *is* God's will, that He will grant our prayers for the salvation of our children.

d. <u>Pray that HE is the One Who answers our prayers</u> – when we pray we have to remember that Jesus said that it is GOD Who answers our prayers, when Jesus said, 'If you ask *Me* anything in *My name, I* will do it' (emphasis added)(John 14:14). Of course, as previously mentioned, that prayer will only be answered with a 'yes,' *if* it's in accordance to His will (Luke 22:42; John 6:38-40; etc). However, throughout Scripture, Jesus, as well as the New Testament writers, are very explicit that when we pray, we are to pray directly to God <u>through</u> Jesus (John 14:14), Who is our 'Advocate with the Father' (1 John 2:1), our '*ONE* mediator also between God and men, the man Christ

Jesus' (emphasis added)(1 Timothy 2:5), 'who also intercedes for us' (Romans 8:34), and Who when we pray to God through Jesus, the '[Holy] Spirit Himself intercedes for us' (Romans 8:26-27). In this way, all three 'Persons' of the Godhead (the Father, the Son, and the Holy Spirit) are each involved in the prayer process: the Holy Spirit 'intercedes for us with groanings too deep for words' (Romans 8:26), Who sort of 'interprets' and 'fine tunes' our prayers more specifically and sends them to our 'Advocate' and 'Mediator,' Who is our 'High Priest' Who takes our prayers before God the Father (Hebrews 3:1), similar to the high priest in the Old Testament who was the <u>only</u> one who was 'appointed on behalf of men in things pertaining to God, in order to offer both gifts and sacrifices for sins before God' (Hebrews 5:1). So, when we pray that God is the One Who answers prayers, that means He is the ONLY One Who does. Therefore, God – all three 'Persons' of Godhead – is the ONLY One Who should be involved in the prayer 'process' – not anyone else.

2. **Take the initiative** – don't rely on your Church leadership to teach your children. Educate them *yourselves*. We have to remember that the average child sitting in the pew only gets 'spiritual exposure' from their spiritual leaders one hour a day, one day a week. So, essentially, they are only being 'spiritually fed' ***one hour per <u>week</u>!*** In order to put this into perspective, imagine only consuming physical food and water one hour per week – we would literally starve to death, wouldn't we? So, what makes

us think that our children can survive *spiritually* on one hour per week of the 'spiritual food and drink' of Christ (1 Corinthians 10:4)? Without this additional 'food and drink' our children are literally starving spiritually. Now, that doesn't mean that I'm saying, 'Don't take your kids to church, and only teach them the Word of God yourselves,' or simply plop them down in front of 'Christian television.' In fact, Scripture actually *commands* us 'to stimulate one another to love and good deeds, *not forsaking our own assembling together*, as is the habit of some, but encouraging one another; and all the more as you see the day drawing near' (emphasis added)(Hebrews 10:24-25). Rather, I'm saying not to *merely* depend on the leaders of your church for the *sole* source for the spiritual 'feeding' of your children. And it's worse for "C and E" Christians (those who only attend service on Christmas and Easter) – they only get 'fed' **two hours per year!** That's not nearly enough! Unfortunately, that's what a lot of Christian parents do – they solely rely on their Church leadership, or T.V. preachers, to teach their children the Word of God, thinking 'that's sufficient.' However, Scripture makes it explicitly clear that it is the role of both the father AND the mother to teach the Truth of the Gospel on a *daily* basis.

As previously mentioned, the apostle Paul commands fathers to 'bring them up in the discipline and instruction of the Lord' (Ephesians 6:4). However, that also includes mothers as well. The mistake I have seen so often in Christian families is that they think that the father is the only one who should teach the Word of God and the Truth of the Gospel to their children, because that is one of his primary responsibilities in his family. However, Scripture also states that the children's *mother* is also expected to teach them. Paul reminds Timothy that he was 'mindful of the sincere faith within you, which first dwelt in your grandmother Lois and your mother Eunice, and I am sure that it is in you as well' (2 Timothy 1:5), who it was 'from childhood you have known the sacred writings' (2 Timothy 3:15), because although Timothy's mother was a believer, his father was a Greek (Acts 16:1), which means that his father wasn't a believer. It is so crucial that children of Christian parents should be taught Scripture not only by their fathers but **also** by their mothers as well, especially if the father is an unbeliever or absent, such as in the case of Timothy, whether due to death, divorce, or abandonment. This is why the apostle Paul commands older women about '*teaching* what is good, so that they may *encourage young women*' (emphasis added) (Titus 2:3-4). So, the more teaching of the Word of God and the Truth of the Gospel that children hear from their Church leaders, their fathers, AND their mothers and grandparents, the more 'spiritually fed' our children will be, so that when they do 'hunger' and 'thirst,' they will have the desire to 'come' to Jesus through His Word and 'believe' in Him (John 6:35,37), and less likely to have their 'hunger' and 'thirst' be unsatisfactorily 'fed' by temporary ungodly, worldly 'deceitfulness' that will never permanently satisfy them (Matthew 7:22).

So, 'how' is a Christian parent supposed to 'take the initiative' and teach their children?

a. **LEARN the Word of God** – begin by reading Scripture daily to become doctrinally sound, which includes comparing what you're being taught to Scripture (Acts 17:11). Remember, the *primary* responsible party who God has entrusted to teach your children is YOU - the parent – not their Church leaders who only get them for one hour per week, nor the 'T.V. Christian preacher.' And the only way that a parent will be able to teach Scripture accurately to their children, is if they have a strong grasp of it themselves, which requires daily reading of the Word of God on their own, so that they can be like Timothy's mother and grandmother who taught the Old Testament Scriptures to Timothy, which is 'why' Timothy's faith was sound. So, even if you don't have a lot of time due to 'real world' responsibilities, **make time** by reserving a specific time period each day – even if it's only ten or twenty minutes, and even if you have to completely rearrange your 'busy' schedule. Your children, and their eternal destination after death, *are* worth that sacrifice, and it will glorify our Lord!

b. **TEACH the Word of God** – once you have enough of a grasp of the Word of God, begin teaching what you have learned to your children. Although there's no such thing as an 'expert' on the Word of God (myself included), once you understand the basics of sound Biblical doctrine, such as the depravity of man which resulted from the Fall of Adam (Genesis 3:1-24; Romans 5:12,17,19), the Atonement and the *need* for a Savior to reconcile us before God (Romans 5:6-10; 2 Corinthians 5:14-21), belief in Jesus for eternal life (John 3:16) and salvation by grace through faith and not of works (Romans 5:1; Ephesians 2:8-9), and *genuine* repentance ('the changing of one's mind') by turning <u>away</u> from our sinful lifestyle and mindset and turning <u>towards</u> God (Matthew 3:2; 4:17; Mark 1:15; 6:12; Luke 13:3,5; 15:7,10; Acts 2:38; 3:19; 8:22; 17:30; 26:20) which is demonstrated BY our works (James 2:18) – but not the MEANS of our salvation – you will then be able to at least teach basic, sound, fundamental Christian doctrine and the Truth of the Gospel to your children, as you continue to learn the Word of God yourself. No one ever 'graduates' from learning God's Word – even those who preach and teach Scripture or have written study Bibles – it's a life-long learning process that extends beyond the grave. However, as you continue to grow in your knowledge of the Truth and teach it to your children, you should begin to grow spiritually and more knowledgeable of His Word, rather than remain in spiritual 'infancy.' However, this takes effort and discipline to set aside time each day to study the Word of God and then teach what you've learned to your children. Unfortunately, many Christian parents don't take this effort and remain as the apostle Paul states, 'I gave you milk to drink, not solid food; for you were not yet able to receive it. Indeed, even now you are not yet able' (1 Corinthians 3:20).

Being able to 'receive' spiritual 'solid food' is imperative for not only your own spiritual growth, but also that of your children. It's no different than a parent who is only able to help with their child's education up to the sixth grade. If the child doesn't receive the help from their parents beyond a sixth grade level, they may lag behind and have difficulty with higher education. Likewise, if the parent is still 'nursing on the milk' themselves, they will be unable to be 'teachers' to their children, as the writer of Hebrews warns us, 'For though by this time you ought to be teachers, you have need again for someone to teach you the elementary principles of the oracles of God, and you have come to need milk and not solid food. For everyone who partakes only of milk is not accustomed to the word of righteousness, for he is an infant. But solid food is for the mature, who *because of practice* have their senses trained to discern good and evil' (emphasis added)(Hebrews 5:12-14). So, the key to teaching your children is *practice* which should be done *daily*, and then teach what you've practiced and learned to your children, and begin when they are <u>young</u>. There are many age-appropriate aids at your church, Christian bookstores, and elsewhere that can aid you in continually teaching your children as they grow, while at the same time aiding you in your own spiritual growth. And as your child grows, getting more age-related resources to aid them in their spiritual growth and help them to understand Scripture at a more deeper level, such as the MacArthur Study Bible³,

---

³ Ibid.

as well as other Christian apologetic sources (which we'll cover later in this chapter), will help them to learn, as well as to objectively believe in and trust in what they are learning.

c. **TRAIN them in the Word of God** – when the apostle Paul tells us that after we are saved by grace through faith and not of works (Ephesians 2:8-9), he goes on to say that we are God's 'workmanship, created in Christ Jesus *for* good works' (emphasis added)(v.10). Another wards, the whole purpose of our existence and 'why' God created us, and then saved us, is to be His 'workmen' to *do* good works, which includes training up the next generation to be fellow 'workmen' for Christ themselves. And the way a parent 'trains' them is to explain to them that the *source* of 'training in righteousness' and 'good work' is through Scripture. As the apostle Paul writes, 'All Scripture is inspired by God and profitable for teaching, for reproof, for correction, *for training in righteousness*; so that the man of God may be adequate, *equipped for every good work*' (emphasis added)(2 Timothy 3:16-17). So, the primary way a Christian parent 'trains' their children to be 'equipped for every good work' is by emphasizing that the *source* of good work is Scripture, because ALL Scripture is Inspired, or 'God-breathed' – which includes both the Old Testament Scriptures (2 Timothy 3:15) AND the New Testament Scriptures, such as: Paul's epistles (2 Peter 3:15-16), the Gospel of Luke (1 Timothy 5:18; cf. Luke 10:7) - which would also include the book of Acts which was also written by Luke – as well as the 'word of Christ' that our 'faith comes from hearing' (Romans 10:17) which are spoken in the other Gospels (Matthew, Mark, John), as well as the book of Revelation which is 'self-authoritatively' Authored by Jesus Christ also (Revelation 1:1,3,5,8-11), as well as the rest of the New Testament that is Inspired, which Jesus is the 'author' of (Hebrews 12:2). So, this Scriptural 'training' should begin just as early for your children, as their 'teaching.' Another wards, have them apply what they have been taught. It's not just enough for them to read and learn Scripture – that's just memorization, and as we've witnessed in the book, memorization doesn't mean a child will remain in the faith as they get older. Children need to be trained 'why' those verses are important. They need to believe and be convinced that all Scripture *is* God's Word, which involves not only reinforcement of *reading* it to them, but also having them *apply* God's commands, which includes, 'whoever slaps you on your right cheek, turn the other to him also' (Matthew 5:39); 'If anyone wants to sue you and take your shirt, let him have your coat also' (v.40); 'love your enemies and pray for those who persecute you' (v.44); 'Do not store up for yourselves treasures on earth...But store up yourselves treasures in heaven' (v.19-20); and 'In *everything*, therefore, treat people the same way you want them to treat you, for that is the Law and Prophets' (emphasis added)

(Matthew 7:12).[4] These are self*LESS* values that are largely in opposition to worldly, self*ISH* ways of thinking and acting towards others, as well as being unique to the Christian faith, which demonstrates to others that your beliefs, actions, and attitudes – as well as those of your children – towards others that they 'will know that you are My [Christ's] disciples, if you have love for one another' (John 13:34-35) are not of man but of God, even if they reject these values.

---

4 Some people may attempt to point out that Jesus' command to 'treat people the same way you want them to treat you' (the 'Golden Rule') is merely a variation of much earlier 'golden rules' from the past. However, the 'Golden Rule' that Jesus taught was spoken and commanded <u>positively</u>: 'In everything, therefore, treat people *the same way* you want them to treat you, for this is the Law and the Prophets' (emphasis added)(Matthew 7:12). Other 'golden rules' prior to, and contemporary with, the time of Jesus were spoken and commanded to avoid <u>negative</u> behavior that may result in negative retaliations. For example: 'What is hateful to yourself, <u>*do not to someone else*</u>." – Rabbi Hillel (100 years before Jesus). '<u>*Never impose on others*</u> what you would <u>*not choose for yourself*</u>' – Confucius (China). '<u>*Do not do to others*</u> what would anger you if done to you by others." – Isocrates (Greece). 'Expect from others <u>*what you did to them*</u>.' – Seneca (Rome). Jesus' *positively-commanded* 'Golden Rule' is different than these *negatively-avoiding* 'golden rules,' because it was based on the 'Law and the Prophets' (ie: the Old Testament Scriptures)(Matthew 5:17) which also commanded God's people to have an attitude of forgiveness towards, and prayer for, our enemies in this same way. When Jesus was asked what the 'greatest commandment' is, He quoted Deuteronomy 6:5 and Leviticus 19:18, which tells us not only to 'love the LORD your God,' but <u>also</u> to 'love your neighbor as yourself' (Matthew 22:36-40). Jesus also corrected some of the false teachings of the scribes and the Pharisees, who although taught correctly to 'love your neighbor,' they incorrectly taught to 'hate your enemies' (Matthew 5:43), while Jesus taught to 'love your enemies and pray for those who persecute you' (Matthew 5:44). <u>Jesus</u>' 'Golden Rule' commands us to 'love one another, even as I have loved you' so that '*all men will know that you are My disciples*' (emphasis added)(John 13:34-35).

3. **Provide assurance and love** – this point can't be emphasized enough, because I have personally seen Christian parents not do this enough with their children, which is desperately needed. However, this assurance should not only include that the Christian faith is <u>based</u> on evidence (Hebrews 11:1), including the assurance that our salvation is <u>based</u> on what's 'written' (1 John 5:13), but also the assurance to children of Christian parents that they are *truly* loved and accepted, just as Jesus assured those who *truly* 'believed *in Him*' that God loves them and they <u>will</u> have 'eternal life' (John 3:16). Just as we need assurance from God that we can (and will be saved), children also need assurance from their parents that they love and accept them. What all children – including children of Christian parents – want more than anything is to <u>know</u> they are loved and accepted. And if they don't feel they have this 'love' and 'acceptance' from their parents, they'll seek it elsewhere by others, who may not be Christians, and as a result they may begin to embrace the false worldviews of those who 'accept' them.

Notice, I didn't say that they would embrace false worldviews that would 'accept *AND love*' them, because by definition, 'God *IS* love' (emphasis added)(1 John 4:16). So, unless the affection that a child receives from someone else is a *Biblically*-based Christian, then the perceived 'love' they are receiving from that individual will never be that close, personal, intimate 'God-love' that can only be shared between Christians. And it is this kind of 'love' that God has for His *true* children, whom He saves and 'gave the right to become children of God, even to those who believe in His name' (John 1:12).

Unfortunately, too many times I've heard the words 'I love you,' used so frequently in Christian circles, that it almost loses its meaning. It's almost like a thoughtless, knee-jerk response, such as "you're welcome." Mom has repeatedly said that those words are so precious to her that that is the reason she doesn't say them all the time, so when you hear those words from her, you'll know they aren't 'just words,' but that she truly means that she <u>loves</u> <u>you</u> deep down in her heart. Also, saying the words 'I love you,' doesn't automatically convince children that their parents love them. Children – even very young children – pick up on non-verbal actions very quickly. I have personally seen parents slap their child across the face for being disobedient to them, send them to their room, and then almost immediately the first words out of their mouth to their child is 'I love you!'

How is a child supposed to react to that? What are they supposed to think? What parents don't understand is that when they do that, they send mixed and confusing messages to their children, and they actually begin to build up doubt – not only regarding their parents' genuine love for them, but it may also begin to plant seeds of doubt in the validity of the reality of the Christian faith that their parents taught them. Now, as mentioned earlier in this book, that doesn't mean that parents shouldn't discipline their children when they are disobedient. After all, a *lack* of discipline – as well as a lack of following through on promised discipline – gives the child the message that their disobedience is 'okay,' and also receive the message that disobedience will only result in empty promises of discipline that will never happen, and thus encourage further disobedience. So, discipline needs to be balanced – the 'punishment' must fit the 'crime,' but neither be too severe nor too permissive – sort of an 'eye for eye' type punishment (Exodus 21:24), while at the same time assuring their children that their parent *truly* loves them, beyond just saying the words. And part of providing their children the assurance they need that their parents truly love them is to demonstrate that their love for them doesn't change even 'when' they are disobedient. The apostle Paul reminds us, 'But God demonstrates His own love toward us, in that *while we were yet sinners*, Christ died for us' (emphasis added)(Romans 5:8). Notice that God's love for us isn't conditional, because He 'demonstrated' His love 'towards *us*' when 'we were *yet* sinners.' So, although God doesn't condone us sinning against Him, anymore than a parent doesn't condone their own children willfully disobeying them, that sinning against God and that disobedience against parents doesn't diminish God's love for His children, nor a parent's love for their children – or at least it *shouldn't*. And it is 'this' kind of 'assurance of love' that children are looking for.

Growing up, Mom disciplined me when I was willfully disobedient to her and refused to listen, but she also balanced that with assuring me that she never stopped loving me, not only because she said so, but also because she demonstrated that through her actions. When children are young, they fear disappointing their parents, because they fear that their parents might stop loving them. And if they perceive that has happened, that can actually damage their relationship with their parents, even if their parents are not aware of it. And that is why it's important to not just *say* the words 'I love you,' but also *demonstrate* that love to them, even when they are most 'unlovable' – which is when they need that assurance the most, just as Jesus did when He <u>died</u> for sinners out of **love** for them. And if parents don't do that, their children will attempt to find that assurance from someone – or some*thing* – else, like alcohol, illegal drugs, or illicit sex with someone who doesn't actually love them, because they are so used to the 'words,' they don't know the difference between *genuine* love, and someone simply using the words to just get the child to do what they want. If a person *truly* loves you, they'll love God even <u>more</u> than you, which demonstrates being obedient to Him through their thoughts, words, and actions (James 2:18) – otherwise, it's not actual love. It's actually something worse – disobedience to God and disrespecting <u>you</u>.

Lastly, this 'unconditional love' also needs to be assured even if they abandon the Christian faith. I've seen too many times where parents threaten to disown their children if they walk away from Christ. However, what if Jesus would have done that with us the first time we sinned against Him, or during a period of our lives when *we* questioned the Christian faith or even abandoned it ourselves? We need to have the same 'long-suffering' patience with our children that Christ did with us, because we don't know when the Holy Spirit is going to regenerate their hearts and convict them of the Truth of the Gospel, and then they'll come back. It's not at all helpful to 'force' an ultimatum on our children ('either accept Christ or you're disowned.') Remember, they are already rebelling. Threatening to disown them isn't going to help – it's only going to push them further away, especially if they have already established a 'support-system' of individuals who accept them just as they are. However, the reality is that that 'acceptance' from their 'support-system' is also based on <u>conditions</u>, because what rebelling children don't realize is that if they begin to rebel against their 'support-system,' especially if their rebelliousness conflicts with something foundational to their support system, their support-system may also threaten to disown them as well, which is what you find in many cults, as well as non-religious groups. So, again, unconditional love – including acceptance of your unbelieving child – is imperative to letting them know you *truly* love them and accept them, while at the same time, pray for them and share the Truth of the Gospel with them, when they are open to it.

4. **<u>Explain the difference between 'opinion' and 'truth'</u>** – I can't tell you how many times I've heard, "You have your truth and I have my truth, so we'll just have to 'agree to disagree'" or "You have your truth and I have my truth, so how can you say your truth is right and my truth is wrong?" The problem with these statements is that the incorrect word is being used – truth. By definition, 'truth' is something that isn't false. In fact, truth is the *opposite* of false. Anyone who has ever taken a 'True or False' quiz knows that. Therefore, if something is true, then the exact opposite is false. Opposite beliefs can't be both be true, nor can they be both false, because they are opposite.

One belief MUST be true and one belief MUST be false, because they are opposite and contradict each other. So, what the person is actually attempting to say in the above comments is "You have your *opinion* and I have my *opinion*" – not your 'truth' and my 'truth.' Now, someone's opinion 'can' be true, but it can also be false, because the validity of a person's opinion is based on whether their opinion is <u>factual</u>. So, if one person's opinion is factual, then the opposite opinion of someone else is *not* factual, and therefore *not* true.

Now, the unbelieving child might ask their Christian parent, "Then how can you say your 'opinion' is right and my 'opinion' is wrong?" The answer to that is that unlike other religious and secular worldviews, the Christian faith is backed up on <u>factual</u> evidence – historical, scientific, archaeological, logical reasoning, and HUNDREDS of LITERALLY fulfilled prophecies about future events written dozens, hundreds, and even sometimes <u>thousands</u> of years before the events actually happened in the real world. The confusion that the unbelieving child runs into is that with the thousands of religions and worldviews out there, they refuse to accept that any one worldview, let alone the Christian faith, can be true with the vastness of 'opinions' in the world. However, what they don't realize is that they *are* accepting a worldview – theirs. But, most of the time, it's a worldview that is either based on absolutely ZERO evidence outside of 'their' opinion, which is just circular reasoning, or it's a blend of opinions that they 'pick and choose' what to accept and what to reject, in order to justify their lifestyle. They are also not accepting

that – logically – ONLY ONE worldview (or 'opinion')
can – and <u>must</u> – be true, because 'something' *has* to be
true. Therefore, since only one worldview is true, then –
logically - all the other worldviews (religious and secular)
are false, because their 'opinions' are opposite of the only
one, factual worldview that is true. And as previously
mentioned, the Christian faith is based on fact, not
falsehood, therefore, any other worldview that contradicts
the Christian faith is <u>not</u> based on fact, but on falsehood,
and is therefore <u>not</u> true. You can't have opposite 'opinions'
both being true. That's illogical, yet so many children of
Christian parents will, and have, embraced this illogical
way of thinking, by incorrectly referring to their and other
people's 'opinions' as 'truth,' when in reality – logically –
there can be ONLY ONE 'truth.' In fact, the apostle Paul
refers to the Christian faith as the 'truth of the gospel'
(Galatians 2:5,14; cf. Ephesians 1:13; Colossians 1:5).

5. **<u>Be examples/be consistent/be honest</u>** – children,
including children of Christian parents, closely observe
their parents, including what they say, how they act, and
what they profess. And too many times, the old adage
'Don't do what I do, do what I say' is either enforced or
implied, even by Christian parents. So many times, I've
heard Christian parents condemn their children for using
the Lord's Name in vain or use other curse words, only
for the parent to do the same. Don't be a hypocrite, but
rather imitate the apostle Paul, who imitated Christ (1
Corinthians 4:16; 11:1). When you read Paul's epistles,
what clearly comes across in them is his extreme humility
and humbleness as a follower of Christ, as well as his

honesty and consistent theology, including rebuking not only the churches he wrote to, but also well-respected and established Church leaders when they were wrong, including the apostle Peter (Galatians 2:11-14). Paul was never afraid to 'mix it up,' even with other apostles and elders in the Church, but he never considered himself 'above' them, nor 'inferior' to them by stating, 'For I am the least of the apostles, and not fit to be called an apostle, because I persecuted the church of God' (1 Corinthians 15:9) and 'Therefore I am well content with weaknesses, with insults, with distresses, with persecutions, with difficulties, for Christ's sake; for when I am weak, then I am strong...for in no respect was I inferior to the most eminent apostles, even though I am a nobody' (2 Corinthians 12:10-11).

It takes an incredible about of humility for an apostle such as Paul – who wrote one-third of the New Testament (more than any other writer of it) – to express that kind of humbleness and honesty, especially to the churches he was writing to who were beginning to allow false doctrines to creep in. And it is this kind of humble example that Christian parents should show towards their children. I remember when I was growing up, Mom was usually right about most things, because she was one to really check things out ahead of time before claiming something to be true, rather than just assuming something is true and reacting with emotion (something I freely admit I used to be guilty of, which Mom would most certainly agree). However, she was also one to admit when she was wrong, too – something she does to this very day. And I think this is the big mistake that parents, including Christian parents, make with their children. They love their children so much that they don't want them to make the same mistakes they made, to the point that they're afraid to admit to their children 'when' they are wrong, because they are afraid that they will lose credibility with their children. However, by not doing that, when their children do find out something wrong about their parents and their parents refuse to acknowledge it, that dishonesty actually *loses* credibility with their children, and eventually, their children begin to question the validity of other things their parents have taught them to be true, including the validity of the Truth of the Christian faith. So, it is essential that Christian parents admit when they are wrong, especially to their children. Honesty is not only the best policy, but also the best teacher and witness of truthfulness and will actually earn respect and trust from your kids. Whatever behavior you exhibit and examples you demonstrate to your children – good or bad – your children will likely mimic, even as adults.

And don't act like one of those 'smarmy' televangelists. You know the ones I mean – the ones who scream and yell on T.V., and repeatedly say "IN JESUS' NAME" about every other sentence, and virtually 'thump' their Bibles on the people in the front row of their church, who then reply with 'Amen!' in response to every "in Jesus' name." The ones whose phony smiles never leave their faces, and never stop raising their arms up to Heaven with their 'church-bought' Rolexes on their wrists, while that nineteenth century organ music intermittently hits that loud chord for just the right emotional effect. I realize I'm being quite a bit stereotypical and dramatic, but only for the purpose of helping you to visualize the impressions that certain televangelists and pastors have on your children, who are already questioning the legitimacy of the Christian faith. I also realize that not *all* televangelists and pastors act this way. Most of them do an exceptional job faithfully teaching the Word of God accurately with passion and zeal, without the unnecessary dramatics found in others, like the kind previously mentioned. But when it comes to impressions, your children tend to remember the most eccentric ones – including those preachers who 'act like televangelists.' Unfortunately, this way of talking and behaving can actually 'rub-off' on Christian parents too, and when they act that way around their own children, this phoniness bleeds through.

The apostle Paul wrote about similar experiences he had with the Jewish leaders of His time, who, although, were 'entrusted with the oracles of God' (ie: teaching the Old Testament Scriptures)(Romans 3:1-2), did not truly have a heart for Christ, but instead were caught up in their own dramatics and legalism, when Paul had to 'testify about them that they have a zeal for God, but not in accordance with knowledge. For not knowing about God's righteousness and seeking to establish their own, they did not subject themselves to the righteousness of God' (Romans 10:2-3). Now, these particular televangelists and pastors might argue that they are in no way like the Jewish leaders of Jesus' and Paul's time who rejected Christ, because they accept Jesus as their 'Lord and Savior.' But, we have to remember that Jesus didn't have a problem with the Jewish leaders teaching the Old Testament, but rather with their legalism and theatrics that they *added to* the 'oracles of God.' For example, when the Pharisees and scribes approached Jesus and criticized His disciples for not washing their hands before they eat (Matthew 15:1-2), they weren't addressing their hygiene, but rather the fact that they were 'break[ing] the tradition of the elders' (v.2), which involved a very visual and ritualistic process that was not a commandment of God found in the Old Testament, but rather for others to witness their pious behavior. The actual Old Testament commandment was for *priests* ('the sons of Aaron') who 'bathed his _body_ in water' (emphasis added) before he could 'eat of the holy gifts' (Leviticus 22:1-7). However, the Pharisees and the scribes applied this commandment to *everyone* and turned it into an elaborate, visual production for everyone to see how 'righteous' *they* were.

Unfortunately, even in many churches today, you see this visual, ritualistic 'washing of _hands_' before touching the communion bread. In fact, as an altar boy in my former parish, it was only necessary for the priest to have us pour the water on his _fingertips_ – not his entire hands. Yet, the specific commandment given was for the *priest* to wash his entire _body_, not just his hands or fingertips, nor to have *someone else* wash his hands or fingertips either. So, the Pharisees and the scribes were actually being hypocritical for criticizing Jesus' disciples for something they themselves didn't do. This is why Jesus fired back by asking them why they 'transgress the commandment of God for the sake of *your* tradition?' (emphasis added) (Matthew 15:3), which involved *dis*honoring their <u>parents</u> (Exodus 20:12), by making the excuse that they were unable to financially assist their parents (even though they had the means to do so), because their financial resources 'has been given to God' (Matthew 15:4-6). Essentially, they were making God out to be the scapegoat in order to justify their *extra*-scriptural tradition, which involved 'TEACHING AS DOCTRINES THE PRECEPTS OF MEN' (v.9), which is what Jesus had a problem with – not when they were teaching and applying God's Word properly and in context, which wasn't that often.

Sadly, even many Christian preachers do this in the form of their *extra*-Scriptural rituals and traditions that are also 'not' found in either the Old nor the New Testament Scriptures, and it is this confusion that can actually lead your children *away* from Christ because they don't know who is teaching the Word of God correctly, which is why it's important to read the Scriptures *daily* and compare what's being taught TO it (Acts 17:11). And this includes the eccentric, loud 'televangelistic-style' screaming that goes on in many churches and on television, particularly those who encourage you to 'send your money,' which, sadly, for some of them goes onto those televangelist's Rolexes, expensive robes, and wardrobe. Now, there's nothing wrong with being 'on fire' for the Lord or tithing to the Church. In fact, the apostle Paul actually *encourages* Christians to tithe at least every <u>week</u> (1 Corinthians 16:1-2; cf. Galatians 2:10), but when they tithe to 'do just as he has purposed in his heart, not grudgingly or under compulsion, for God loves a cheerful giver' (2 Corinthians 9:7). However, it should be clear by the demeanor and intent of the pastor or televangelist 'what' and 'who' the tithe is to benefit. Most God-honoring churches will have no problem supplying you with their year-end annual financial statements, so you can see where every dime the Church tithes goes in order to advance God's kingdom on earth. Those churches don't have anything to hide. That's how you, and your children, can discern between God-honoring Christian leaders who humbly encourage you to give your tithes in a Biblically-supported manner verses greedy, false prophets who blaspheme the Name of our Lord by stealing 'His' money for their own selfish purposes (like how many private jets they purchase). And by doing that they breed dishonesty and distrust, and hinder the advancement of the 'true' kingdom of God on earth.

Regarding the 'screaming' and 'phoniness' of certain televangelists, unfortunately, I've seen it rub off on Christian parents and others who teach the Word of God. For example, I've heard people ask them, 'How are you doing?' and instead of the normal response like, 'I'm doing well today,' or 'I'm feeling a little under the weather,' they consistently make responses like, 'I'm eternally blessed because my Savior lives, Who shed His precious blood on the cross for my worthless sinful soul! Praise Jesus!' Although that's all 100% true, the person who asked them that already *knew* all that about them, so his question is based on wondering about their *physical* or *emotional* condition *at that time*, which that person is <u>not</u> aware of – not their salvation status, which they <u>are</u> aware of. Plus, that kind of flamboyant response can actually be a poor testimony for Christ and actually lead children and others *away* from Christ, because they may be thinking, 'If this is the way people start to act and talk when they convert to Christianity, that's a little too strange for me. I don't want to get that way!' However, most Christians I've met don't actually act that way, but that is the impression they will remember and view all Biblically-based Christians as being that way, like the street-preacher who yells and screams prayers on street corners which Jesus told us 'not' to do: 'When you pray, you are not to be like the hypocrites; for they love to stand and pray in the synagogues and on the street corners so that they may be seen by men. Truly I say to you, they have their reward in full' (Matthew 6:5). Pusa and I were looking through an old photo album from Florida and came across a picture I took of some guy's car that he had Scripture verses hand-written all over it, a cross attached to his front bumper, and a bull horn on his roof that he used to 'preach' as he road down the street. It is *this* kind of strange and flamboyant street-preaching and praying that Jesus was against, because although the intent might be to bring positive attention to Jesus, in reality – to the unsaved – it's actually bringing *negative* attention to the street-preacher, as well as to Christ. People (like me at that time) will actually be turned *away* from Jesus, not towards Him. So, if you're a pastor, preacher, or any other kind of teacher of the Word of God and display this kind of phony, flamboyant demeanor towards Christian children or others – PLEASE STOP! Speak more like a normal human being while spreading the Gospel, rather than the 'stereotypical' televangelist who unnecessarily uses all that 'Christian lingo' if you want to win souls for Christ. Children, including children of Christian parents, can easily detect phoniness and will be turned away from it – just don't compromise the Gospel message by 'watering it down' in an effort to 'pack the pews.' Children can also detect that bait as well. Instead, be honest, be consistent, and be godly examples to your children. There are many good examples to emulate on Christian churches and programming, like Pastor John MacArthur, Dr. David Jeremiah, Pastor Greg Laurie, Pastors Charles and Andy Stanley, Pastor Kerry Shook, and several others.

One last, and very important, example of being consistent is with Christian doctrine. As the apostle Paul wrote to the Corinthian church, 'Now these things, brethren, I have figuratively applied to myself and Apollos for your sakes, so that in us you may learn *not to exceed what is written*, so that no one of you will become arrogant in behalf of one against the other' (emphasis added)(1 Corinthians 4:6). This 'not to exceed' or 'do not add, nor take away' Biblical concept is repeatedly and consistently reinforced throughout the Word of God from the very beginning of the Bible (ie: the Torah) to the very last page of the book of Revelation (Deuteronomy 4:2; 12:32; Proverbs 30:6; Ecclesiastes 3:14; Isaiah 30:1; Jeremiah 26:2; Matthew 15:1-9; Acts 17:10-11; 1 Corinthians 4:6; Revelation 22:18-19), which aids in promoting God's will and desire to have His Church teach and promote <u>trust</u> and credibility in the sufficiency of God's Word. The problem with 'exceeding what's written' in the Bible, is that you will *lose* credibility and trust with your children. As they grow and begin to think for themselves, they will become skeptical of anyone (and anything) which is not consistent in what they believe and teach. Trust is built on consistency, and trust in Christianity is no different. That is why it's important for your family to belong to a Biblically-based church that believes in, and teaches, the sufficiency of Scripture in matters of Christian doctrine (2 Timothy 3:16-17), and not to exceed it. It's bad enough that there have been so many 'divisions' within Christendom, and the reason for that is because most of them *have* exceeded Scripture in defining their doctrines. The effect of these lack of strict, Biblical guidelines will confuse your children, who will not understand how there can be so many different 'variations' of Christianity, yet so many of them don't agree with each other on essential doctrines, and even contradict each other doctrinally. It's even worse when the parent teaches their child one thing, their pastor teaches them something else, and their Christian teacher teaches them something else. That doesn't show unity, but *dis*unity in the Church. And it is this kind of 'disunity' that makes a child begin to question the faith. If the Church cannot convince each other what is Biblically true, then how is the child supposed to trust it? Of course, I'm not talking about certain 'non-essentials' of the Christian faith which allow for 'Christian liberty,' like how frequently a Christian should celebrate communion, but rather the 'essentials,' especially those related to salvation. That is why it is <u>vital</u> to be actively involved in a Biblically-based church, which believes and trusts in the sufficiency of the Word of God for Christian doctrine, rather than 'exceeding' it or 'taking away' from it. Being involved in a doctrinally-sound, Scripture-sufficient church will demonstrate consistency and trust in your child, as well as build their trust in the Christian faith, and provide a proper and effective spiritual defense when they are engaged by false religions and worldviews that are 'not' consistent with, nor provide reliable evidence for, 'their' beliefs.

6. **Wait for a 'window'** – just as God had the apostle Paul wait patiently in prison, before He 'opened a window' for Paul to share the Gospel and lead his jailor to Christ, and eventually his entire household (Acts 16:27-34), Christian parents, too, should wait on God to 'open a window' for their children who have abandoned the faith. It's understandable that when a child abandons the faith that the Christian parent frantically attempts to tell their children to repent and provide them evidence of the Christian faith at every opportunity they get. This may be in the form of providing them gospel tracts, devotionals, referrals to sermons, and apologetic sources. However, we have to remember that a child who has been raised in a Biblically-based Christian family, church, and/or education, usually already knows everything their parent is trying to 'push' on them – and, unfortunately, 'pushing' or 'thumping' is exactly the way they are viewing your attempts. Of course, what they don't realize is what they are 'pushing away' is the Truth, because, based on their personal 'opinion,' they don't *believe* it's true. They have the same view about the Christian faith as a Christian would have about Islam, Hinduism, Buddhist, or atheism.

In fact, the child may actually use that as an argument, much to their Christian parent's dismay.

For the sake of argument, in order to understand what they are thinking, imagine you wake up to a knock on your front door, and you are greeted by two Jehovah's Witnesses (just as I have been – twice) attempting to spread *their* 'good news.' The first reaction most Christians have is the same reaction that the non-believing child of Christian parents has when they attempt to witness to their unbelieving children with the 'true' Gospel. They usually don't want anything to do with it, because they 'think' it's not true, and in fact, they won't take the time to engage in a conversation with them about whether or not it's *actually* true, much like the 'Wayside Child' did in Chapter One, who wouldn't even take the time to *listen* to find out if the Christian faith is indeed true. So, although it's a command from God to share the Truth of the Gospel with others, especially, our children, we also have to wait on God to open a window for us to share it. Otherwise, if we attempt to share it with our unbelieving children whose window is 'closed,' then it's no different than 'throw[ing] your pearls before swine' because 'they will trample them under their feet, and turn and tear you to pieces' (Matthew 7:6). And unfortunately, that is exactly how I've seen a lot of unbelieving children react to their Christian parents. They have an almost violent, emotional outburst towards their parents, partially because their initial disbelief was fueled by emotion and subjectivity, rather than by objective inquiry. If that was not true, they would attempt to at least question their parent's belief calmly, rationally, and objectively, using the same apologetic techniques used by Christians. But many times the reason they don't is because outside of their personal 'opinions,' they know deep down that they <u>can't</u> defend their worldview, which is the actual source of their emotional outburst – not their parent's witnessing attempt. So, until God opens that window of opportunity for the Christian parent, they will choose to allow their heart to remain hardened like the Egyptian Pharaoh was with Moses' attempts to free the Israelites from slavery, and any attempt to share the Truth of the Gospel with them will be futile and in vain. So, wait for that 'window' from God – don't try to 'force it open' yourself. And regardless of whether that window is opened or not, if your unbelieving child continues to reject the Truth of the Gospel, remember the command from Jesus, 'Whoever does not receive you, nor heed your words, as you go out of that house or that city, shake the dust off your feet' (Matthew 10:14). However, that doesn't mean to *disown* your children, just not to continue 'throwing your pearls' at them, because telling the Truth to someone who is purposely and willfully rejecting it, will only make matters worse. Plus, you never know when God will 'open a window' of opportunity with your children later, when they *will* be open-minded enough to at least listen to the Truth, which can't happen if they've been disowned. Yet, at the same time, they need to know and accept that what you believe is something you're not going to just 'not talk about,' because you're afraid of 'offending them,' anymore than when *they* <u>don't</u> refrain with sharing things with you that you, frankly, either don't have interest in hearing or don't believe in. Even if you don't agree with each other, it needs to be kindly reminded to your children that an *adult* relationship is a <u>two</u>-way street – including between an adult child and their adult parents – not <u>one</u>-way like when your children were still underage, immature adolescents. This outlook of this kind of relationship is the difference between someone being an 'adult' verses being a 'child.'

7. **Give a 'defense'** – once God opens that 'window,' and the unbelieving child begins to question you, because they are legitimately seeking answers, then it's time for the Christian parent to provide them with those answers. Unfortunately, too often, this is where the Christian parent doesn't know what to say beyond, 'It's true because the *Bible* 'says' it's true.' We have to remember, that when most of us became believers, it wasn't based on clever, apologetic techniques used by someone else, but by the Holy Spirit regenerating our hearts and opening our eyes, so we could see clearly to accept the Truth. But what the unbelieving child is asking is if the Christian faith – like the life, death, and resurrection of Jesus – is based on actual real-world events. And the answer to all of this is an unequivocal 'Yes!' However, too many times the average Christian parent is either unaware of this themselves, or they are unable to provide these real-world, historical evidences for the Christian faith, such as the examples in Appendix B of this book.

The apostle Peter wrote, 'but sanctify Christ as Lord in your hearts, always being ready to make a defense to everyone who asks you to give an account for the hope that is in you, yet with gentleness and reverence' (1 Peter 3:15). The Greek word Peter uses for 'defense' ('apologia') means 'verbal defence, speech in defence; a reasoned statement or argument.'[5] It basically means to provide an answer or an explanation. It's where we get our English word 'apologetics,' which Christians use to defend the Truth of the Christian faith. And it is this kind of 'defense,' or 'apologetics,' that the inquiring non-believing child is asking for. So, if this is what they are asking from you, provide it to them. However, as mentioned previously, a Christian parent can provide all of the apologetics in defense of the Truth for the Christian faith to their unbelieving child, but it isn't until the Holy Spirit has regenerated their heart that they'll be willing to accept the Truth. So until then, they are willfully and spiritually 'blinded' to it, so apologetics won't work with them, because they are both unwilling and unable to accept the Truth.

What I usually do when I come across someone who questions me about my faith, the first question I ask them is "Are you asking me, because you really want to know if the Christian faith is true, and if I can provide you objective evidence that it is true, will you be willing to believe in it and accept Jesus as your Savior and Lord?" If they say anything other than 'yes,' then they aren't actually willing to accept the Truth, even if you provide them all the evidence they need. Their 'window' is still 'closed.' Therefore, that isn't the right time to share the

---

[5] Blue Letter Bible. "Dictionary and Word Search for *apologia (Strong's 627)*". Blue Letter Bible. 1996-2014. 6 May 2014. < http:// www.blbclassic. org/lang/lexicon/lexicon.cfm?Strongs=G627&t=NASB >

Truth of the Gospel with them, and my usual response to them is, "Then since no amount of evidence I could provide you would convince you, then, essentially, you're saying you would rather choose to disbelieve the Truth and evidence, because it disagrees with what your personal 'opinion' is. So, there's no real point of providing you the Truth that you're going to reject anyways." It is also helpful to let them know that when they will be willing to accept and believe in the Truth when it's heard, that you would be readily available and more than happy to share the Truth with them. But until then, it's fruitless, because you can't 'force' someone else to believe – including your unbelieving child. Only the Holy Spirit can convict and convince them of the Truth, as well as the desire to want to know the Truth.

However, once they are willing to objectively listen, and not just for the purpose of arguing and debating with you, then your job is what the apostle Paul states as 'accurately handling the word of truth' (2 Timothy 2:15). Some Bible versions, like the NKJV, translate it '*rightly dividing* the word of truth.' The Greek word here ('orthotomeō') means 'to cut straight, to cut straight ways; to proceed on straight paths, hold a straight course, equiv. to doing right to make straight and smooth, to handle aright, to teach the truth directly and correctly.'[6] Another wards, it means to rightly explain Scripture and teach it accurately. There are two types of apologetics

6 Blue Letter Bible. "Dictionary and Word Search for *orthotomeō (Strong's 3718)*". Blue Letter Bible. 1996-2014. 6 May 2014. < http:// www.blbclassic. org/lang/lexicon/lexicon.cfm?Strongs=G3718&t=NASB >

that Christians employ. The first is the kind that Paul refers here to Timothy, which involves allowing Scripture to explain Scripture, rather than what an individual personal's 'opinion' believes Scripture means. This latter personal view is called 'interpretation,' which the apostle Peter states, 'no prophecy of Scripture is a matter of one's own interpretation, for no prophecy was ever made by an act of human will, but men moved by the Holy Spirit spoke from God' (2 Peter 1:20-21), just as Joseph asked Pharaoh's officials in the Old Testament 'Do not interpretations belong to God?' (Genesis 40:8). And since ALL Scripture is Inspired, or 'God-breathed,' (2 Timothy 3:16), then in order to objectively and 'accurately handle' (or, 'rightly divide') the 'word of truth,' we must appeal to Scripture and allow *Scripture* to explain *Scripture* to our inquiring, unbelieving child, as well as teach it to them. And as previously mentioned, there are several reliable, Christian sources in Biblically-based churches, Christian bookstores, and elsewhere to aid the Christian parent. However, whatever 'source' you use – even if it's from a reputable Christian source – we must still compare these 'sources' TO the Word of God, emulating the Bereans to be 'more noble-minded than those in Thessalonica, for they received the word with great eagerness, *examining the Scriptures daily* to see whether these things were so' (emphasis added)(Acts 17:11), because although ALL *written* Scripture is Inspired ('God-breathed')(2 Timothy 3:16), *written* (as well as oral) Christian sources aren't, but rather are attempts at 'accurately handling the word of truth' (2 Timothy 2:15). This discernment requires diligent study of God's word, prayer to God for discernment, as well as regular attendance in a Biblically-based church, whose desire is to 'accurately handle' and teach Scripture, without imputing their 'opinions' into Scripture, but rather allowing *Scripture* to explain *Scripture*, as well as using it 'for reproof, [and] for correction' (2 Timothy 3:16).

The second kind of apologetic techniques used by Christians in defending the Christian faith are extra-biblical sources which support that the Christian faith is true and historically accurate, again, such as what's found in the Appendices of this book. However, it needs to be emphasized that no one ever accepted Christ as their Savior and Lord and the Bible as the inerrant, Inspired Word of God *solely* on extra-biblical apologetic sources, but rather solely through the saving power of the Holy Spirit. But the benefit of extra-biblical, apologetic sources is that they provide additional support for the Truth of Scripture (see the quotes from Lee Strobel in the Epilogue of this book). So, although the Christian is not *dependent* on these extra-biblical, apologetic sources, they do *reinforce* what is already established Truth, rather than the Christian faith just being another 'religion,' based on 'fairy tales,' like other religions and secular worldviews. Therefore, it's important when your inquiring, unbelieving child asks you to 'defend your faith,' it's not only important to explain *what* you believe, but also *why* you believe it.

8. **Don't use Paschal's Wager** – 'Paschal's Wager' is based on the idea that 'Given the possibility that God actually does exist and assuming the infinite gain or loss associated

with belief in God or with unbelief, a rational person should live as though God exists and seek to believe in God. If God does not actually exist, such a person will have only a finite loss (some pleasures, luxury, etc.)'[7] Now, on the surface, this seems like a decent argument for believing in God. However, it actually shows very 'little' faith, because it appears that the Christian is encouraging others to base their belief on the *possibility* that God exists, rather than on the *confidence* in the <u>reality</u> that God's existence which is based on objective evidence. And this is something unbelievers will gladly point out. In fact, they'll use this same argument for believing in the absurdity that the universe is made up of invisible pink unicorns or that the universe was created by the Flying Spaghetti Monster. The problem with this analogy is that unlike the existence of the *Biblical* God, there is ZERO objective evidence for invisible pink unicorns or the Flying Spaghetti Monster.[8] However, when given this false analogy, many Christian parents aren't equipped to explain 'how' it's false, and that's because (sadly) many Christian churches and schools aren't equipped to explain it either. So, they default to the 'Paschal's Wager' argument, which isn't really a good argument at all. Rather, get yourself educated in Christian apologetics (refer to Point Seven and Appendices A and B) by attending a Bible-based church that teaches Christian apologetics, use valuable Christian apologetic resources found in Christian bookstores and on Christian Web sites,

---

[7] "Blaise Pascal," Columbia History of Western Philosophy, page 353.

[8] S. Michael Houdmann, CEO, GotQuestions.org. *"How is belief in God any different from Flying Spaghetti Monsterism?"* http://www.gotquestions.org/flying-spaghetti-monsterism.html

and **avoid** using Paschal's Wager. It will only backfire and leave you sounding like your faith is based on a 'possibility' rather than on reality. There's more than enough solid evidence for the Christian faith being true than to rely on a weak philosophical argument like Paschal's Wager.

9. **Don't exceed your role** – this point is just as important as, if not more important than, the previous eight points put together. As previously mentioned, it is the <u>Holy Spirit</u>, Who is the One Who 'regenerates' the soul of an unbeliever (Titus 3:5), 'convicts' them (John 16:8), and permanently 'seals' believers (Ephesians 1:13), Who then 'opens a window' for us to 'preach the gospel to all creation' (Mark 16:16). Unfortunately, many Christians take it upon themselves to attempt to do the job of the Holy Spirit, and spend all their time attempting to 'regenerate' the hearts of unbelievers. I once heard of an evangelical church who told its members that God didn't merely want Christians to preach the gospel, but also to <u>convert</u> people *themselves*, and if they didn't, then they weren't obeying God, God was not happy with them, and they should question 'their' true conversion. This heretical kind of thinking borderlines on apostasy, because as mentioned throughout this book, ONLY the Holy Spirit can regenerate and convict an unbeliever (John 16:8; Titus 3:5), not another regenerated individual. Rather, our job is merely to preach to others the Truth that 'will make you free' (John 8:32), and then it is up to the Holy Spirit to do the 'regenerating' and 'convicting,' and ultimately, the converting. But, since we don't know 'to whom' or 'when' the Holy Spirit is doing this, we are to follow the Great

Commission of Jesus to 'be My witnesses' (Acts 1:8) and 'make disciples of all nations' (Matthew 28:19), but for 'Whoever does not receive you, nor heed your words, as you go out of that house or that city, shake the dust off your feet' (Matthew 10:14), and for Christian parents, that applies to their willfully, unbelieving children who reject the Truth of the Gospel, until the Holy Spirit opens their eyes. However, that doesn't mean disowning them, but loving them unconditionally (see 'Point Three,' above).

10. **Pray** – you might be thinking to yourself right now, 'Umm...didn't you mention that already?' Yes, I did. However, it's worth mentioning again, because we should <u>begin</u> AND <u>end</u> with prayer. In fact, the apostle Paul emphasizes that we should 'pray *without* ceasing' (emphasis added)(1 Thessalonians 5:17). Of course, this doesn't mean bowing down on one knee to pray and never standing up, or perpetually closing your eyes and bowing your head to pray (especially when you're driving!) All this means is that we should desire to be continually in communion with our Lord, and keep all unregenerated souls, including our unbelieving children, in our prayers. I often hear people say, 'I'll keep you in my prayers,' but is that always true, or are those just words Christians just 'say?' I have said it over and over again, that Pusa is one of the greatest 'prayer warriors' that I have ever known, because when she says she's going to pray for you – she <u>means</u> that. Same with Mom, as well as with me. When we say 'I'll pray for you' – you can confidently take that to the bank! I have prayed with Pusa countless times, and her prayers are so genuine and so sincere, that I can attest

that when she prays, she prays with the genuine hope that that prayer is granted with a 'yes,' but she also trusts God enough that if it isn't God's will, then the prayer isn't in accordance with His eternal Sovereign desire – at least not at 'that' time. However, that doesn't inhibit her to 'draw near with confidence to the throne of grace, so that we may receive mercy and find grace to help in time of need' (Hebrews 4:16), because whatever the outcome, Pusa <u>knows</u> that God is in control of *everything*, including the salvation of those who she loves. And it is 'this' kind of praying and trust God expects from us, not the empty, superficial 'I'll pray for you' reply so often heard – even among Christians – that is nothing more than a phrase in order to make someone 'feel better,' because they are *thinking* about them, but who never actually *pray* for them. But as previously mentioned in 'Point One,' that doesn't mean that <u>every</u> time we pray to God for something, He's going to answer it in the way or timing that we expect – including prayers related to our children's salvation. So, it's imperative to trust God's Judgment and eternal Sovereignty (Psalm 103:19; 1 Timothy 6:5), including His Authority in 'whom' He wills to save, as well as 'when,' and in the meantime, to continue praying as Jesus did, for God the Father's will to be done, not ours (Luke 22:42).

These are just a few things that Christian parents can do, who have children who have abandoned the faith, while waiting on God. And each 'point' is just as important as the others. Too many times, I've seen that all Christians do is pray (which *is* vitally important), but they forget to do 'points two through nine,' which are <u>also</u> things that God wants us to do, in addition to prayer. And on the other end of the spectrum, I've seen Christian parents do 'points two through nine,' but they forget to pray – perhaps, because they don't think prayer will 'work.' However, if prayer doesn't work, then 'why' would God <u>command</u> us to pray? And I have personally seen the power of prayer work in literal, real-world time including *answered* prayer for a person's salvation – not because prayer, in and of itself, actually does anything, but because it is *through* prayer that God responds to us, provided (again) that it is in accordance with *His* will and not *ours*.

One of the concerns I hear most often from Christian parents whose children have abandon the faith is, "I'm getting older, and I'm worried that my kids won't come to Christ before I die!" As a parent ages and begins to see more years behind them than in front of them, they may start to become more anxious, because they'd at least like to see their child accept the Truth of the Christian faith before they die, so they can 'rest in peace.' They would like nothing more than to reestablish that close, intimate spiritual relationship they once had with their child when they were young that they don't currently have now. One of their concerns is that once they are gone, then they feel there will be no way of them knowing whether or not their child will ever accept Christ, which can fill them with a tremendous amount of worry, because they feel that they have somehow 'failed.' However, we have to remember that in terms of salvation God doesn't work on *our* time-table, but on *His*. So, although 'waiting on God' might seem like 'forever,' as the apostle Peter reminds us: 'that with the Lord one day is like a thousand years, and a thousand years like one day. The Lord is not slow about His promise, as some count slowness, but is patient toward you, not wishing for any to perish but for all to come to repentance' (2 Peter 3:8-9, cf. Psalm 90:7). From *our* perspective, waiting our entire life-time – and even beyond – seems 'slow,' but from *God's* perspective it's not, because He isn't affected by the passage of time like we are. His timing and will is *always* perfect. And even if a parent doesn't live to see their child come to Christ before they die, that doesn't mean they never will if it's the will of God. An adult child of a Christian parent is never 'too old' to accept Christ. I remember hearing about a gentleman who didn't accept Christ until he was in his <u>mid-seventies</u>. This would put his parents, at a minimum, in their mid-to-late nineties or more probably in their hundreds, which would mean that most likely they never got to see their son accept Christ before they died. In my former church, I remember hearing about an even older gentleman in Brazil who heard the Gospel and accepted Christ in his <u>mid-nineties</u> – ten days later, he died! So, there's no 'age limit' to hearing the Gospel and accepting the Truth of the Christian faith. But even if your child never does accept Christ, be comforted by the words of our Lord who speaks about Heaven and the soothing and consoling hand of God: 'and *He will wipe away every tear from their eyes*; and there will no longer be any death; *there will no longer be* any *mourning, or crying, or pain*; the first things have passed away' (emphasis added)(Revelation 21:4, cf. 7:17; Isaiah 25:8). Once we are in Heaven and free from the bonds of our sinful bodies, we will experience no more sorrow or worry, but only experience joy and happiness, because we will be eternally bonded with our heavenly family, and <u>all</u> of our earthly worries and concerns – even about our unbelieving loved ones – will be of the past, because we will be in the presence of our loving, caring, and compassionate Creator for all eternity! So, never give up praying for your children, because you don't know if God will answer your prayer while you are living or after you are 'at home with the Lord' (2 Corinthians 5:8). That is up to God's *perfect* will and timing.

The most personal example is my own salvation. As I illustrated in the Introduction, I wasn't raised in a home that taught the Bible. In fact, I don't even remember hearing the word 'Bible' even at my parochial school, or explained what it was. All I heard was that the book that was held up during Mass (which actually wasn't the Bible, but rather called the Lectionary that *contains* 'certain' Scripture passages, but not all of them) was called 'The Word of the Lord,' which as a youth, I didn't really understand what that meant. So, it was safe to say that I had little, if any, exposure to the Bible throughout my youth, adolescence, and young adulthood. Yet, when Mom began attending Bible studies, and the Holy Spirit regenerated her heart and convicted her of the Truth, she immediately began praying for my salvation, as well as continuing to employ the other 'points' previously listed. And it was because of her answered prayers, which were in accordance with God's will, as well as her unconditional love and patience for God to 'open a window' to share the Gospel Truth with me, and submission to not exceed her role, that in August 2004, I *finally* accepted the Truth of the Gospel, the legitimacy of the inerrancy and Inspiration of the Bible, and Jesus as my Savior and Lord, which I was 'unable' to before that moment. But, those prayers didn't happen overnight. Mom prayed diligently for well over a year, before God answered those prayers – perhaps to assure her that God allows things to happen in *His* timing, not *ours*, as God tells us in His Word, "'For My thoughts are not your thoughts, Nor are your ways My ways,' declares the LORD. 'For as the heavens are higher than the earth, So are My ways higher than your ways And My thoughts than your thoughts'" (Isaiah 55:8-9). And God's 'thoughts' and 'ways' were for me to accept the Truth of the Gospel and His Son as my Savior and Lord in August 2004, and neither before nor after that time. However, that doesn't mean that God *always* answers our prayers in a year, nor does He always answer with a 'yes,' but as previously mentioned, He answers them in *His* time, according to *His* will. And in the meantime, we should continue to employ the 'Ten Points' listed earlier in this chapter, while we wait and trust in His perfect, Sovereign will.

Some Christians may ask, 'since God predestines His 'elect' anyways, then aren't we demonstrating a *lack* of faith by not simply trusting in Him when we pray?' If that were true, then why do we even bother to pray for our children's salvation, since God has predestined the salvation of His 'elect' anyways? As just previously mentioned, as well as in 'Points One and Ten" God actually <u>commands</u> us in Scripture <u>to</u> <u>pray</u> to Him (1 Thessalonians 5:17), which *demonstrates* an action of faith and *trust* in what God commands us (James 1:5-6). Likewise, in addition to praying, God wants us to do ALL of the 'Top Ten' things previously listed – as well as everything else He commands and instructs us to do in Scripture – not just the things related to salvation – which *also* demonstrates an action of faith and trust in what God commands us.

So, continue to pray but don't forget to employ 'points two through nine.' And, likewise, employ 'points two through nine' and don't forget to pray!

Chapter Six

A word to the unbelieving child

I f you are a child who was raised in a Christian home and have abandoned the faith, as someone who once shared your 'unbelief,' there's a few additional points I'd like to make. If you've read this far, I'm guessing that you may have a wide-range of thoughts and reactions, anywhere from genuine inquiry, to continued disbelief, to outright anger, depending of which kind of 'soil' you represent that the Gospel was originally 'seeded' in your heart during your Christian upbringing. But, if you have read this far, I'd encourage you to keep reading. And if you haven't read the rest of this book, but instead jumped to this chapter, I'd encourage you to go back to the very beginning, and read through the Prologue, Introduction, and all the previous chapters, just as I encouraged your Christian parent to do in Chapter Five, in order to fully appreciate this chapter. But regardless of whatever reason you left the Christian faith, what you have in common with 100% of other children, who abandoned their Christian upbringing, is that you have some kind of 'rift' between you and your Christian parents. Now, that doesn't mean that you don't love them or don't have a relationship with them (many of you may, many of you may not), but it's no longer the same kind of close spiritual, intimate relationship you had with them when you were younger. Something 'ripped,' just like it did with Rachael and her father in Chapter Three. But, whatever happened, and no matter how close you feel you are with your parents, it's not the same kind of intimate closeness you once had. Do you engage in conversations about the Lord with your parents, or just conversations that 'you' want to talk about? Do you go out of your way to listen to your parents talk about Jesus, Christianity, and the Bible because they have a real joy and desire to talk about them with you, or do you go out of your way to let them know that you "don't want to hear it, because 'that offends me!'" but expect them to listen to things they either don't want to hear or even offends *them*? Even if you are not active in a church, do you at least attend church out of love for your parents when they ask you to attend *with them* – at the very least on Christmas and Easter – even if you don't believe in that anymore or don't get anything out of it, yet expect them to attend events 'you' are interested in?

Even if you're not a Christian, relationships are supposed to be a two-way street, and what I've found in my experiences with non-christian, adult children with their Christian parents is that in terms of their relationship, the 'street' is more 'one-way,' with the parent doing more of the giving, even when the unbelieving child enters adulthood. Now, I'm not implying that non-christian children are *always* the takers, and that Christian parents are *always* the givers, but it's very rare that I ever see an unbelieving child, who has abandoned the faith, engage in the type of conversations and participate in the kind of events with their parents as the ones previously mentioned, or suggested to their parents about attending church (ie: the 'giving'). Do you know how much joy that would bring them? A similar kind of joy it brings you when your parents choose to engage in conversations and attend events that you are interested in. Now, I'm not saying that the two of you should share in EVERY experience (that would be a bit unrealistic). However, the specific things that will bring you both the most joy, that won't make you horribly uncomfortable or violate your core beliefs (like taking your Christian parent to a strip club), is worth the trouble. At the very least, it'll bring you a step closer together, which is - in part - what this book is about: attempting to re-establish a relationship between the unbelieving child and the Christian parent, as a first step in opening the lines of communication, and perhaps engage with each other civilly to discuss with each other 'why' you left the Christian faith, and what depth and closeness of a relationship you are both able to have – at least at this point.

For example, I have close friends who are members of the same 'denomination' of Christianity that I was brought up in, which I am no longer a part of for Scriptural and other reasons. However, a few years ago when I visited them one weekend, that didn't stop me from worshiping there, when they invited me to their church. I could have said, 'Thanks, but I no longer believe in that particular denomination. I'll just find another church to worship in,' but I didn't say that.

Instead, I went with them to their church, out of respect for our friendship and because they invited me. I realize there are those in certain churches who would say I shouldn't have done that, but keep in mind that Luke, who wrote both the Gospel that bears his name as well as the book of Acts, wrote, 'The God who made the world and all things in it, since He is Lord of heaven and earth, does not dwell in temples made with hands' (Acts 17:24; cf. 2 Corinthians 5:1; Hebrews 9:11,24). The 'true' God Who made and rules the heaven and the earth can be worshiped *anywhere*, because He is 'Omnipresent' (ie, 'ever-present'). And out of respect for me, when my friends came to visit, they attended the church that I was attending at that time, even though it wasn't the same 'denomination' that they belonged to, plus, they were able to hear the Truth of the Gospel, which was preached there that day. Now, of course that doesn't mean that I'm going to begin worshiping there all the time, because while I was there, there were so many things (words spoken, actions, rituals, traditions, etc.) that were performed there that were not supported by the Word of God (and even contradicted it) that it wasn't a place where I felt that I could perpetually worship faithfully that represented the God of Scripture. However, the point is that even though I didn't *share* the exact same belief in Christianity as my friends, I attended there out of *respect* for them, and at the same time I maintained my faith, and I was able to objectively compare what was being preached TO Scripture (Acts 17:11), and then discuss it with them afterwards when they asked me. And that is another benefit of the unbelieving child to actively engage in conversations and attend a Christian service with their Christian parents – if there's something you don't agree with, it'll give you the chance to discuss what you don't agree with them and 'why.' Otherwise, without talking about it, the lines of communication stay closed and the 'rift' remains wide open.

You may be thinking to yourself at this point, "So, if I was raised in an atheist home, or brought up in another religion, like Islam, and I converted to Christianity but my parents didn't, are you saying that 'out of respect for them,' if they asked me to come attend an atheist 'convention,' or worship in their mosque, that I should do that since God is 'Omnipresent' and 'can be worshiped anywhere'?" No, I'm not saying that because the God of Scripture isn't being worshiped or honored in a secular or non-christian religious gathering like He is in a Christian church (in fact, He's actually being blasphemed in those kind of gatherings), even if not everyone in that particular church is a Biblically-based Christian, because as Jesus said, 'For where two or three have gathered together *in My name, I am there* in their midst' (emphasis added)(Matthew 18:20). And the 'name' of Jesus is not worshiped nor honored in a mosque, and definitely not in an atheist gathering, like He is in a Christian church. However, that should not inhibit a Christian child from talking about the differences between their faith and the religious (or nonreligious) beliefs with their unbelieving parents, because it opens the lines of communication and the opportunity for the Christian child to share the Truth of the Gospel with them.

Throughout this book, particularly in the Introduction, I have attempted to relate to **you** - the unbelieving child – by sharing some of the same thoughts and denials I had about the Christian faith when I was unbeliever, which now "I" hear other unbelieving children express, because as I mentioned in

155

the Introduction, I think it's difficult for someone who was raised Christian but never abandoned the faith, to be able to empathize with someone else, who was also raised Christian and with the Bible, and to understand why a person with that same exposure to the Truth would abandon the faith. Therefore, I would like to take some time to share ten of the common arguments and comments I have heard from unbelieving children towards their Christian parents – most of them I once used myself when I was an unbeliever:

1. **'They're just a bunch of stories'** – yes, that's true. They are a 'bunch of stories.' But, they are 'a bunch of *true* stories.' And the reason I can say that with utter confidence, is because there is <u>nothing</u> in the Bible that can be disproven, either scientifically, historically, archaeologically, nor prophetically. Of course, not everything can be *proven* using science (such as miracles, the *scientific* existence of God, angels, or demons, etc), history (the physical conditions of the pre-Flood world), or with archaeology (like the physical remains of Adam and Eve), nor does everything have to be, because the inability to prove something doesn't automatically make it false. In addition, they can't be *dis*proven either, which is what you would have to do to justify the claim that 'they're just a bunch of (untrue) stories.' Another wards, to verify the claim that those 'stories' aren't true, the burden of proof is on the one making that claim – not the person who says they are true, because the evidence that those 'stories' are true, are based on the fact that: 1) <u>many</u> of those 'stories' *have* been proven scientifically, historically, prophetically, and archaeologically to be true over the last

two-thousand years, and 2) Jesus, Himself, *verified* that all of those 'stories' from the Old Testament are true, like the Creation account of Adam and Eve (Matthew 19:4-5; cf. Genesis 1:27; 2:24), and the days of Noah and Lot (Luke 17:26-29,32; cf. Genesis 6:1-7:24; 19:24-26), which He proved His claims by rising bodily from the dead three days later and appearing to His disciples and 'more than five hundred brethren at one time' (1 Corinthians 15:5-8; see also Appendix A). Anyone can claim to be the promised Messiah, and can even go so far as to attempt to prove it by willfully being nailed to a cross, but the *real* proof is the ability to bodily rise from the dead after being deceased for three days and buried in a sealed cave, which is exactly what Jesus did, which proved everything that He said prior to that – including His claim that the Old Testament Scripture 'stories' were true, because they were actually about *Him* (John 5:46-47). So, there's no real objective reason to believe the Bible is 'just a bunch of (untrue) stories,' but there are many, many objective reasons to believe the Bible is 'a bunch of *true* stories.'

2. **'I believe in science, not a 'god-of-the-gaps' religion**
   – that's good that you believe in science, because as a Biblically-believing Christian, so do I. In fact, you'll be hard-pressed to find *any* Bible-believing Christian who doesn't believe in science. The idea that believing in science and believing in Christianity are mutually exclusive is a false dichotomy, as well as a false assumption. As we'll see, most very educated people actually believe in Christianity, as well as science. The problem comes from believing that Christianity is *dependent* on science to be true. However,

there are many things that can't be proven using science, such as historical beliefs, like George Washington being elected the first President of the United States of America. You'd have some real difficulty finding an American who doesn't believe this historical fact, despite the fact that Americans living today were neither alive when President Washington got elected in order to verify the legitimacy of that 'belief,' nor could they produce any empirical *scientific* evidence for his election to the Presidency. We take it on 'faith' based on the overwhelming evidence from multiple, reliable *historical* sources that this is true – but then again, this same kind of 'faith,' based on this same kind of overwhelming *historical* evidence (Hebrews 11:1) is what Christians rely on to believe in the claims of Christianity. In fact, there is more reliable, historical evidence for the Resurrection of Christ, than there is for the historical existence of the Greek philosopher, Socrates (470/469 to 399 B.C.), because outside of the writings of some of his students, like Plato, there are ZERO copies of Socrates' actual writings, let alone his originals. However, compared to other ancient writings, the number of their available written copies, such as those by Caesar (10), Plato (7), Thucydides (8), Tacitus (20), Suetonius (8), Homer ('Iliad')(643), are exponentially and significantly less than the number of available written copies of the New Testament which are in excess of **24,000**![1] In fact, not only do the number of available written copies of the New Testament far exceed those of these other historical

[1] Rich Deem, "Is Our Copy of the Bible a Reliable Copy of the Original?" http://www.godandscience.org/apologetics/bibleorg.html Last updated December 13, 2005

writings, but they are also much *closer* to their original writings (25 to 50 years), compared to the next closest – Homer ('Illiad') – (500 years after the originals).[2] Yet, many people who believe in the legitimacy of these much *fewer* available written copies of non-biblical historical writings (as well as copies that are much more *distant* from the originals), are the same people who reject the available written copies of the New Testament, despite there being exceptionally *more* of them, as well as the copies having a much *earlier* date to the originals. So, not everything that is true is dependent on being able to 'prove' it's reality on science, but rather on reliable 'evidence' which is based on faith.

The other issue is this 'god-of-the-gaps' mentality, which is rooted in the theory that when Christians don't have a scientific answer to account for something – like an explanation for 'why' the universe exists – they simply say 'God did it.' Well, aside from the fact that the Bible does say 'God created the heavens and the earth' (Genesis 1:1), the truth is that science *can't* explain 'why' the universe exists, because since science explains what happens *within* the boundaries of our space-time universe, science is unequipped to explain 'why' the universe exists in the first place, because that would require science to exist *prior to* the existence of space-time, as well as *prior to* the existence of the universe, which there is no evidence for, nor is it logical, because science requires 'cause and effect,' which requires the passage of time, which would not have

---

[2] Ibid.

existed *prior to* the existence of the space-<u>time</u> universe [See Appendix C].

And although there are Christians who do (sadly) have a 'god-of-the-gaps' mentality, most Biblically-believing Christians are able to discern between simply not having a current scientific explanation to account for something verses acknowledging the reality that there are some things that science <u>can't</u> explain, because science is the wrong 'means' to account for 'why' the universe exists, for the reasons previously mentioned. This 'belief' in 'scientism' that 'empirical science is the only way to be sure about anything' is both self-refuting and therefore illogical.[3] However, as mentioned previously, science <u>can't</u> explain everything that is true, such as: what actions and thoughts are and are not moral; historical claims; whether a work of art is good or bad; etc. Therefore, the absence of a scientific explanation for something, like the legitimacy of the historical truth for the Christian faith, is not *dependent* on science, even though it is *supported* by science based on the evidence.

Lastly, since the 'god-of-the-gaps' is an argument for 'religious people' to account for what they don't know, keep in mind that there are plenty of things that the God of the Bible 'knew' hundreds, even *thousands*, of years before 'science' was able to prove it, such as:

---

[3] S. Michael Houdmann, CEO, GotQuestions.org. *"What is the New Atheism?"* http://www.gotquestions.org/new-atheism.html

- 'In the beginning God <u>created</u> the heavens and the earth' (Genesis 1:1)(before 1450 B.C.) – the universe had a beginning. Therefore, it is not eternal.
- the <u>circular</u> shape of the earth (Isaiah 40:22)(~700 B.C.)
- 'He has <u>inscribed a circle</u> on the surface of the waters <u>At the boundary of light and darkness</u>' (Job 26:10) (~2000 to 1800 B.C.) – both the circular shape of the earth as well its 'curvature' *at* the 'boundary' between 'light and darkness' describes a three-dimensional sphere, rather than a two-dimensional disk or flat earth.
- that the earth 'stretches out' over '<u>empty space</u> And hangs the earth on <u>nothing</u>' (Job 26:7)(~2000 to 1800 B.C.)
- 'He [God] <u>wraps up</u> the waters in the <u>clouds</u>, and the cloud <u>does not burst</u> under them" (Job 26:8), and 'with moisture He <u>loads the thick cloud</u>' (Job 37:11) (~2000 to 1800 B.C.) – describing evaporation and the earth's hydrologic cycle.
- 'It [the earth] is <u>turned</u> as clay to the seal; and they stand as a garment' (Job 38:14)(KJV)(~2000 to 1800 B.C.) – describes the rotation of the earth, rather than being motionless.

There are many more scientific explanations in the Bible than these, but this is to demonstrate that this 'alleged god-of-the-gaps' had actually *closed* these and other 'gaps' long before science was able to 'close' them itself and explain these <u>scientific</u> phenomena. So, not only do Christians believe in science, but they don't actually believe in a 'god-of-the-gaps,' because the Biblical God has been 'closing scientific gaps' for thousands of years, long before a scientific explanation could explain them. Believers in the Word of God have merely been waiting for science to 'catch up' to what they've always known for hundreds, even *thousands* of years.

3. **'People aren't believing in Christianity anymore, because it's based on an old myth like Thor or Zeus'**
   – although mentioned in the Prologue that as many as two-thirds of *youth* growing up in the Church leave it in their twenties, the common misconception that people aren't believing in Christianity anymore, implying that the number of Christians – AS A WHOLE – are decreasing rapidly, is based on very, poor research, because statistically, this is simply not true. Dr. David Jeremiah quoted George Weigel by stating:

> "As of mid-2011, there will be an average of 80,000 new Christians per day…but *300 fewer atheists* every 24 hours [italics added]."[4]

So, not only are the number of people who believe in Christianity *increasing* daily, but the number of atheists are actually *decreasing* daily – rapidly! Some people may attempt to argue, 'Well, that's because with the rapid explosion of the world population, the number of atheists are simply *dying* at a quicker rate. However, how does that

---

[4] David Jeremiah, "I never thought I'd see the day!: culture at the crossroads," 1st ed. (October 2011), p.26. FaithWords, Hachette Book Group: New York, NY. [italics in Dr. Jeremiah's text]

explain the <u>rapid</u> *increase* of daily Christians? What this statistic actually demonstrates is that the reason for the rapid increase in the daily number of Christians and rapid decrease in the daily number of atheists is that people are simply not believing in atheism anymore, due to all the evidence for the Christian faith that they finally <u>accepted</u>. Not only that, but the vast majority of educated people in America actually embrace specific, supernatural religious beliefs as well. Dr. David Jeremiah quotes from "NPR Commentary by Steven Waldman September 4, 2003," regarding the supernatural and religious beliefs held by the majority of well-educated Americans:

> "Listen to these numbers – 55% of people with post-graduate degrees (lawyers, doctors, dentists, and the like) believe in the Devil…. Remember these are people with post-graduate educations. 60% believe in the virgin birth. And 64% believe in the resurrection of Christ."[5]

And <u>ALL</u> of these 'supernatural religious beliefs' are <u>Christian</u> beliefs! And the reason why all these 'well-educated, post-graduate degree Americans' believe all of this, isn't because they are believing in a 'myth' that are 'just a bunch of (untrue) stories,' but because they are convinced in the overwhelming, reliable historical *evidence* (as well as other kinds of evidence) that it's true, such as the fact that Jesus was an actual real-life *historical* Person,

[5]   Ibid, p.9. Quoting from Steven Waldman, "NPR Commentary by Steven Waldman September 4, 2003," The Brights, accessed April 19, 2011, http://www.the-brights.net/vision/essays/waldman_futrell_geisert_npr.html.

Who really lived and died, unlike the stories of Thor or Zeus which are actually based on myths. In reality, the real 'myth' is a worldview based on atheism, which was legally declared by the 7th Circuit Court of Appeals in an appeal from a prison inmate in Wisconsin, as 'the [inmate's] religion.'[6] So, as of 2005, which is when the article was published one day after the Wisconsin ruling, atheism is now just as much of a 'religion' as Christianity is – only not based on evidence. Now, some atheists may say, 'Atheism isn't a religion, because I don't <u>believe in</u> anything, that's the point.' However, that's not true, because 'not' believing that God exists or 'not' believing that Christianity is true, is the same thing as *believing* that God does 'not' exist or *believing* that Christianity is 'not' true. So, the atheist DOES 'believe *in*' something – the denial of the real existence of God and the rejection of the Truth of the Christian faith. So, atheism 'is' a '*religious* belief system,' just not a religion that worships God or believes in Christianity, much like people mentioned in the New Testament whose religion involved the 'worship of angels' (Colossians 2:18), rather than God. Also, keep in mind, that it was an <u>atheist</u> in prison – not a 'religious' person – who sued to declare atheism a <u>religion</u>.

4. **'The Bible was written by men; what about all the errors and contradictions in it?'** – this is probably the one I hear most often, and, ironically, the one I used to use. However, just because mankind writes something,

---

[6] "Court rules atheism a religion. Decides 1st Amendment protects prison inmate's right to start study group." Published 08/20/2005. http://www.wnd.com/2005/08/31895/

should it be automatically assumed that it's full of errors and contradictions? Of course, it becomes more probable when you're dealing with a nearly 800,000 word document that was written by forty different writers and is actually the compilation of sixty-six individual books and letters, written over approximately 1,500 years. However, unlike other large volume pieces of literature, the Bible is also Inspired (God-breathed), so it *without* error or contradictions. Yet, that will not stop people from making the erroneous claim that it has errors and contradictions in it, and search the Internet endlessly to find as many as they can. For instance, they will be more than happy to point out that if you Google 'errors and contradictions in the Bible' in the search engine, that over a half of a million sites pop up. However, what they fail to tell you is that on the <u>first</u> <u>page</u> which lists the first ten links, *three* of the links actually <u>defend</u> and <u>answer</u> these 'alleged' Bible errors and contradictions found on the other sites. And when you compare these links to the other ones that claim that there are errors and contradictions in the Bible, the links defending the Bible are actually more detailed and argue in context. Another wards, they give much more thorough, objective explanations for their arguments than the others do. Also, if you type 'Bible difficulties' in the Google search engine, you actually find *more* links <u>defending</u> the Bible on the first page that pops up. In fact, the first two links are from The Christian Apologetics and Research Ministry which has seven whole pages that addresses some of the most popular 'alleged' errors and contradictions in the Bible – which prove that they don't actually exist after reading them.[7],[8] So, the question must be asked, "Since anyone is able to easily find for themselves links on the Internet that list both 'alleged' errors and contradictions in the Bible, as well as links that effectively defend against and answer these 'alleged' errors and contradictions, why do those who claim that the Bible has them <u>only</u> quote from the accusing sites and not the defending sites? Why do they merely 'cut and paste' from the accusing sites, and completely ignore the defending ones?" If one is honest, you have to wonder if they are really interested in finding out the Truth, or are they just trying to maintain their disbelief in the Bible and the Truth of Christianity? Sadly, through experience with atheists and other skeptics, the latter seems to true, because when I have pointed these defending links out to them, they don't even take the time to look at them, much like the 'Wayside' child from Chapter One who doesn't even make the effort to *listen* to the arguments for the Christian faith. Objectivity and open-mindedness involves listening to ALL sides, including the ones you don't believe in or agree with, which is what led me to eventually believe in the Truth of the Christian faith, based on ALL of the available evidence. That is the only way to make an informed decision. Otherwise, you are basing your worldview on a very small and limited outlook of the world that 'might' not actually be based on fact, but instead based on poor, sloppy secular apologetics.

---

[7] Matt Slick, http://carm.org/bible-difficulties/genesis-deuteronomy

[8] Matt Slick, "Introduction to Bible Difficulties and Bible Contradictions" http://carm.org/introduction-bible-difficulties-and-bible-contradictions

However, the major 'roadblock' that I have noticed with skeptics is that since the Bible is a 'religious' book, rather than a secular one, they don't believe that it can be 'inerrant,' so we're back to 'scientism' again, which we covered in 'Point Two' of this chapter is a self-refuting and limiting belief. However, is that even a valid argument to disbelieve something? What makes something 'inerrant' is, by definition, if it doesn't contain any errors in it. And the Bible contains none. In fact, the Bible is without error, without contradiction, contains hundreds of literally fulfilled prophecies that have come to pass in the real world, and is actually supported by science, history, archaeology, and logic, as mentioned repeatedly throughout this book and the Appendices, and backed up with a careful, objective studying of Scripture, and not just 'quote-mining' the Bible out of context, which is the standard ploy of atheists and other skeptics. And 'this' is the *real* reason why skeptics don't want to acknowledge the inerrancy of the Bible, but instead frantically scurry to find alleged errors and contradictions in it, because if they acknowledge that such a large volume of a collection of independent writings which were written over a millennia and a half by fishermen, shepherds, desert dwellers, professed prophets of God who had no real political or religious clout, etc.; written in three different languages and on three different continents; again, didn't contain <u>any</u> errors and contradictions, under these unique conditions that the Bible was written in and placed under one cover, it would be a rather pretty big pill to swallow that it was written without Divine intervention – which the reality is that **it _was_**! (2 Timothy 3:16; Hebrews 12:2). So, although other religious and secular writings do indeed have errors and contradictions in them, to be really objective, we shouldn't just 'assume' that because a large volume of writings are 'religious,' that it's necessarily not true or Divinely Authored.

5. **'The events of the Bible that Christians base their faith in were written over 2,000 years ago during an age of superstition and other false religious beliefs. It couldn't possibly be true'** – is longevity a fair criterion for judging if something is true or not? Unfortunately, many people seem to think so. Let me ask you this, when it gets to be 2,000 years since George Washington was elected President of the United States, should we begin to question the written documents from his era that says he was? If not, then based on the previous arguments in this chapter, then why should we question the legitimacy of the testimonies of the writers of the Bible – many of which, in the New Testament, were *eyewitnesses* to the Resurrection of Christ? Whatever criteria we use to believe that something is true or false, we need to be <u>consistent</u> with that criteria with *everything* – not just those things we subjectively 'believe' to be true or false, which applies to things that are both secular AND religious in nature. Otherwise, we are establishing a double-standard in order to justify a philosophy or worldview, which is hardly objective. Our ultimate goal should be seeking Truth, not trying to maintain a worldview, whether it be religious OR secular.

6. **'There are so many denominations of Christianity and interpretations of the Bible. If Christianity was true, wouldn't all Christians agree with each other?'** – secularists and other non-christian religious people don't all agree with each other on why the universe exists. In fact, most of them contradict each other, yet you've embraced one of these. Why is that? Why have you abandoned the Christian faith that is based on Truth, as well as supported by the evidence that we know about our universe through science, yet you've embraced a different worldview – whether it be secular or religious – that is 'not' based on Truth, nor on observable, testable, and repeatable scientific evidence (ie: the 'scientific method'), which contradicts other non-christian 'beliefs' that are 'also' not based on Truth, nor the 'scientific method'? Therefore, diversity among people who may share a common core belief (or disbelief) isn't evidence that something is not true. The fact that there are a wide variety of views about Christianity, as well as different and often conflicting interpretations of the Bible, only demonstrates that even Christians can be no different than the secular world or other religions for accounting for 'why' things are, like why the universe exists. You might ask, "Then 'why' do you believe your view of Christianity and interpretation of the Bible is true?" This is a branch of apologetics that is really beyond the scope of this book, but one of the core beliefs shared by all Christians is that <u>God</u> is the reason for the existence of the universe (Genesis 1:1). So, whatever conflicting views that Christians have with each other, we all share many of the same core, fundamental beliefs, including 'Who' Jesus was/is – 'the Christ [Messiah], the Son of the living

God' (Matthew 16:16). In fact, it may surprise you that there are things that I share with the secular world that I disagree with other Christians. But, that's not because I don't believe in the claims of Christianity or the inerrancy of the Bible. Rather, it's because I believe in <u>Truth</u>, which much of what we see in the world is supported *by* the claims of the Bible, while many of the beliefs of other Christians are not. For example, the book of Mormon makes a lot of statements that contradict the Bible,[9],[10],[11],[12] as well as other theological and historical errors.[13]

The same is true with other non-christian religions. However, my point is that a Biblically-based Christian's faith is based on evidence and Truth, not religion. So, the 'problem' within Christianity why all Christians don't agree with each other, is that many Christians are no different than people in the secular world – the part of their worldview that isn't in agreement with Biblical Christianity is 'not' based on evidence or Truth, but on the desire to maintain 'their' particular interpretation of the Bible, which is either largely based on 'their' opinion or

[9] Matt Slick, "Is Mormonism Christian?" http://carm.org/is-mormonism-christian

[10] Matt Slick, "Mormon Beliefs, are they Christian?" http://carm.org/mormon-beliefs

[11] S. Michael Houdmann, CEO, GotQuestions.org. *"What is Mormonism? What do Mormons believe?"* http://www.gotquestions.org/Mormons.html

[12] S. Michael Houdmann, CEO, GotQuestions.org. *"How should Christians view the Book of Mormon?"* http://www.gotquestions.org/book-of-Mormon.html

[13] Matt Slick, "Problems with the Book of Mormon." http://carm.org/problems-with-the-book-mormon

that of their particular church, rather than on 'accurately handling the word of truth' (2 Timothy 2:15), by allowing *Scripture* to explain *Scripture*, including using it 'for reproof, for correction' (2 Timothy 3:16) and compare what's being taught TO it (Acts 17:11). Therefore, even though there are differing and often conflicting views of Christianity, as well as those of other religions and worldviews, logically, only <u>one</u> worldview can (and must) be true, because they can't all be right, since they all contradict each other. And since the claims of Biblical Christianity are *based* on fact and evidence, rather than on opinion or 'religion,' then it would logically follow that any other religion or worldview that contradicts Biblical Christianity would automatically be false. Now, I'm certainly not asserting that 'everything' that other religions and worldviews teach is false, but rather any specific belief or teaching that contradicts Biblical Christianity is false, since views that are in opposition to each other can't both be right at the same time. Therefore, since it can be demonstrated that all religions and worldviews contradict Biblical Christianity in some way, then the belief in those contradictions are false, and therefore those religions and worldviews are also false, because when a religion or worldview that claims something to be true turns out to be false, then that religion or worldview is professing falsehood. So, since it's been demonstrated throughout this book that Biblical Christianity is based on Truth, then why are you embracing a worldview, which is in opposition to it, that's not, and is false?

7. **'I realize all this, but I still believe the Christian faith isn't true'** – based on what? You're opinion? This question may sound a bit too direct, but it's only meant to get you to ask yourself, 'why do I believe it's not true?' And just as important, 'why do I believe that my *disbelief* in the Christian faith is true?' I was having dinner one evening with Pusa and another couple who did not share our faith – at least not in the Inspiration and inerrancy of the Bible which Christians should believe and follow, and we were discussing politics. The gentleman I was talking with actually shared a particular view with me about a particular politician. However, the difference between 'why' we believed it was true was quite different. I shared with him some objective evidence for 'why' I believed it was true. However, when I asked him why he believed it was true, his response was 'well, I just believe it is.' When I asked him 'why' he believed it was true and to elaborate on this, he just repeated his response 'because...I just believe it is.' I could tell he was getting uncomfortable, so I didn't press it any further. Although we shared a common belief which was probably true, he realized that his belief was based on nothing more than his opinion. In apologetic circles, this is called 'circular reasoning' (*"I believe 'A' is true because 'B' says so, and I believe 'B' is true because 'A' says so."*) Some people may claim that Christians employ 'circular reasoning' too, by believing in the Bible, because the Bible says it's true. However, although the Bible does profess itself to be the Inspired Word of God, as demonstrated throughout this book that isn't the sole reason why Christians believe that. However, I have seen quite frequently among non-christians, including children

who have abandoned the Christian faith, that *they* are the ones who are actually using circular reasoning to maintain their worldview, and many of them don't even realize it.

To continue the story from Chapter One, I was reading the Bible once during my lunch break, and an atheist co-worker came up to me and asked me if 'I really believed that.' My response was, 'Yes, don't you?' (I figured it was a good 'window' of opportunity, since *she* was the one who approached and asked *me* <u>first</u>.) Her response was 'no, because I believe in science.' My response to her was the same thing I wrote in 'Point Two' of this chapter: 'That's good that you believe in science, because as a Biblically-believing Christian, so do I.' I remember she looked kind of puzzled with my response, and then began to ask me how I could believe in science *and* the Bible. I asked her if it would be okay if I could explain it to her. After she agreed, I explained many of the Christian apologetic techniques previously discussed in this book in defense of the Christian faith, and how only the Biblical explanation for why the universe exists is both logical and supported by science [See Appendix C]. After I finished, I asked her that since she doesn't believe in the Biblical explanation for why the universe exists, which is supported by both science and logic, then what does she believe to account for its existence, and why? I vividly remember her response, 'It came from a black hole.' I quickly asked her if she knew what a black hole was and what accounted for the existence of that black hole. How did the black hole come to exist, before the universe did? After thinking for a moment, she ended up not actually answering my question, but responded with "Well, you have your opinion, and I have mine, and we can just 'agree to disagree.'" Notice, that she was quick to end our discussion when she realized that when her standard answer didn't work, and although she was able to provide an answer to 'what' she believes, she wasn't able to answer 'why' she believes it. I ended up responding to her, "Yes, we can 'agree to disagree.' But keep in mind that the reason we don't agree is because what I believe, I'm able to explain it and base it on evidence which is *supported* by science, while you are unable to give an explanation using science for 'why' you believe what you believe." In fact, she still didn't actually know what a black hole was. And then it hit me. She didn't *understand the science* behind a black hole – which is not an actual, literal 'hole' in space that many people incorrectly assume it is based on the term 'black <u>hole</u>.' She merely heard that argument, but didn't make the effort to find out if that explanation was a plausible one, which many scientists today don't agree it is, because based on what we know about black holes being very dense and having an extremely heavy mass, since it's made up of matter and energy, that it too would require an explanation for 'its' existence as well, otherwise, you have the same 'infinite regress' you have for the alternative arguments covered in Appendix C, which are unscientific AND illogical. So, in a sense, she was actually being more 'religious' than I was in her 'belief' for why the universe exists, the main difference being that her opinion was neither supported by science nor by any other objective evidence, nor did she understand 'why' she was believing 'what' she was believing. She was merely basing her 'belief' on what other people told her – nothing more.

Unfortunately, this sort of 'non-answer' is what I've come to experience in conversations with people who have a worldview that is in opposition with Biblical Christianity, including children of Christian parents who have abandoned the faith. And yet, it's Christians who are so often falsely accused of basing their faith on 'religion' and a lack of evidence. (Hopefully, by now, we have put that false assumption to rest for good.) So, again, since the Christian faith is based on and supported by fact, evidence, and Truth, and your 'opinion' that contradicts it isn't, then 'why' are you embracing it and rejecting Biblical Christianity? From my experience with others, for them, opinion is more important than Truth, because they feel they are entitled to their opinion – I couldn't agree more! Everyone is entitled to their opinion, regardless of whether their opinion is based on facts or fiction. But, that doesn't really address my question, 'why' do you want to maintain an opinion that is not based on Truth, but on falsehood? What I've seen is that just like the 'Wayside' child in Chapter One, the *desire to listen* to the Truth isn't even there, let alone the willingness to accept it. This is what I experienced with the gentleman who I spoke with at dinner. He was content with his opinion and that it was true, but had no desire to learn if it wasn't true, nor explain 'why' he believed it was true. This lack of desire is in complete opposition with what the apostle Peter tells us: 'always being ready to *make a defense to everyone who asks you* to give an account for the hope that is in you, yet with gentleness and reverence' (emphasis added)(1 Peter 3:15). Christians are more than happy to 'make a defense' and explain not only 'what' they believe, but also 'why' they believe it, because they are <u>confident</u> that what they believe is true, not because of a personal or religious 'belief,' but because the evidence actually *supports* that belief. However, the same is normally not true for non-christians, because they <u>don't</u> desire to give a defense 'why' they believe what they believe, because deep down, they know they <u>can't</u>, so that's why they refrain from responding, or if they do, they respond with anger. So, if you are unable or unwilling to 'make a defense to everyone who asks you to give an account' for 'why' you believe 'what' you believe, then 'why' do you continue to believe in something you are unable to defend?

Why is 'opinion' more important to you than 'Truth'?

8. **<u>'Christianity is no different than any other religion, which is based on fear'</u>** – although other religions, like Islam, *are* based on fear, the Truth of the Christian faith is <u>not</u> based on fear, but rather, as explained throughout this book, is based on evidence – the evidence that Jesus was a real historical Person, Who really lived, really died, and really rose bodily from the dead. The idea that it's based on fear is because of New Testament passages where Jesus states that unless you believe in Him (and what He did *for us*) you won't have eternal life (John 3:16), and those who have refused to 'has been judged already' (v.18), and as a result, will be cast 'into the outer darkness; in that place there will be weeping and gnashing of teeth' (Matthew 8:12; 22:13; 25:30; etc), as well as other Old Testament verses about God that are 'quote-mined' completely out of context by skeptics. Although on the surface, statements

like these may 'seem' to be intended to be fearfully-motivating, making a factual statement is not the same as an attempt to force someone to believe something based solely on fear. So, although other religions may actually use fear as their primary motivation to get people to believe in their religion, that is not the intent of the Christian faith, because those pronouncements spoken by Jesus are based on fact and Truth, which He was able to back up by rising bodily from the dead – something no other religious leader from other religions were either able to do, nor claimed to.

Also, just a cursory overview of comparing the Christian faith to other religions should make it quite obvious that Christianity is nothing at all like other religions. Christianity *solely* declares that we have 'been justified by faith' (Romans 5:1) and 'by grace you have been saved through faith; and that *not of yourselves*, it is the gift of God; *not as a result of works*' (emphasis added)(Ephesians 2:8-9), while with all other religions and false forms of Christianity, salvation is based on some combination of faith AND good works. On CNN's "Larry King Live," in less than 30 seconds, Pastor John MacArthur summed up the uniqueness of the Christian faith and how it differs from every other religious and spiritual worldview of getting to Heaven, as well as how all these other worldviews are the same:

> "There are two religions in the world – just two. One is the true Christian religion of Divine accomplishment; you can't be good enough – nobody can – you only get there through Christ's goodness being applied

when you believe in His death and resurrection. Every other system in the world: Hindu, Muslim, spiritist, you name it, believes you get there by your works. Those are the only two. Make your choice. You can pick from all the religions of the world. It's all the same thing. Christianity stands alone based upon the authority of Scripture."[14]

If you watch that part of the interview, you can see the shocked look on the face of the spiritist, when Pastor MacArthur places spiritism in the same category of Hinduism, Islam, as well as all other religions. In fact, I'd be willing to bet that any religion would disagree that their religious views on 'good verses evil,' 'right verses wrong,' and attaining Heaven are no different than any other religion. Although they don't all agree with *what's* 'good and evil' or *what's* 'right verses wrong,' what they all have in common, as Pastor MacArthur points out, is that they all believe – at least in part – that if you're 'good enough,' you'll attain joy and happiness in the afterlife, whether that refers to Heaven or something else, which is in complete conflict with the Christian faith.

9. **'I believe Jesus existed, and I believe that he was a good moral teacher. I just don't believe He was the Son of God and was raised from the dead'** – this line of thinking goes hand-in-hand with the things we just covered in 'Point 7' – opinion verses Truth. Ironically, even many

---

[14] John MacArthur, "God and Good vs. Evil" (Larry King Live) || 4/22/2005 | INT-LK-04 http://www.gty.org/video/interviews/INT-LK-04/god-and-good-vs-evil-larry-king-live?term=larry%20king

well-known and educated atheists, like Richard Dawkins, freely admit that Jesus really existed [See Appendix B], and that's because they base their belief on the historical evidence that He existed and died. However, they are *in*consistent in their *dis*belief in His Resurrection, because they are 'not' basing their disbelief on the historical and logical evidence for it, as they do with His life and death. When it comes to the Resurrection, they suddenly 'switch gears' in their objectivity, because the Resurrection not only can't be proven with science, more specifically, it contradicts 'their' worldview. However, as mentioned in Appendix C, it also can't be *dis*proven either using science, just as His life and death can neither be proven nor disproven using science, which is why science is the wrong means of deciding whether or not the Resurrection actually happened or not and whether the Truth of the Christian faith is legitimate or not. Think about it - let's say that the Resurrection was an undisputed, universal historical fact that everybody believed. Exactly, 'how' would you go about using *science* today to prove a vanished body in an empty tomb from 2,000 years ago? It's impossible if your only instrument is based solely on science, just as it is for many other historical events that you accept as 'fact' but also can't be proven nor disproven using science. And that is where skeptics of the Christian faith are inconsistent with the criteria they use in determining if something is historically true or not. As mentioned previously, there is more historical evidence – both secular and religious – for the life, death, and bodily resurrection of Jesus, than there is for the existence of Socrates. Yet, as previously mentioned in 'Point Two' of this chapter, skeptics of the

Resurrection have no problem believing in not only the existence of Socrates, but also what he allegedly wrote, even though there are ZERO original writings of his around, as well as ZERO copies of his writings still in existence. Rather, we must rely on the writings of his students, like Plato, that he even existed. Another wards, we base our historical evidence for them on faith, which is the same thing that Christians base their faith on the Resurrection, which also is a historical <u>fact</u>. So, saying 'I just don't believe He was the Son of God and was raised from the dead,' is nothing more than a personal opinion that is based on nothing more than a personal opinion, which is just circular reasoning and is merely subjective, not objective.

And as far as believing Jesus was a 'good moral teacher,' keep in mind the words of Jesus, Himself, when He addressed the rich young ruler who, when he referred to Jesus as 'Good Teacher' (Luke 18:18), Jesus replied 'Why do you call Me good? No one is good except God alone' (v.19). Jesus points this out, because Scripture states that only God is righteous and can do good (Psalm 14:1,3; 53:1,3; Romans 3:10,12). Obviously, Jesus wasn't denying His Deity, since elsewhere in Scripture, Jesus affirms it (John 8:58; cf. Exodus 3:14; John 10:30-33; etc). Rather, Jesus was pointing out to the rich, young ruler the implication of his use of the word 'good' that refers to God alone, which he was using to describe Jesus. So, if you're denying that Jesus was the Son of God, Who was raised bodily from the dead, then how can you also believe that Jesus was 'good' – a term used solely to describe God? If

He wasn't God Who 'became flesh' (John 1:1,14), then He'd have to be something else. One of the most famous quotes from C.S. Lewis addresses this very important and significant issue about the 'goodness' and 'moral character' of Jesus, and the implication of referring to Him this way:

> "I am trying here to prevent anyone saying the really foolish thing that people often say about Him: 'I'm ready to accept Jesus as a great moral teacher, but I don't accept His claim to be God.' That is the one thing we must not say. A man who was merely a man and said the sort of things Jesus said would not be a great moral teacher. He would either be a lunatic – on a level with the man who says he is a poached egg – or else he would be the Devil of Hell. You must make your choice. Either this man was, and is, the Son of God: or else a madman or something worse. You can shut Him up for a fool, you can spit at Him and kill Him as a demon; or you can fall at His feet and call Him Lord and God. But let us not come with any patronizing nonsense about His being a great human teacher. He has not left that open to us. He did not intend to."[15]

So, when people state that they believe Jesus was a 'good moral teacher,' but also deny His Divinity and

---

[15] C.S. Lewis, "Mere Christianity: a revised and amplified edition, with a new introduction, of the three books, Broadcast talks, Christian behavior, and Beyond personality," p. 52. Copyright 1952, C.S. Lewis Pte. Ltd. Copyright renewed 1980, C.S. Lewis Pte. Ltd. HarperCollins Publishers: New York, NY. Harper Collins Publishers, New York: NY

Messiahship, I don't know how they can claim both, based on what Jesus claimed about Himself. As C.S. Lewis logically pointed out, Jesus was either crazy, satanic, or the Son of God. There is not 'fourth option.' So, if you believe Jesus was a 'good moral teacher,' but deny His claim to Deity, then you're also believing He was either crazy or satanic. But how can someone be 'good and moral' and also be satanic at the same time? Let's assume that you believe He was crazy. Again, how can someone be crazy and 'good and moral' at the same time? As Jesus pointed out previously to the rich, young ruler, only *God* is good, therefore, only *God* can be completely moral. So, how can God be 'good and moral' and crazy at the same time? Although many skeptics view God as being crazy, they are basing that belief on 'their' opinion of Him, not on Who He actually is, which at one time even Jesus was accused of by His own earthly family of having 'lost His senses' (Mark 3:21). However, a crazy person doesn't make logical statements, nor could have done and said the things that Jesus did and said. When Jesus argued with the Pharisees, Sadducees, and the scribes about God, Jesus – not them – was the One Who accurately professed the Truth about God. When you hear crazy people claim to be God, their self-profession of Deity isn't based on anything other than their own self-deluded, grandiose beliefs. Another wards, they can't back it up. However, when Jesus declared things about God, Who He was, and what He was sent by the Father to do, He backed up all of His claims with the Word of God, when He made statements, like 'It is *written*...' (emphasis added)(Matthew 4:4-10; 11:10; 21:13; 26:24; Mark 7:6; 9:13; 14:21,27; Luke 4:4-10; 7:27;

24:46; John 6:45) and 'Have you not *read…?*' (emphasis added)(Matthew 12:3-5; 19:14; 22:31; Mark 12:10,26; Luke 6:3). In fact, Jesus even makes it a point to convict the Jews with their own Scriptures by stating, 'For if you believed Moses, you would believe Me, for he wrote about Me. But if you do not believe his writings, how will you believe My words?' (John 5:46-47).

I realize that Jesus' claim that He was going to bodily rise from the dead after three days does seem to sound pretty 'crazy' to non-christians, but keep in mind two things: 1) bodily resurrection of the dead was something that the Jews always believed, based on their Old Testament Scriptures (Daniel 12:2), which the Jewish leaders of Jesus' time, like Nicodemus and Joseph of Arimathea, would have also believed and taught, including Saul of Tarsus who became the apostle Paul, who continued to teach it to the Church (1 Corinthians 15:12-23), as well as other New Testament Jewish writers like the apostle John (Revelation 20:5-6,11-13). In fact, many Old Testament passages actually prophesy about the coming Messiah's death and resurrection (Psalm 16:10; Isaiah 53:5-10; Daniel 9:26), which both the apostle Peter and the apostle Paul, as well as the evangelist, Philip, quoted in reference to Jesus' death and Resurrection (Acts 2:25-27; 8:32-33; 13:32-35). So, Jesus wasn't preaching anything anymore 'crazy' than what had already been taught for over a thousand years before He was even born; and 2) Jesus was actually able to back up what He said *by* bodily rising from the dead, which is physically impossible for a crazy person to do. Professing something to be true is a far cry from actually going out and *doing* it. This is the clear distinction between being 'crazy' and being <u>truthful</u>: a crazy person can't back up the crazy things they say, while a truthful person *can* back up what they say. So, Jesus was no more crazy than He was satanic, which leaves only one option left – that He was Who He claimed to be: the Son of God.

One last thing to think about: do you believe Jesus is in Heaven? Before you respond, take some time to really think about that. If Jesus was satanic, why would He be in Heaven? If He was crazy, He would have actually led literally billions of people over the past two-thousand years *away* from God. So, why would He be in Heaven if He willfully and knowingly did that? However, as previously mentioned, when Jesus affirmed to the rich, young ruler that He was 'good,' He was also professing that He was 'good enough' for Heaven, unlike us, thus also affirming His Deity and Messiahship. So, if your answer is 'yes,' then, logically, you are also affirming His claims about Himself, as well as the Truth of the Christian faith. If you answer, 'no,' then you are declaring that Jesus was either satanic or crazy, and therefore <u>not</u> a 'good moral teacher.' However, neither of those claims can be substantiated about what we know about Jesus, and what He actually did to prove both what He said about Himself, as well as what He came to do *for us*, which He was able to back up. So, once again, what is the 'real' reason for your abandonment of the Christian faith?

10. **<u>'I know a lot of Christians who are immoral and don't 'practice what they preach.' They are hypocrites, like</u>**

**the scandals involved throughout Church history.
The God of the Bible is a blood-thirsty monster. He
is immoral. Therefore, Christianity is immoral, so it
can't be true'** – there are a lot of immoral physicians,
attorneys, mechanics, as well as other people, so does
that mean you are going to stop believing and trusting
in <u>all</u> physicians, attorneys, mechanics, etc.? Are you
going to start believing that their *entire* professions are
'immoral,' because of the *individual* ones who are? If
not, then why are you applying that reasoning towards
the Christian faith? There is no doubt that many self-
professed 'Christians' throughout Church history have
been involved in immoral behavior, including murder and
various forms of abuse. However, that is not a reflection of
the Christian faith, any more than a physician who violates
the Hippocratic Oath is a reflection of the intended
morality and well-being of the medical community
towards its patients. People who violate the commands
of Jesus are actually *disobeying* Him, and, therefore, not
true examples of genuine followers of Christ, Who said,
"You have heard that it was said, 'AN EYE FOR AN EYE,
AND A TOOTH FOR A TOOTH.' But I say to you, do
not resist an evil person; but whoever slaps you on your
right cheek, turn the other to him also. If anyone wants to
sue you and take your shirt, let him have your coat also.
Whoever forces you to go one mile, go with him two"
(Matthew 5:38-41), and "You have heard that it was said,
'YOU SHALL LOVE YOUR NEIGHBOR and hate your
enemy.' But I say to you, love your enemies and pray for
those who persecute you" (vv.43-44).

Unfortunately, what we so frequently find in the secular world, as well as the Christian community, are examples of people who 'resist' the needs of others, engage in retaliation rather than forgiveness, and 'claim' to love God but not mankind Who God created - particularly our enemies, Who God also created them 'in His own image' (Genesis 1:27). They claim that they love God by following 'the great and foremost commandment' to 'LOVE THE LORD YOUR GOD WITH ALL YOUR HEART, AND WITH ALL YOUR SOUL, AND WITH ALL YOU MIND' (Matthew 22:36-37), but they fail to demonstrate this, by not following the second commandment He also gave them to 'LOVE YOUR NEIGHBOR AS YOURSELF' (v.39b), which Jesus stated, 'The second is like it' (v.39a). Another wards, a person can't claim to love God, but not also love other people, including their enemies, which the apostle John points out when he wrote, "If someone says, 'I love God,' and hates his brother, he is a liar; for the one who does not love his brother whom he has seen, cannot love God whom he has not seen. And *this commandment we have from Him*, that the one who loves God *should love his brother also*" (emphasis added)(1 John 4:20-21). So, hypocritical 'Christians' who don't obey <u>both</u> of these commands from Jesus, and even go so far in becoming involved in immoral activity, are not true representatives of Jesus, nor the Christian faith. In fact, they don't even reflect the practices of the vast majority of Christians and Christian leaders whose behavior *is* representative of Jesus and Christianity. As Pastor John MacArthur corrected Nancy Grace's erroneous assumption of 'Christian evangelical leaders' who are involved in sex scandals in the Church 'over and over and over':

> "First of all, the 'over and over' concerns me a little bit. I think 98% of the men who are out there pastoring in churches are serving the Lord with integrity and honesty and living good, wholesome, moral, righteous lives and trying to honor Christ. Those that fall from the heights of these high-profile ministries, obviously *garner the media*. I could give you a theological reason, Nancy. I think the enemy of our souls, Satan, assaults the Church and assaults the *truth* and counterfeits it, and places people in ministry *who have no business being there*. I think very often when guys get to the top of an empire, they begin to believe in a certain level of invincibility, and corruption creeps in and goes from there. But I really believe it's an inability or unwillingness to deal honestly and spiritually with your life before God. I just think it's a huge case of hypocrisy. You have people in ministry *who have no business being there*."[16] (emphasis added)

As pointed out in the interview, unfortunately, whatever the media chooses to focus on about Christianity, as well as its leaders, is the impression that people have about the Christian faith. However, what the media chooses to 'garner' are usually the bad examples and *exceptions* of

---

[16] John MacArthur, "Pastor vs. Prostitute Sex Scandal" (Nancy Grace) || 2/2/2007 | INT-NG-01 http://www.gty.org/video/interviews/INT-NG-01/pastor-vs-prostitute-sex-scandal-nancy-grace?term=nancy%20grace (italics added in the quote for emphasis)

Christian leadership, rather than the norm. As a result, the public, including children of Christian parents, begin to erroneously believe that the core of Christianity is 'immoral,' when in reality, the teachings and commands of Jesus are both 'God-centered' as well as 'other-centered,' rather than 'me-centered.' Christians who truly have a desire to serve Christ, also have an equal desire to serve others, which Jesus gave Himself as an example, 'For even the Son of Man did not come to be served, but to serve, and to give His life a ransom for many' (Mark 10:45) and 'For I gave you an example that you also should do as I did to you….If you know these things, you are blessed if you do them' (John 13:15,17). This is the 'true' picture of what Christian living and interactions with others is actually about – serving God and serving others, as Christ served us. However, just as there are immoral physicians who refuse to follow the Hippocratic Oath, there are also immoral 'Christians' who refuse to follow Christ, but that doesn't mean that the medical and Christian communities are immoral. Rather, those *particular individuals* in those communities are immoral. So, it's important to distinguish between those *professions and movements* verses the *individuals* in those professions and movements.

In fact, <u>only</u> the Christian faith is truly moral, because, unlike other worldviews, religions, and movements, Christianity provides absolute justice, while at the same time offering absolute mercy and grace. And the reason why it's truly moral is because Christian morality is based on <u>God's</u> perfect standards of morality, which are *objective* and *external* for the individual, rather than <u>man's</u> imperfect standards which are *subjective* and *internal* which is found in every other religion and worldview [See Appendix D]. Another wards, for the Christian faith, morality and Truth do not begin and end with the individual, but rather with <u>God</u>, Who is Himself completely moral and the source of all Truth (John 14:6). An example of this is when Jesus gives the 'Parable of the Sheep and the Goats' (or the 'Parable of the Judgment of the Nations')(Matthew 25:31-46). Jesus states that at that time, He will look to the 'goats' on His 'left' (ie: those who rejected Him and refused to repent) and sentence them eternally 'into the eternal fire [ie: Hell] which has been prepared for the devil and his angels' (v.41), because 'to the extent that you did not do it to the one of *the least of these* [ie: His other disciples ('sheep') on His 'right' (v.34)], you did not do it to Me' (emphasis added)(v.45). Another wards, an outward sign that a person is *genuinely* obedient to God is 'how' they treat ***other people***. In fact, Jesus goes so far as to warn us that 'Whoever causes one of these little ones who believe to stumble, it would be better for him if, with a heavy millstone hung around his neck, he had been cast into the sea' (Mark 9:42). This vivid and very serious warning is intended to make us aware that Jesus will judge us accordingly, as well as our faithfulness and devotion to Him, by how we treat our fellow human beings. Compare the 'morality' of other religions and worldviews to the morality of the Christian faith:

- **Islam** – although Muslims insist that Islam is the 'religion of peace,' the Qur'an actually commands that if a Muslim leaves their religion, the family has the obligation to murder that 'infidel.' However, in Christianity when the apostle Paul discusses an unbelieving spouse who abandons them, 'Yet if the *unbelieving one leaves, let him leave*; the brother or the sister is not under bondage in such cases, but God has *called us to peace'* (emphasis added)(1 Corinthians 7:15). This is because <u>God</u> Himself – not His followers – will deal with the abandonment of the unbeliever. This is how a *true* 'religion of peace' deals with those who abandon the faith or the marriage of a believer.

- **Judaism** – although Christianity unquestionably has its roots engrained in Judaism, and devout Jews would never use God's Name in vain, since Jews reject Jesus as their promised Messiah, Lord, and God, they do not believe using Jesus' Name as a four-letter curse word would violate the Third Commandment (Exodus 20:7). However, both the New, as well as the Old, Testaments affirm that Jesus *is* God (John 1:1,14; 8:58; cf. Exodus 3:14; John 10:30-33; etc.), as well their promised Jewish Messiah (Matthew 1:22-23; cf. Isaiah 7:14). Therefore, regardless of the fact that they reject Jesus as their Messiah, when Jews do use His Name as a curse word, they are committing blasphemy, which although is not the 'unpardonable sin' (Matthew 12:31-32) provided *genuine* repentance and acceptance of Jesus as their Savior and Lord, blasphemy of Jesus' Name is still immoral in the eyes of God – something that a *genuine* Christian would not have the desire to do, because, for the Christian, blaspheming Jesus' Name equates with blaspheming the Name of God, because they are the <u>same</u> God. Also, have you ever noticed that Jesus is the <u>*only*</u> leader of a religion whose Name is blasphemed? You never hear Jews blaspheming the name of Moses, Muslims blaspheming the name of Muhammad, Buddhists blaspheming the name of Buddha, etc. Blaspheming the Name of Jesus is unique, which is something you would expect the world to do, because the world actually *hates* the One True God. If the world did not hate God, people wouldn't use His Only Begotten Son's Holy Name as a curse word. But as Jesus points out, 'He who hates Me hates My Father also' (John 15:23). A Jew, or anyone else, cannot claim to love God, while at the same time 'hate' Jesus, by blaspheming His Name.

- **Buddhism/Hinduism** – on the surface, Buddhism and Hinduism 'appear' to be non-threatening, non-judgmental religions. However, in Buddhism and Hinduism, morality is based on what the *individual* considers 'moral' – and that is where the deception begins. Since there are no *objective* and *external* boundaries for what 'moral' is in Buddhism and Hinduism, and the individual can decide 'morality' for themselves, this allows a wide, open door to advocate immorality on the most innocent and defenseless of human beings – the unborn. Although many Buddhists, Hindus, and other religions and worldviews don't equate abortion with murder, both Biblically <u>AND</u> scientifically, human life *begins* at <u>conception</u>[17] – not 'at a later developmental stage in

---

[17] Matt Slick, "Chronological development of a baby." http://carm.org/chronological-development-of-a-baby

the womb.' That's because at the moment a human egg is fertilized, *he* or *she* is *alive* because the cell is <u>actively</u> dividing, and has *human* DNA and *human* sex chromosomes, which are different from *his* or *her* parents. Therefore, at the moment of conception, the fertilized egg is a <u>*living, human being*</u>. So, a Buddhist, Hindu, or anyone else who advocates abortion is actually advocating murder of the most innocent and defenseless of all human beings, who 'should' be in the safest place in the entire world – their mother's womb. I acknowledge and certainly empathize with the fact that many people – particularly women – would emphatically object to this by obviously pointing out that I'm a man and that I don't have the right to tell a woman 'what to do with *her* body.' However, I would also like to point out that **<u>who</u>** is growing in '*her* womb' isn't actually 'part' of '*her* body,' but rather a separate, **living human** being, who has just as much right to live as any other separate, living human being, regardless of their 'geography.' Also, my gender is completely irrelevant to the Biblical and historical facts, which state that life *begins* at <u>conception</u>. So, 'how' they came into the world is less important than the fact that they are now currently **living** in the world – a reality that the Biblically-based Christian acknowledges the truth of. God told the prophet Jeremiah, 'Before I *formed you in the womb I knew you*, And *before you were born I consecrated you*' (emphasis added)(Jeremiah 1:5). Jeremiah later laments before God by saying, 'Because he did not *kill me before birth*' (emphasis added)(Jeremiah 20:17).

You can't 'kill' something in the womb if he or she is not alive. King David stated, 'Behold, I was brought forth in iniquity, And *in sin* my mother *conceived me*' (emphasis added)(Psalm 51:5). King David is stating that sin is a *human* quality that takes place at *conception* – not 'at a later developmental stage in the womb.' Job even laments to God, "Let the day perish on which I was to be born, And the night which said, 'A *boy is conceived*'....Why did I not *die at birth*, Come forth *from the womb and expire*?...I would have slept then, I would have been at rest....Or like *a miscarriage* which is discarded, I would not be, *As infants that never saw light*...there *the weary are at rest*" (Job 3:3,11,13,16-17). Job is clearly stating that a male child is considered a 'boy' at *conception*, at that if he 'died at birth,' he would have *already* been considered <u>alive</u>, because even a 'miscarriage' is defined as an '*infant* that never saw life.' These truths are all things that Christians consider 'moral,' both Biblically <u>AND</u> scientifically, about keeping the unborn human being alive. Christians also teach that abortion is also not the 'unpardonable sin,' provided *genuine* repentance before God and accepting Jesus as their Savior <u>AND</u> Lord. Jesus died and offers forgiveness and love to anyone who committed that sin too.

- **<u>Atheism/agnosticism</u>** – like Buddhism and Hinduism, atheism and agnosticism also 'allow' the *individual* to determine what is and what is not 'moral,' based on the *subjective, internal* standards of <u>man</u>, rather than the *objective, external* standards of <u>God</u>. However, this 'allowance' for *individually*

193

defining 'morality' is exponentially more threatening to the well-being and safety of mankind than even 'organized religions' like Hinduism and Buddhism are, because since there are no *objective, eternal* godly boundaries to what 'good' and 'bad' are in atheism and agnosticism, the *individual* can decide for <u>himself</u> or <u>herself</u> what 'good' and 'bad' behavior and treatment <u>*towards*</u> another individual is. The atheist or agnostic can determine if murder, rape, abuse (physical, emotional, mental, or sexual), or any other action, speech, or attitude is 'good' or 'bad,' based solely on *their* 'standards.' Now, the atheist or agnostic may say that they 'personally' base morality on what their society defines as 'moral.' However, is that a fair, objective criterion to judge what is 'moral' and what isn't? Was it 'moral' for Nazi Germany to attempt to exterminate the Jews, because their 'society' believed their behavior was 'moral'? What if society changes its mind, like in the case of The United States Supreme Court's judgment in 1973 that made it legal to murder defenseless, innocent, living human beings in the womb? Was it '*im*moral' to murder them before 1973? Can 'morality' change? If so, then if someday 'society' makes it legal to murder, rape, or abuse other people, then how will we be able to say *at that time* that those actions are 'immoral,' if 'society' deems it 'moral'? However, for the Christian, morality does <u>not</u> change, because *God* does not change (Malachi 3:6).

- **Self-religion** – also known as not believing in 'organized religion' is the individual's way of saying that they don't 'define' morality based on anyone else's 'definition' other than their own, including society's. However, they run into the same moral dilemma that 'organized religions' and atheists and agnostics do. If they base their 'definition of morality' beginning and ending with themselves, rather than with God, then 'they' are the determiners if something is moral or not, and in order to be consistent, since morality can't change, then neither can their 'definition of morality,' which is *subjective* and *internal*, rather than *objective* and *external*. Some may say that their 'definition of morality' would exclude the 'harming' of an individual or society, even if society allows for it. However, how to you objectively determine what 'harmful' is? And what if someone else's 'definition of morality' and behavior conflicts with theirs? How can they say that the other person's behavior is 'immoral,' because then they are being no different than the one who belongs to an 'organized religion'? So, 'self-religion' is really no different than 'organized religion,' because it is the 'organized religion of <u>ONE</u>.' The only real difference is that they have no objective support that their 'morality' is truly moral and 'non-harming' to other individuals and society, because that 'morality' is based on nothing other than their personal opinion which is subjective, and can be very dangerous. In fact, since they are basing 'morality' beginning and ending for themselves, what prevents them from violating the laws of a society that actually *protect* individuals, if they don't believe that those laws are 'moral'? Since the individual defines 'morality' beginning and ending with themselves, there is nothing preventing them – 'morally' – from breaking a law that society deems 'moral' if the individual thinks it's '*im*moral.' However, the Christian faith bases its morality beginning and ending with *God*, Who *alone* is the <u>definition</u> of 'good' and 'righteous' (Mark 10:18; Romans 3:1-12), as well as the Christian faith being of 'moral excellence' (2 Peter 1:5).

So, if a person accuses the Christian faith of being 'immoral' or that God is a 'wicked monster,' all they are basing that on is their *own* 'morality' that is *subjective* and *internal*, rather than on something that is *objective* and *external*.

Many children, who have read the Bible - particularly the Old Testament, insist God is a 'blood-thirsty monster.' This is largely based on particular passages that, when taken out of proper context and with a *very*, basic surface-level reading of them, seem to support this accusation. However, this kind of 'quote-mining' of Scripture does not take into consideration the surrounding passages of these particular quotes nor the real intention of God's actions and commands, such as when we examined Rachael Slick's 'deconversion' from her Christian upbringing in Chapter Three, and her confusion of who God's commandments were applied to, how they affected them, and her misunderstanding that sins don't 'stop being sins' simply because Jesus died for His 'sheep.' It is this same kind of 'quote-mining' of Scripture taken out of proper context why skeptics view God as a 'blood-thirsty monster.' However, these 'straw-man' arguments against God, as well as Christianity, are based on poor Biblical hermeneutics, or an inaccurate interpretation of the text. A careful exegesis of those particular passages – or interpreting Scripture simply based on what it says, not merely 'reading into' it – reveal that God's intention was to protect His chosen people – <u>Israel</u>, that the promised Jewish Messiah and Savior of the world was going to be born from (Revelation 12:1-2; cf. Genesis 37:9-10). And any individual or people-group who would attempt to annihilate them – either at that time or in the future – were enemies of God attempting to prevent <u>OUR</u> salvation. So, as a just and merciful God, throughout both the Old and the New Testaments, God has provided the means and availability of salvation and repentance for <u>anyone</u>. However, anyone who rejected His gracious gift, and instead willfully and violently attempted to thwart His salvation plan by attempting to destroy Israel was dealt with justly. To do otherwise, would make Him an *un*just God, Who wouldn't care about our eternal destination after death. However, Scripture explicitly states that God 'is patient toward you, not wishing for any to perish but for all to come to repentance' (2 Peter 3:9). That doesn't sound like an 'immoral, blood-thirsty' god to me, but rather a patient, loving God, Who desires the absolute best for us, and willfully offered His 'Best' to us – His Son's shed blood on the cross to atone for our salvation. But, it's up to <u>us</u> to accept it on *His* righteous terms, not our *un*righteous ones.

Incidentally, these baseless, subjective accusations against God and the Christian faith cut to the core of the *real* reason for 'why' children of Christian parents abandon the faith: an emotional reaction towards Christianity, which was either based on God 'allegedly,' or a Christian either 'allegedly' or genuinely, disappointing them at some point in their early Christian lives, or a desire that began to slowly build from within them to live a self-fulfilling lifestyle rather than a God-fulfilling one. As an unbelieving child of Christian parents, you might be quick to deny this, but let's quickly review the other 'reasons' why children of Christian parents claim they abandoned the faith, as well as 'why' they aren't legitimate reasons for abandoning it:

- **'They're just a bunch of stories'** – yes, but they are a 'bunch of *true* stories,' many of which have been proven. Plus, the inability to 'prove' something doesn't automatically make it false, otherwise, <u>anything</u> we are unable to prove through eyewitness testimonies is also false, which would not apply to Christianity, which <u>is</u> <u>based</u> on eyewitness accounts. So, this is a poor argument to abandon the Christian faith.
- **'I believe in science, not a 'god-of-the-gaps' religion'** – so do Christians who also do not believe in a 'god-of-the-gaps.' In fact, there are many 'gaps' that Christianity has 'closed' hundreds, even thousands of years, before the scientific community could 'prove' it with science. Also, 'science' verses 'Christianity' is a false dichotomy, because they are not opposed to each other, but rather the former is supported by the

latter, and vice versa. So, this too is a poor argument to abandon the Christian faith.

- **'People aren't believing in Christianity anymore, because it's based on an old myth like Thor or Zeus'** - this is simply not true for multiple reasons mentioned previously, including Jesus being a real live historical Person, while Thor and Zeus were not. So, this too is a poor argument to abandon the Christian faith.

- **'The Bible was written by men; what about all the errors and contradictions in it?'** – although written by men, the Bible is Inspired ('God-breathed') by God and Authored by Jesus, which is free from errors and contradictions – something you would expect from such a complex grouping of independent texts of literature, placed under one cover to be, if it was Divinely revealed by God. So, this too is a poor argument to abandon the Christian faith.

- **'The events of the Bible that Christians base their faith in were written over 2,000 years ago during an age of superstition and other false religious beliefs. It couldn't possibly be true'** – something written in antiquity is not objective criteria for determining if something is true or not. Verifying its historical, scientific, and most importantly, spiritual and prophetic accuracy does, which the Christian faith in the Bible is based on. So, this too is a poor argument to abandon the Christian faith.

- **'There are so many denominations of Christianity and interpretations of the Bible. If Christianity was true, wouldn't all Christians agree with each**

other?' – in a world of countless conflicting beliefs, only <u>one</u> can be true, because 'something' <u>must</u> to be true, and they can't *all* be right. This is also true for conflicting beliefs within Christianity, and the reason for this lack of conformity is the lack of commitment to the sufficiency of Scripture, by so many denominations, which is the *source* of Truth. So, this too is a poor argument to abandon the Christian faith.

- **'I realize all this, but I still believe the Christian faith isn't true'** – one's personal 'belief' is not the source of Truth, because what if someone else's 'belief' conflicts with yours? Rather, Truth is based on objective <u>evidence</u>, which is what the Christian faith is based on, while all other 'beliefs' that conflict with it, are based on subjective <u>opinions</u>, either by the individual, their religion, or their worldview. Opinions can be wrong; Truth can't. So, this too is a poor argument to abandon the Christian faith.

- **'Christianity is no different than any other religion, which is based on fear'** – although many other religions, and even secular beliefs and regimes, have been based on fear and 'forcing' to convert to their religion or secular worldview, the Christian faith is not. In fact, many of these worldviews use fear *because* of a <u>lack</u> of evidence, while Christianity is 'based' on evidence, not fear. So, this too is a poor argument to abandon the Christian faith.

- **'I believe Jesus existed, and I believe that he was a good moral teacher. I just don't believe He was the Son of God and was raised from the dead'** – if you believe Jesus was a 'good moral teacher,' but deny He was the Son of God, then you must believe that He was either satanic or crazy, which would not make Him a 'good moral teacher.' And if you believe He wasn't a 'good moral teacher,' then you're rejecting the objective evidence that He was Who He said He was, and did what He said He did, demonstrated throughout this book. So, this too is a poor argument to abandon the Christian faith.

- **'I know a lot of Christians who are immoral and don't 'practice what they preach.' They are hypocrites, like the scandals involved throughout Church history. The God of the Bible is a blood-thirsty monster. He is immoral. Therefore, Christianity is immoral, so it can't be true'** – how individuals act is not a reflection of the religion, profession, or movement they are a part of. Rather, the core teachings and beliefs of them are. And when you study the core teachings, beliefs, and commands of Jesus, they are truly and objectively moral, because only the Christian faith offers absolute justice, while also offering mercy and grace, which is lacking in all other religions and worldviews. So, this too is a poor argument to abandon the Christian faith.

I'm sure there are other arguments that I've missed, but for the purpose and scope of this book, these are arguments I wrestled with before I accepted the Truth of the Christian faith, and now I continue to hear these same arguments by children of Christian parents who abandoned the faith that I once used myself. So, I completely understand where you are coming from, because it wasn't that long ago that I shared your same 'disbelief.' However, over the past ten years through conversations with Christians, people of other religions and worldviews, as well as atheists, my faith has only been strengthened, because I <u>know</u> the Christian faith is true – not because of arrogance or a personal 'belief' (or personal 'disbelief' in something else), but because the Christian faith is based on <u>evidence</u>. This reminds me of an exchange between Professor Richard Dawkins, who is an atheist, and Dr. John Lennox, who is a Christian, who participated in a friendly debate called 'The God Delusion Debate,' which really reinforced what Christians mean by 'faith' is *based* on evidence:

> <u>Dawkins</u>: "…we only need to use the word 'faith' when there isn't any evidence."

> <u>Lennox</u>: "No, not at all. I presume you've got faith in your wife. Is there any evidence for that?"

> <u>Dawkins</u>: "Yes, plenty of evidence."[18]

Notice how Dr. Lennox managed to get Prof. Dawkins to admit that faith is *based* on evidence! And if you continue to watch the debate, Prof. Dawkins catches himself and realized what he just did, and then attempts to squirm his way out of it by 'redefining' what he means by 'evidence.' However, it doesn't change the fact that faith <u>is</u> based on evidence (which Prof. Dawkins readily admitted). And for the Christian, his

---

[18] *The God Delusion Debate*, featuring Richard Dawkins and John Lennox. (2007). Fixed Point Foundation. All Rights Reserved. (DVD)

or her faith in Christianity and Jesus Christ is based on the same kind of 'evidence' that Prof. Dawkins has in his wife, because like Prof. Dawkins, the Christian is basing his faith in a <u>Person</u>, not a religion or worldview. And that faith in that Person is based on the <u>evidence</u> of what Jesus did *for us* on the cross, which is supported by the <u>evidence</u> of His Resurrection, based on the <u>evidence</u> of 'more than five hundred eyewitnesses at one time' (1 Corinthians 15:6a), most of whom were still alive when Paul wrote his first epistle to the Corinthian Church (v.6b), who were available to verify Paul's claim of their *individual* eyewitness accounts.

I realize that this particular chapter has turned into a sort of 'Christian apologetics' chapter. However, I felt the need to not only address most of the same arguments that I used when I was a skeptic, but also to address 'why' those arguments are invalid. So, once again, I ask you, since the above ten arguments are not decent, plausible arguments for why you abandoned the Christian faith, what is the **real** reason for abandoning it? Was it because of a prayer that God didn't answer with a 'yes'? Was it because of either an alleged or real disappointment with another Christian – perhaps even a parent? Did something begin to build up in you, possibly influenced by others, to fulfill some internal desire that you knew Christ is opposed to? Or did you simply buy into one of the ten poor arguments previously mentioned in this chapter? I know of a lot of people who converted to the Christian faith, who later admitted that the main thing that 'blocked' them from repenting and accepting Christ was that they knew their lifestyle was in direct opposition to God, and they didn't want to feel convicted (see the quotes from

Lee Strobel in the Epilogue). But how is that any different than someone who is a thief or some other kind of criminal, who is told that they need to stop their lifestyle, because it's 'wrong'? That truth doesn't change the fact that the thief, or other criminal, still desires to engage in that lifestyle, because they perceive some sort of benefit for *them* (such as the free acquisition of money or 'stuff') by continuing to engage in that immoral lifestyle. But as Pastor Craig Groeschel points out too well, 'Sin is fun – at least for a while. But it never fails to come back to haunt you, usually when you least expect it. Like a sneeze, sin feels good at first, but it leaves a huge mess.'[19] And that is something that I learned, which children who abandoned the Christian faith don't realize, that there are long-term consequences for rejecting the Christian faith and engaging in a sinful lifestyle. You may not feel the long-term, negative effects at first, like the analogy I used with the woman in her early twenties who has been smoking for a few years, who believes she can 'quit at any time I want to' (yet, is still smoking), but I can guarantee in time you will feel those negative effects of sin. So, just as today is the day to end any other bad habit that will produce long-term negative effects, "behold, *now* is 'THE DAY OF SALVATION'" (emphasis added)(2 Corinthians 6:2). Don't wait. You have no guarantee past your next breath that you will live another minute. Repent of your sin against God, and ask Jesus into your life as both your Savior <u>AND</u> Lord over every aspect of your life. Do it <u>today</u>!

---

[19] Craig Groeschel, *"The Christian atheist: believing in God but living as if he doesn't exist,"* p. 22. Zondervan: Grand Rapids, MI: Zondervan, 2010.

Another reason I have heard is that the Christian faith is 'too hard.' I wouldn't argue with that. However, no one said the Christian faith is easy. Like Mom says, "Becoming a Christian is the 'easy' part. Living the Christian life can be hard." I can attest to that. I have actually lost long-term friendships because of my profession of my Christian faith. Some of them have dated back twenty-five-plus years all the way to high school. However, Jesus warned us that He was going to bring 'division,' even within households (Matthew 10:34-36; Luke 12:51-53). In fact, James, the Lord's brother, wrote that a Christian's faith will be tested through trials, 'Consider it all joy, my brethren, when you encounter various trials, knowing that the testing of your faith produces endurance' (James 1:2-3). It was these kinds of 'trials' and 'testing' that the apostle Paul experienced that actually strengthened his faith, as an example for us to follow when we experience trials of our own, 'Therefore I am well content with weaknesses, with insults, with distresses, with persecutions, with difficulties, for Christ's sake; for when I am weak, then I am strong' (2 Corinthians 12:10; cf. 11:23-28). So, whatever 'trial' you might be going through, it will be for 'Christ's sake,' because Jesus tells us that it is <u>Him</u> Whom the people of the world hates, which is why they reject you and take it out on you, 'If the world hates you, you know that it has hated Me before it hated you. If you were of the world, the world would love its own; but because you are not of the world, but I chose you out of the world, because of this the world hates you' (John 15:18-19). So, if the world accepts and 'loves' you, Jesus says it's because you are *of* the world, and if you are 'of' the world, then you aren't 'of' Christ, nor in terms of His Church, you are "not really *'of'* us" (emphasis added)(1 John 2:19). No one said being a Christian is 'easy.'

But, the eternal rewards for maintaining the faith, rather than abandoning it, far outweigh any temporary trial or persecution you experience in this life. The apostle Paul enforces this point, 'For momentary, light affliction is producing for us an eternal weight of glory far beyond all comparison' (2 Corinthians 4:17). So, if this is part of the reason you have abandoned the faith, because you can't see the forest for the trees, the eternal rewards far exceed the temporal 'benefits' that this world 'attempts' to offer you, which will only lead to long-term disappointments and consequences.

So, whatever your reason for abandoning the Christian faith: an alleged disappointment of God, alleged or real disappointments from Christians, worldly desires, or one of the ten erroneous reasons previously mentioned in this chapter, none of them are legitimate, rational reasons for abandoning the Christian faith, because they are either not true and/or will not benefit you in the long-run. Not only will that reluctance in accepting the Truth of the Christian faith damage your long-term relationship with your Heavenly Father Who loves you and desires an eternally joyful relationship with you that mere words are incapable of expressing, but your reluctance also damages your relationship with your Christian parent(s) who also love you, and has loved you, even before you were born – even to the point of loving you enough to share the Truth of the Christian faith with you. You can't measure nor buy that kind of love. I hope you truly take some serious time to think about all this, pray about it (even if you don't pray anymore or not that often), and at the very least ask yourself these questions: "What 'kind' of relationship would I like to have with my Christian parents?" "What do I want to base my life on – opinion or Truth?" "What is the 'real' reason I abandoned the Christian faith?" "Was/were that reason(s) legitimate?" "What kind of relationship do I want with God – one based on Truth or falsehood?" "Once I die, 'where' do I want to end up for all eternity?" Once you answer these questions, I hope you realize the reality that once you *truly* repent and genuinely accept Jesus as your Savior and Lord, you can have a much closer, intimate, and fulfilling relationship with God and your parents, than you ever could with anyone, or any*thing* else. You will also find yourself free from so many things, like the bondage of sin that you won't even realize that you were trapped in until afterwards, the bondage of anger that will no longer enslave you, as well as other bondages that are holding you down and back from experiencing true joy and happiness that is only available through a genuine and intimate relationship with Jesus Christ. And I can honestly say, I have never once regretted doing it, and I'm SO thankful to my Lord for regenerating my heart and convicting me of my sin. I am honestly the better for it. I pray that you accept the Truth and 'abandon' opinion, just as I did ten years ago. The reality of your eternal destination depends on it.

Epilogue

Jerry and I were talking earlier today after a Bible study he leads at my mom's work. (Jerry is my mom's boss). We were discussing the youth at his church, and he was expressing his concern and frustration over some of them, who were refusing to accept the Truth of the Christian faith, even after faithfully preaching the Gospel, and backing it up with support with very, strong Christian apologetics. Although Jerry has been my Bible study teacher for nearly ten years, out respect for him, I humbly reminded him that no one was ever saved using Christian apologetics, but rather through hearing the Gospel <u>after</u> the Holy Spirit regenerated and convicted their hearts, and that all apologetics does is reinforce that Christianity is true. I reminded him about what former atheist Lee Strobel stated in his DVD "The Case for Christ" (which is based on his 1998 book of the same name), that it wasn't all the extra-scriptural evidence that he had researched over the previous two years to determine whether or not the Christian faith and the Resurrection of Jesus was true that convinced him. Rather, it wasn't until after he read a particular passage written by the apostle Paul in <u>Scripture</u> that convinced him:

"My research took me to a letter that the apostle Paul wrote to the church of Corinth, and it contains the earliest passage of all about what happened to the resurrected Jesus."[1]

Mr. Strobel was of course referring to the passage in 1 Corinthians 15 where the apostle Paul listed all the eyewitnesses to the Resurrection of Christ, including the fact that at the time Paul wrote it, many of those eyewitnesses were still alive to verify that the Resurrection actually happened. I think this really helped Jerry, because even though he knew that, I believe hearing it from a fellow 'brother-in-Christ' helped alleviate some of his frustration. However, I'm confident that his concern was still there, because the consequence of them willfully refusing to accept the Truth of the Gospel, and continuing to cling to false worldviews is eternal separation from God. And if they die in that perpetual state of doubt, there is no 'second chance' after death. Our 'second chance' is *right now*. However, as Lee Strobel points out, what delayed him from accepting the Truth of the Christian faith was one personal and significant stumbling block – accountability:

> "This was not just an intellectual journey. There was a very real emotional component to this, because I would find things along the way that would challenge me and my worldview on a very deep level. And I would recoil from it, and I wouldn't want to believe it. There was so many reasons why I didn't want

[1] Lee Strobel, "The Case for Christ: a journalist's personal investigation of the evidence for Jesus" (2007). La Miranda Films. All Rights Reserved. (DVD)

there to be a God, because I did not want to be held accountable for my life."[2]

I believe that *this* is the <u>real</u> reason so many children of Christian parents begin to doubt, and when they abandon the Christian faith later, they are resistant to accept it – personal conviction and accountability for one's life. I also believe this is one of the contributing factors to Rachael Slick's 'deconversion' too. And it's apparent that the seeds of doubt are beginning to take root in some of the hearts of the youth of Jerry's church, which are starting to become visible. However, this can be a good thing, because as Christians we have to make sure that our faith is *our* faith, and not merely us believing what our parents believe, like children of parents from other religions and worldviews, regardless if what we believe is true or not.

In Chapter Two, I discussed a little of my experience being involved on the Missions Committee of the first church I attended after accepting the Truth of the Christian faith. As I interviewed each teenager who was applying for consideration to go on a missions trip, I began to notice the answers that were given by each candidate were oddly similar. *Too* similar. For one particular older teen, I decided to diverge a bit from my usual round of questioning, and asked him about his Christian faith. I asked him, 'Can you say with 100% certainty that what you believe isn't just because you were born into a Christian family and attend a Christian church?' I think that really stumped him, because his response was 'That's a good question. Honestly, I really don't know, but I know what I

---

[2] Ibid.

believe is true.' Now, my intention wasn't actually to stump him, nor cause him to question his faith (that would be pretty counterproductive as a Christian if I did it for that reason!) However, since that is the kind of questioning our children are going to be exposed to in droves when they get out into the 'real world,' they really need to be prepared for that kind of questioning ahead of time, while they are still under the protective spiritual care of their parents and church leaders. This kind of 'practice testing' will actually *strengthen* their faith and help them to be better equipped later to deal with the satanic deception of 'the god of this world [who] has blinded the minds of the unbelieving so that they might not see the light of the gospel of the glory of Christ, who is the image of God' (2 Corinthians 4:4), which they'll be exposed to and will be fired at them from every direction when they enter the 'real world' – sadly, even from other 'Christians.'

A few years ago, I was at local 'mega-church' where a few dozen people were being baptized that night – at least one of them was as young as five years old. I was really excited to hear about the different backgrounds each of them had and how the Holy Spirit worked in each of their hearts to convict and convince them of the Christian faith. However, what I noticed was a sort of 'cookie-cutter' response from each of them. Most of them used similar 'Christian lingo' to describe their conversion process, and nearly all of them whose testimonies were viewed on the 'big screen' quoted John 3:16, and the 'dunking' process seemed to move along rather swiftly, more like an assembly line than the quality time that should be given to express the intimate, mutual joy shared between the baptismal candidate and the rest of the congregation, while they are sharing their testimony before being baptized that I've seen in three of the churches I've attended since becoming a Christian. Somehow, this seemed to be 'missing' during this 'mass baptism.' Now, I'm aware that at Pentecost, three thousand souls were baptized that day (Acts 2:41), so I'm sure that they didn't give long speeches. However, it's apparent from Acts that there was a real intimate, mutual joy shared between those who were being baptized and those who witnessed them, because 'They were continually devoting themselves to the apostles' teaching and to fellowship, to the breaking of bread and to prayer' (v.42). There was a real, intimate 'connection' felt among the Church body that day at Pentecost that I didn't really feel that day at the 'mass baptism.' It seemed almost 'rehearsed.' That's not to say that they aren't just as legitimate of Christians as I am, and I acknowledge that a newly 'born again' Christian isn't going to be as 'versed' as someone who has been a Christian a long time – particularly the five-year-old. However, I can honestly say that when I first became a devoted follower of Jesus Christ, I wanted to share it with whoever was willing to listen, as well as share every detail in my 'road to salvation,' especially during my baptism. The quickness of the baptisms coupled with the 'standard' comments seemed kind of 'stiff' and impersonal. In fact, the pastor who walked out 'on stage' didn't even open the Bible to read a single passage from Scripture, in order to explain the meaning and Christian significance of 'believer's baptism' before the baptisms started, like I've seen in every other church where I've witnessed 'believer's baptism' – including my own. Again, I'm **not** saying that their conversions and commitment to Christ weren't as legitimate as mine was. All I'm saying is that this kind of 'swift, impersonal, rehearsed, cookie-cutter, assembly line' profession of faith (ie: emotionally and/

or superficially saying a 'sinner's prayer,' making a 'decision for Christ,' making an 'altar call,' etc) can place a child in risk of abandoning the faith later in life if they didn't really understand, deep down, what it means for Jesus to be their *Lord* (ie: 'Master'), and not just their *Savior*, including 'what' Jesus 'saved' them *from*.

What I also see too often from Christian parents when their child begins to question the faith, they respond with comments like 'if they weren't actually Christians, they wouldn't worry about being one.' (Really? That didn't seem to be true for Rachael Slick!) Or, they simply dismiss it and make comments like 'Don't worry, God is in control. Just trust Him, and everything will be okay.' Of course, we should trust Him, and He *is* 'in control,' however, when our children are coming to us, because they are questioning the faith and are doubting whether they are a true Christian or not, that needs to be taken seriously and addressed – NOW! Although God is in control, He also doesn't 'force' His will on people, including forcing them to believe. He merely regenerates our hearts and convicts us to the Truth, so that we can have the *ability* to believe. So, constant reassurance, as well as explaining 'why' they should be assured that the Christian faith is true and not just another one of the countless religions out there, is something every parent needs to be doing with their child, at least on a <u>daily</u> basis, as well as assuring them that they are *unconditionally* loved, just as God loved us and 'while we were yet sinners, Christ died for us' (Romans 5:8).

Another thing I see often are the "mini-me's" mentioned in Chapter Two who are seen too often in churches today.

I remember one teenager who not only repeated the same 'Christian lingo' of his parent, but also used the same Bible version that his parent used (including sharing the same frame of mind that this 'version' is the only 'legitimate' version, as well as the only one that should be read). Unfortunately, these kinds of 'Christian kids' are just as likely to abandon the faith later on when they begin to be influenced by others, because skeptics will attempt to point out that the only reason they believe in the Christian faith – including which version of the Bible is the 'only' one to be used – is because *their parents* believe that, and they are merely believing what their parents believe – just as children from other religions believe in it, because *their parents* believe in it – and not being encouraged by their parents to use their own minds to legitimize the faith later, in order to determine its authenticity. I've seen this too often with children of Christian families who abandoned the faith, who later say, 'The only reason I believed this is because my parent(s) did. I never made up my own mind, until later, which is why I abandoned it.'

Last week when I met Mom for dinner, and we were talking about how much different she was from her brothers, as well as how much different they are from each other. [And by 'different,' I'm not implying 'better' or 'self-righteous,' since – Biblically – there's no such thing as a '*self*-righteous' Christian, but rather, in terms of their perception of their relationship (or lack of it) with Jesus]. And what Mom simply shared was that unlike her brothers, she always had a *desire* to know what is true about God. Whatever was true, she wanted to find out. When I asked her why she thought that was, her response was, for her, knowing what is true has always been more important to her than maintaining a personal belief, because she has always acknowledged that she is capable of being wrong, while the Truth can't be wrong. I remember a comment by her 'younger' older brother who stated that when he dies, he wants it to be just like it was when they were all younger – his parents and his brother and sister all together again. Although this is a very sentimental belief, in reality that is all it is – a sentimental belief based on a personal opinion, because there is absolutely no evidence for that being true. But as repeated throughout this book, 'opinion' and 'Truth' are not the same thing, because the former is simply based on nothing more than a personal belief, while the latter is based on evidence. And it is this 'avalanche of evidence' that Lee Strobel finally accepted that convinced him that Christianity was true:

> "In light of this avalanche of evidence, pointing toward the Truth of Christianity, it would require more faith for me to maintain my atheism, than to become a follower of Jesus Christ."[3]

However, for my mom's brother, this desire to believe in his *lack of* evidence-based opinion is drastically stronger than his desire to believe in what's actually evidentially true, including his lack of desire to even *listen* to what's true, much like the 'Wayside' child in Chapter One. I often wonder why not everyone has this 'desire' to know the Truth, or at least the desire to listen. But, as I'm reminded by Scripture, it's only by the power of the <u>Holy Spirit</u> that a person even acquires that desire, because it is based on the will of God and His eternal

---

[3] Ibid.

216

Sovereignty to convict, such as what happened to Lee Strobel when he accepted the Truth of the Resurrection, after reading Paul's first epistle to the Corinthian church – something he could have never done through his own will, particularly being a devout atheist. Although I don't have a clue why God convicts some and not others, I'm comforted by the fact that God's purposes are always just, all of the time, which is why He states, "'For My thoughts are not your thoughts, Nor are your ways My ways,' declares the LORD. For as the heavens are higher than the earth, So are My ways higher than your ways And My thoughts than your thoughts'" (Isaiah 55:8-9), including His Will regarding Who He saves and Who He doesn't: 'For if the ministry of condemnation has glory, much more does the ministry of righteousness abound in glory' (2 Corinthians 3:9). Another wards, God's infinite 'ways' and 'thoughts' are perfect and just, even if our finite minds are unable to comprehend them.

These, and other reasons, are why I decided to write this book. This is something that has been weighing heavily on my heart in the last few years. Last year after Pusa and I returned from California, when we went to visit Grace Community Church to listen to Pastor John MacArthur preach, I felt led by the Holy Spirit to address this ever-important issue in writing. This project has taken nearly a year to complete, because much of what I have written in this book has been taken from individual Bible studies that I've led over the last couple of years – most of them that were done weren't even finished until this current year, as well as being involved in other projects, including my own home Bible studies I lead out of my basement which Pusa affectionately nicknamed

"Toledo *Underground* Church," as well as my full-time job as a male nurse (or 'murse'), and investing in my own loving relationships with Pusa and my Mom, and other friendships, as well as keeping up the responsibilities of a house, etc. But as it's frequently stated, 'Anything worth while takes a lot of hard work' – but it's worth it, and that includes the 'hard work' of serving our Lord – it's *worth it!* I've also been blessed to have read numerous books by Christian authors that I felt have invaluably aided in effectively communicating certain key points I have made throughout this book. I would also encourage you to read the Appendices if you haven't already, as well as some of the footnotes, such as 'Point Four' of Chapter Five, because as you read the Appendices and footnotes where they are referenced in each of the chapters, they help reinforce what's being expressed and defended throughout the book.

My prayer is that after you have read this book, whether you are a Christian parent, a child of one who has abandoned the faith, or simply a Christian who is concerned about the spiritual future and well-being of our youth, that you have taken away something from this writing that is helpful that you can use. If you have, then this project met its goal. At the very least, I hope this makes you think, including what kind of relationship you want – with God first, and also with your Christian parent or unbelieving child. Remember, the 'rift' that you have between each other is the result of each one of you wanting something in the relationship that you didn't perceive to receive from the other in your past. So, if you decide to make the effort to mend that rift, you might want to begin by exploring with each other where that rift started and go from there, and be sure to engage each other in a loving way. Find out what the other one wants and then decide if you can offer it. And if you don't feel you can, then at least offer what you are able to. Remember, genuine love isn't based on what the other person can do *for you*, but what you can do *for them*. And the greatest example of that is God offering up His Son as the sacrificial, unblemished Lamb to atone for your sins. Jesus said, 'Greater love has no one than this, that one lay down his life for his friends' (John 15:13), which was later echoed by His disciple John, 'We know love by this, that He laid down His life for us; and we ought to lay down our lives for the brethren' (1 John 3:16). Whether or not you have accepted the Truth of the Christian faith, these words couldn't be more true. Genuine love begins and ends with giving, but it's up to *you* to the extent that you want to give. And one of the many ways Christian parents express that love to their children is through sharing with them the Truth of the Gospel. However, your parents won't always be around nor do you know 'when' they will take their last breath and close their eyes for the last time, so don't delay in reestablishing that 'rifted' relationship with them, because once they're gone, they're gone *permanently*, and there is only one way to ever see them again – repenting and believing in the Truth of the Christian faith that Jesus is the <u>ONLY</u> Way to the Father (John 14:6). There are many familial relationships from my past that I didn't take the time to invest in properly until it was too late, which I regret to this day, which I can tell you, still leaves a gaping hole in my heart. Don't make the same mistake I made by making that mistake with your parents or your children, because your relationship, and the unknown, limited time you have with them is too precious to waste.

Thank you, Mom, that you never stopped loving me, encouraging me, and continued to 'pray without ceasing' (1 Thessalonians 5:17) for my salvation. I can never repay you for that. Thank you, Pusa, for always praying for me and encouraging me, especially during those moments when I needed it the most. Mom and Pusa, your unconditional love through your words and actions go beyond words. And most of all, I thank God that He never stopped loving me, never gave up on me, and that He changed my heart, so that I could see clearly to be open to the Truth and accept it. Although I don't know you personally, I will keep you and your relationship with God and your parents/children in my prayers, because Truth will win out in the end – and 'Truthfully,' it already *has!*

God bless you in Jesus' Name.

"Sanctify them in the truth; Your word is truth." – John 17:17

For Sabina and Iselin, because your mother loves you and prays for you every, single day with every fiber of her being and with her whole heart, and because Jesus loves you even more than that.

For Bob, because it's <u>true</u> *- ALL of it. I love ya, bro!*

And for Grandpa Donald and Grandma Florence – I miss you.

Appendix A

How can we be 'assured' that Jesus rose from the dead?
What about 'alternative theories'?

'Swoon theory' (Jesus didn't die on the cross. He just 'fainted')
– according to the apostle John, who was an 'eyewitness' to
the crucifixion of Jesus (John 19:35), Jesus was clearly dead, as
evidenced by the fact that, unlike the two criminals whose legs
were broken by the Romans to speed up their deaths (v.31-32),
Jesus was *already dead*, even prior to the spear being driven
into his side, which poured out 'blood <u>AND</u> water (pericardial
fluid)' (v.33-34), indicating that He had suffocated on the cross.

'Stolen body theory' – the eleven remaining disciples were
cowering behind locked doors in fear (John 20:19). They
had neither the means nor the motive to steal the body, as
Jesus' body was being guarded (Matthew 27:62-66), which a
prisoner in Jesus' day would have been guarded from anywhere
between *40 to 100 heavily armed Roman soldiers*.[1] So, even 'if'

---

[1] Duke Crawford, "From Skeptics to Martyrs," 2011-04-24, Message 42 of
61, "Discovering the Authentic Jesus: Expositional Study of Luke's Gospel
– Account of the Life & Ministry of Jesus." http://www.emmanuelbaptist.
com/social-media-player (audio from Easter 2011 sermon from Emmanuel
Baptist Church, Toledo, Ohio)

the disciples could have somehow managed to overpower the multiple guards (Matthew 28:11-15) and stole the body - which historically, didn't happen - they would have later been arrested and/or executed.

The tomb wasn't empty/the disciples went to the wrong tomb – both Peter and John went to the tomb, which had Jesus' "linen wrappings, and His face-cloth which had been on His head" (John 20:6-7). Had they went to the wrong tomb, the Romans, who had access to Jesus' body, could have simply produced His corpse by going to the 'right' tomb, which they were not able to do, because the 'right' tomb had Jesus' linen wrappings and face-cloth. Also, both Mary Magdalene and Mary the mother of James and Joseph had followed Joseph of Arimathea to the tomb where Jesus was buried (Mark 15:42-47; 16:1), who then later told the disciples where He was buried (Mark 16:7-8).

The disciples hallucinated/they 'made it up' – psychiatrically, hallucinations are *individual* experiences, not *group* ones. Had the disciples 'made up' the story of the Resurrection, most if not all of them, would have recanted their faith, after being threatened with excruciating, tortuous persecution and death, such as the apostle James, who died without recanting his faith (Acts 12:1-2). Although a person *'might'* die for something they *don't know* to be a lie, a person won't die for something they *know* to be a lie. The disciples were willingly tortured and martyred for their faith, because they knew Jesus rose from the dead, because they were eyewitnesses of Jesus' resurrection (John 20:19-28; 1 Corinthians 15:4-7; 2 Peter 1:16; 1 John 1:1).

The FIRST witnesses were women – if the Church was going to 'make up' the Resurrection, they wouldn't have used first century Jewish women, like Mary Magdalene (Mark 16:6; John 20:1,11-18) and Mary the mother of James and Joseph (Matthew 27:56; 28:1,8-10) as their *primary witnesses*, since the testimony of first century middle-eastern women were considered 'unreliable.' Had they 'made it up' they would have used one of the disciples, like Peter, but since they used the women, that provides stronger and more convincing evidence that the Resurrection actually happened.

The conversion of Saul of Tarsus and Jesus' half-brothers – James and Judas (Jude) – Saul of Tarsus was a persecutor and murderer of Christians (Acts 9:1,21; 22:4; 1 Corinthians 15:9; 1 Timothy 1:13), and he was well aware of the belief of the Resurrection, because he was present when Stephen proclaimed it and was martyred (Acts 8:1). However, on the road to Damascus, he met the resurrected Jesus, and he became a believer (Acts 9:1-20; 1 Corinthians 15:8). Jesus' half-brothers, James and Judas (Jude), originally didn't believe in Him (John 7:5), but after witnessing His resurrection (1 Corinthians 15:7), James, as well as Jesus' other half-brothers (Mark 6:3-4) became believers, and James and Judas (Jude) became New Testament writers (James 1:1; Jude 1:1), and along with Jesus' disciples were present at Pentecost (Acts 1:13-14).

The disciples changed from cowards to martyrs – again, the eleven remaining disciples, *shortly*, went from cowards hiding behind locked doors (John 20:19) to 'preaching everywhere' (Mark 16:20), willingly accepting excruciating torture and even death, because they <u>knew</u> Jesus rose from the dead, because they were <u>eyewitnesses</u> to His resurrection.[2]

[2] S. Michael Houdmann, CEO, GotQuestions.org. *"Does the Bible record the death of the apostles? How did each of the apostles die?"* http://www. gotquestions.org/apostles-die.html

Appendix B

Is there evidence OUTSIDE of the Bible for the life, death, and resurrection of Jesus?

Not only does the Bible record the life, death, <u>AND</u> resurrection of Jesus, so do both <u>non</u>-biblical <u>AND</u> *non-christian sources*:

"When you look at the history, maybe I alluded to the possibility that some historians think Jesus never existed. I take that back – JESUS EXISTED!" – Richard Dawkins, atheist & author[1]

"The doctrine of the Kingdom of Heaven, which was the main teaching of Jesus is certainly one of the most revolutionary doctrines that ever stirred and changed human thought...one is obliged to say, 'Here was a man. This part of the tale could not have been invented.' – H.G. Wells, atheist and author[2]

---

[1] Richard Dawkins, "Has Science Buried God?" Copyright 2009. Fixed Point Foundation. All Rights Reserved. (DVD)

[2] H.G. Wells, "The Outline of History : Being a Plain History of Life and Mankind," '49: The Teachings of Jesus of Nazareth.' (1920). Publisher: George Newnes.

"A man who was completely innocent, offered Himself as a sacrifice for the good of others, including His enemies, and became the ransom of the world. It was the perfect act." – Mohandas Ghandi (speaking about Jesus Christ)[3]

"He [Jesus Christ] was condemned. He was crucified in reality, and not in appearance, not in imagination, not in deceit. He really died, and was buried, and rose from the dead." – Ignatius of Antioch (First Cent. A.D., born ~35 to 50 A.D., died ~98 to 117 A.D.), non-Bible writer, non-disciple of Jesus, and Church leader and pupil of the apostle John[4]

"Let us consider, beloved, how the Lord continually proves to us that there should be a future resurrection, of which He [God] has rendered the Lord Jesus Christ the first-fruits by raising Him from the dead." – Clement of Rome's non-Biblical 'First Epistle to the Corinthians,' member of the church of Philippi (Philippians 4:3), non-Bible writer, non-disciple of Jesus, and third bishop of Rome (fl. 96 A.D.)[5]

"It was by means of sorcery that He [Jesus] was able to accomplish the wonders which He performed…. Let us believe that these cures, or the resurrection, or the feeding of a multitude with a

---

[3] Mohandas Ghandi, "Non-Violence in Peace and War," vol. 2, ch. 166. (1949). A_man_who_was_completely_innocent_offered_ himself. (n.d.). *Columbia World of Quotations*. Retrieved May 01, 2014, from Dictionary.com website: http://quotes.dictionary. com/A_man_who_was_completely_innocent_offered_himself

[4] Roberts, Alexander and James Donaldson, editors, *Epistle of Ignatius to the Trallians, Early Church Fathers Ante-Nicene Fathers to A.D. 325*, Vol. 1

[5] *The Ante-Nicene Fathers Volume I through X: Translations of the Writings of the Fathers Down to AD 325* (1997), Volume 1, page 11.

few loaves.... These are nothing more than tricks of jugglers." –
Celsus (Second Cent. A.D.), non-christian Roman author ('The
True Doctrine') and Greek philosopher (~177 A.D.), confirming
the <u>beliefs</u> of the <u>First</u> <u>Century</u> Christian Church that Jesus <u>rose</u>
<u>from the dead!</u>[6]

---

[6] Hendrik van der Loos (1965). *The Miracles of Jesus*. Brill Publishers. Retrieved 14 June 2012. "According to Celsus Jesus performed His miracles by sorcery (γοητεία); ditto in II, 14; II, 16; II, 44; II, 48; II, 49 (Celsus puts Jesus' miraculous signs on a par with those among men)."

Appendix C

Atheists and other non-christian skeptics will say that neither the existence of God nor the claims of Christianity can be 'proven' using science. They are right. However, science can't 'disprove' the existence of God nor the claims of Christianity either. That's because 'God is spirit' (John 4:24). Therefore, science is the wrong means of proving (or disproving) the existence of God and the claims of Christianity. That would be like proving or disproving that something is red with taste - it's the wrong sense. However, there is 'evidence' (albeit not scientific 'proof') that God exists and the claims of Christianity are true, by objectively examining the other scientific 'theories' for the existence of the universe:

<u>An eternal universe</u> - the universe has always existed. Whether in its present state, in a 'different' form, or an infinite number of "Big Bangs" and "Big Contractions," the problem is that if the 'material' that makes up our universe is eternal, then it would never have a 'first moment.' Therefore, a universe that never had a 'first moment' would never arrive at this moment in time. Therefore, an eternal universe - however, you define it - is both unscientific AND illogical.

The universe created itself - the idea that there was absolutely nothing to begin with and then suddenly, the universe 'created itself.' Some will point out examples of something coming into being from nothing IN our universe. However, the 'creation' of something IN our universe can be theorized that the necessary material needed to create it already existed IN our universe, but just can't be explained yet. This is different than absolutely NOTHING existing, and suddenly the universe 'creating itself' out of this 'nothing.' (0+0=1). That is both unscientific AND illogical.

The universe was created by some kind of 'non-god' – 'multiverses,' some kind of 'Mother Universe,' alternative dimensional universes, etc. would require an explanation for 'their' existence as well, and, therefore, you run into the same problem with the eternal universe. It only backs up the problem having an 'infinite regress' that you have with an eternal universe. Plus, the idea of a 'multiverse' has already been debunked by leading atheistic and other non-religious scientists.[1] Therefore, this is also both unscientific AND illogical.

A deistic 'god' created the universe - this is more plausible than the other three, provided that this deistic 'god' isn't material and isn't bound by the laws of space-time that you run into with an eternal universe, the universe creating itself, or a 'non-god' creating the universe. However, based on what we know about the universe, what kind of deistic 'god' would create

---

[1] Robin Schumacher, edited by Matt Slick. "Atheism and the Multiverse." http://carm.org/atheism-and-the-multiverse

our universe? If it's one that has no purpose, intelligence, or intention, this is similar to the 'non-god,' and the problem is that the universe is too finely tuned to have been created without purpose, intelligence, or intention. And without purpose, intelligence, or intention, the universe either would never have formed, or it could not have stabilized to keep the universe to 'evolve' into the form it is today. And even 'if' this deistic 'god' had purpose, intelligence, or intention, but not personally involved in the universe 'it' created, then 'why' would this kind of 'god' create a universe in the first place, and not be interested at all in the universe 'it' created? What would be the purpose of creating something as large, complex, and amazing as the universe, only to be inactive in it after creating it? There would be no point to create it in the first place, as well as other arguments against the existence of a deistic 'god' to account for the existence of the universe.[2],[3] Therefore, both kinds of deistic 'gods' are both unscientific AND illogical.

<u>A personal God with purpose, intelligence, AND intention created the universe</u> - some will say that God would require an explanation for 'His' existence, but as previously mentioned, 'this' kind of God is not physical, like a 'multiverse,' 'Mother universe,' or alternative dimensional universe, because 'this' kind of God is Spirit, or *non-physical*, therefore, a personal, non-physical God would not require an explanation for 'His' eternal existence, like things that are *physical* which would, <u>because</u> God is *non-physical*, and would not be bound to the

---

[2] Matt Slick, "Debate between Matt Slick and Eddie Tabash on 'Does God Exist?'" (December 5, 2009). http://carm.org/debate-matt-slick-eddie-tabash-does-god-exist

[3] Matt Slick, "What is Deism?" http://carm.org/questions-deism

limitations of the *physical* world, like things that 'are' physical, like the universe and everything **in** it. But before writing this off as a 'fairy tale,' keep in mind that if you remain objective, the only other 'theories' have all been *dis*proven both scientifically AND logically. Therefore, if you eliminate this last option, then you've just eliminated *every* possible explanation for the universe existing. So, since the universe does indeed exist, and since we *need* an explanation for the universe existing (since accepting no explanation would be illogical), then since every other 'theory' has been disproven scientifically AND logically, to 'not' believe that a personal God with purpose, intelligence, AND intention created the universe would be illogical as well. So, it doesn't matter that God can't be 'proven' (or disproven) scientifically, because eliminating the *only* other four 'theories' provides strong, overwhelming evidence that the only other option left is supported logically by what we know about our universe, its laws, as well as science.

And when an atheist or another skeptic denies the existence of God and the Christian faith, even after being exposed to all of this, they frantically use poor arguments to find alternative 'theories' (that are nothing more than modified 'versions' of the other four 'theories'), in order to avoid 'the elephant in the atheist's room' - that God *does* indeed exist and 'created the heavens and the earth,' which supports the Christian faith (Genesis 1:1; John 1:1).

Appendix D

<u>Where is the 'justice' in someone who repents and 'gets away' with murder? How it is 'fair' that an unrepentant murderer and the unrepentant victim of murder will BOTH end up in Hell?</u>

For those who don't *genuinely* repent of their sins against God, they <u>will</u> spend eternity suffering in Hell (Revelation 20:14-15), because they have refused to repent of their sins, which are against <u>GOD</u> (Psalm 51:4). However, those who 'do' *genuinely* repent of their sins against God, He 'transfers' their sins onto His sin<u>less</u> only begotten Son, Jesus, when He died 'for' them on the cross, when God looked upon Jesus as if He had lived their sin*ful* lives, while God looks upon them as if they had lived Jesus' sin<u>less</u> life. God is 'all-powerful' enough to forgive *any* sin and place that sin on Jesus – 'the Lamb of God Who *takes away the sin* of the world' (emphasis added)(John 1:29), so that those sins <u>are</u> paid for, while God's judgment and '**justice**' ('getting what's deserved') is served (John 5:20), as well as the repentant sinner receiving both '**mercy**' ('*not* getting what's deserved') and '**grace**' ('getting what's *not* deserved') by a loving, forgiving, and <u>just</u> God. Also, the Bible implies there are certain 'degrees' of punishment in Hell (Matthew 10:15; Revelation 20:12). Therefore, not everyone who has 'willfully' sinned against God, refused to repent of their sin, and rejected Christ receives the 'exact same' punishment in Hell. So, since *all* sins <u>must</u> be 'justly' judged and paid for, <u>no one</u> is excluded from God's judgment; otherwise, God would be an *un*just God.

<u>Don't other religions and worldviews (like atheism) provide 'justice,' 'mercy,' & 'grace' too?</u>

No. Atheism provides absolutely **no justice** for the victim of an evil act, if the criminal never gets convicted. Atheism also offers **no mercy**, because <u>every</u> 'crime' <u>must</u> be paid for by the <u>criminal</u>, regardless of how 'serious' the crime is, because there is no 'substitute' to pay for the crime 'in place of' the 'criminal,' regardless of how repentant they are, how many 'good works' they have done since the 'crime' has been committed, or even if the victim of the crime 'forgives' that person's crime, because 'justice' <u>must</u> be served. Atheism also offers **no grace** because "everyone's" destiny is the same – death. Also, there are no <u>objective</u> 'standards of morality' in atheism in order to define what does and does not deserves 'justice.'

Other religions also provide **no justice** as well, because unlike Christianity, rewards are based on 'balancing' one's 'good deeds' over 'bad deeds.' So if a criminal gets 'rewarded' in the afterlife because their 'good works' outweighed their 'bad works,' then their crime goes 'unpaid' and the victim receives **no justice**. Other religions also provide **no mercy**, because, like atheism, when a crime is paid, it <u>must</u> be paid for by the criminal even if the victim forgives the criminal, otherwise, there is **no justice** being served for the crime committed.

Likewise, other religions provide **no grace** either, because other religions are based on 'getting what's deserved' – rewards based on 'good deeds' verses punishments based on 'bad deeds' - **not grace**. This includes eastern religions (Karma), because there is **no justice** in Karma for the victim of a crime, which gets 'weighed out' if a person's 'good works' outweigh their 'bad works.' And like atheism, there are no *objective* 'standards of morality' in other religions – it is either based on the individual to *subjectively* decide, or the 'rules' of the particular religion, which leads to *injustice* for those who believe they have been victimized and received **no justice** for being 'violated.'

Made in the USA
Lexington, KY
24 November 2014